100 YEARS OF CHANGE
STYLE & DESIGN

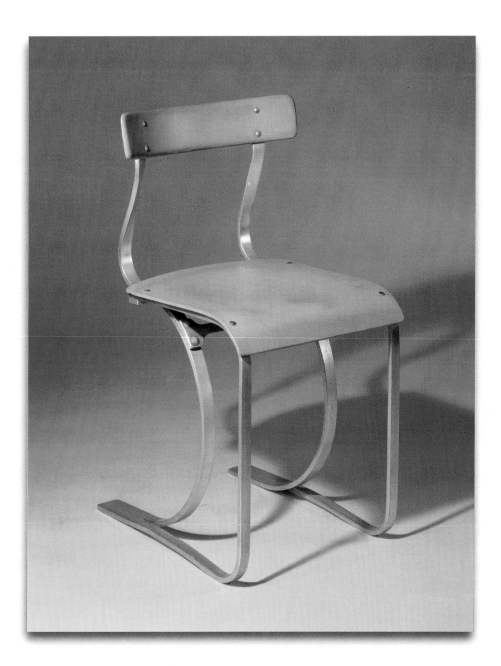

With grateful thanks to Frances Banfield,
Andrea P. A. Belloli, Lucinda Hawksley, Helen
Johnson, Sonya Newland, Ian Powling, Nigel Soper,
and Susan Thompson.

We particularly acknowledge the valuable
comments of Jane Pavitt at the Victoria & Albert
Museum, London.

ISBN 0 75253 145 X

This edition published in 1999 by
PARRAGON
Queen Street House
4 Queen Street
Bath BA1 1HE

Created and produced for Parragon by
FOUNDRY DESIGN & PRODUCTION
a part of The Foundry Creative Media Company Ltd
Crabtree Hall, Crabtree Lane, Fulham,
London, SW6 6TY

100 YEARS OF CHANGE

STYLE & DESIGN

**Deborah Gill, Karen Hurrell, Robert Prescott-Walker,
Martin Raymond, and Vicky Richardson**

Foreword by
Eric Knowles
Presenter of Antiques Roadshow *and* Going for a Song

Introduction by
Kevin Edge

||| ·PARRAGON· |||

CONTENTS

ARCHITECTURAL STYLES HAVE DEVELOPED DURING THE TWENTIETH CENTURY IN RESPONSE TO THE NEEDS OF GROWING POPULATIONS, NEW BUSINESSES AND EXPANDING URBAN CENTRES. AT LEAST ONE TYPE OF BUILDING – THE SKYSCRAPER – HAS BECOME AN ICON OF OUR CENTURY. LESS WELL-KNOWN BUT NO LESS IMPORTANT ARE THE HOMES, GARDENS, LANDSCAPES AND INTERIORS THAT CHART THE EVOLUTION OF THE CENTURY'S ARCHITECTURE.

SINCE THE START OF THE CENTURY, DESIGNERS HAVE HONED THEIR SKILLS AND PRODUCTION METHODS TO MAKE DISTINCTIVE – AND SOMETIMES CLASSIC – ITEMS FOR THE HOME THAT ARE BOTH FUNCTIONAL AND VISUALLY PLEASING. IN THE REALM OF DECORATIVE ARTS CAN BE FOUND SOME OF THE CENTURY'S MOST BEAUTIFUL CREATIONS. EXQUISITE EXAMPLES OF GLASSWARE AND CERAMICS REVEAL THE TALENTS OF THEIR MAKERS.

THE FASCINATION WITH FASHION IS NOTHING NEW. FROM THE FIRST BRASSIERE TO SKIRTS FOR MEN, DESIGNERS HAVE BEEN THRILLING AND SHOCKING US WITH THEIR INNOVATIONS IN CLOTHES AND ACCESSORIES SINCE THE BEGINNING OF THE CENTURY. SOME OF THE FINEST VISUAL ARTISTS HAVE HARNESSED THEIR SKILLS TO PRODUCE STUNNING COSTUMES AND SETS FOR FILMS AND STAGE ENTERTAINMENT.

A HOME'S FURNITURE AND FURNISHINGS CAN SAY A LOT ABOUT THE OWNERS' PERSONALITIES. SIMILARLY, DESIGNERS OF FURNITURE, FURNISHINGS AND ASSOCIATED ITEMS EXPRESS THEIR OWN DESIGN PHILOSOPHIES AND IDEAS THROUGH THEIR WORK. CHAIRS IN PARTICULAR CAN BE REGARDED AS EXEMPLARS OF A DESIGNER'S STYLE, AND MANY REPRESENT KEY MOMENTS IN FURNITURE DESIGN.

ALL AROUND US WE SEE THE WORK OF GRAPHIC ARTISTS AND DESIGNERS. IN ADVERTISING, LOGOS AND PACKAGING, THEIR INSPIRATIONS CAN AMUSE US, MAKE US REFLECT OR PERSUADE US TO BUY. IN THE LATE TWENTIETH CENTURY, NO OTHER AREA OF CREATIVE ACTIVITY IS SO SKILFULLY ATTUNED TO THE SHIFTING CULTURAL TASTES OF SOCIETY.

THROUGH MYRIAD STYLES AND MOVEMENTS, FINE ART HAS BEEN NURTURED, IGNORED AND REDISCOVERED BY GENERATIONS. WITH INCREASING PUBLIC AWARENESS, MANY TWENTIETH-CENTURY WORKS OF ART HAVE BECOME PART OF OUR VISUAL LANGUAGE. ONCE THOUGHT TO BE A THREAT TO THE ART OF PAINTING, PHOTOGRAPHY IS NOW REGARDED AS ONE OF THE CENTURY'S ESSENTIAL VISUAL MEDIUMS.

Some entries that cover designers or works of particular significance have been selected as milestones and are indicated by this symbol

DURING THE TWENTIETH CENTURY, THE URBAN LANDSCAPE HAS BEEN RADICALLY ALTERED BY THE INVENTION OF MACHINES AND PRODUCTS NOW TAKEN FOR GRANTED IN EVERYDAY LIFE: AEROPLANES, CARS AND PERSONAL STEREOS TO NAME JUST THREE. INDUSTRIAL AND TRANSPORT DESIGNERS HAVE CREATED A WORLD UNDREAMED OF A HUNDRED YEARS AGO.

Foreword

The twentieth century witnessed the most radical changes the world has ever known, not only in style and design but also in politics and science. Despite two disastrous World Wars, both the fine and the decorative arts managed to survive and, eventually, to flourish.

The birth of the century brought with it the birth of Art Nouveau, with its combination of symbolism and curvilinear excess – in many respects an artificial style which, by the end of the 1910s, was simply unable to sustain itself. When change came, it did so with a bang, in the 1920s. The 1929 Wall Street Crash put an end to many a party on both sides of the Atlantic. Even so, the Depression years of the 1930s can hardly be regarded as having been fallow, especially in the arts. The seeds of modernism sowed by designers and architects such as Le Corbusier and all those connected with the Bauhaus in Germany had taken root by the advent of the second half of the century, and were beginning to mature, providing the foundations for much of post-war design, especially in architecture.

It is sobering to realize that I have been on this earth to witness most of the advances made during the second half of the twentieth century. I consider myself fortunate in having spent half that time being involved with a premier London auction house with specific responsibility for twentieth-century applied arts. As a result, from time to time I have been fortunate to converse directly with great designers and craftsmen and women, including ceramists Susie Cooper and Dame Lucie Rie. I have also had occasion to meet up with those who were taught by, or worked alongside, such prominent names as Archibald Knox and René Lalique. It is this proximity to those who have played important roles in the development of twentieth-century style and design that continues to keep me enthralled with this remarkable period of change.

Eric Knowles

Introduction

We live in a world in which style and design shapes and colours everything we interact with and see. We respond to seductive images, we desire cleverly-designed products and we are enveloped by architectural spaces.

Whilst many of these styled or designed 'things', big or small, mass-produced or unique, were conceived to meet practical needs, others were given a stylistic veneer so that they might communicate distinctive cultural information amidst the social flux and complexity of contemporary life. Some of these 'things', instead of disappearing at the end of their useful lives, have come to be studied and collected as innovative or quintessential examples of their kind. Many of them – thought of as modern 'icons' – are to be seen in this book.

Style and design, it should be remembered, are not only preoccupations of modern, free-market societies, but have informed human creativity from earliest times. Style and design are deeply embedded human concerns; we have long fashioned tools with which to extend our faculties and express shared values. A copper axe made for an Alpine herdsman 5,000 years ago and a laptop computer built for the 1990s executive, though millennia apart in date, are both complex, highly functional designs and at the same moment 'styled' commodities and cultural icons – desirable signs of status and power to be shown off as well as used. In Europe and America specifically, both style and design have been the preserve of architects and artists for centuries, as they have realized ideas for lordly clients through the acts of sketching, drawing and modelling, using tools as diverse as plaster and knife, parchment and quill and, later, paper and pencil.

Styling and designing emerged in recognizably modern forms in the late eighteenth and early nineteenth centuries as a result of increasing mechanization and division of labour. At that point, the new profession of designer arose, bridging the gap between artistic inspiration, professional know-how and commercial manufacture. Much of the time, these early designers engaged in isolated studio activity, concerned with creating all-purpose flat patterns rather than specific three-dimensional forms and structures.

In the twentieth century, industrial mastery of new materials and technology has led to the conception and manufacture of increasingly complex consumer goods, thus demanding that designers take on the challenge of styling and, more importantly, creating complex, three-dimensional forms such as motor cars and domestic appliances. Today, style and design can be understood as a concern with meaningful surfaces and substantial frameworks, the mutually supportive components of our visual and material environment. Style is a graphically motivated visual language of lines and shapes which communicate several things to us – information about use, about surface appearance and about the enduring human impulse towards beauty. Design exists beneath the surface as the framework for human thought and participation.

Though often quite particular and personal in

origin, the works featured in these pages are to be understood equally as responses to broader social, economic and intellectual currents. The works of many architects, artists and designers like Le Corbusier, Picasso or Peter Behrens have, it might be said, constructed defining portraits of the century. Yet, looking at the bigger picture we become aware of other bodies of work, both old and new and, more importantly, subsequent technical advances and conflicting ideologies which prevent us from discerning a totalizing 'style of the century' which can be ascribed to any one person or movement.

What we do see is a complex weave of innovation, responses, shifting emphases and references. We encounter not one but many movements which have produced equally memorable and influential works. For example, architects and designers of the Modern Movement invested their faith in science, social science and technology, advocating the production of standardized, functional, ornament-free objects. The rationality of machine tools, with their ability to shape products geometrically, was seen to be the preferred source of formal inspiration and practical realization. For other designers, one-off or batch-produced decorative objects inspired by either natural forms or popular tastes provided alternatives to the utopian, universalist solutions of the Modern Movement. These polarities, falling broadly speaking either side of the Second World War, have in fact resonated throughout the century and often run side by side.

Such a plurality of styles has been a consequence of the intellectual and creative tenor of a period populated by thousands of restless architects, artists and designers immersed in an increasingly technological, urbanized, capitalistic environment. The fundamental question so many of them have raised has been: 'What is to be the relationship between humankind and machine, between art and industry?' In other words, what is the value of mechanization from the social or aesthetic perspective? Are twentieth-century houses, as Le Corbusier said, 'machines for living in' – white-washed modernist metaphors pure and simple? Or should they be spaces providing psychological comfort and expressing themselves on an aesthetic level? Should styling and design become adjuncts of national ambition and capitalism, generating the beautiful curve of designer Raymond Loewy's rising sales graph, or should they in the first instance enhance the lives of individuals?

This book presents many of the significant objects and images that have been made in response to such questions as these. The book also aims to show that the twentieth century has given us ample evidence of creativity and intellect, putting style and design to social and environmental use and in so doing, furnishing us with new languages and tools for living. Many of these fascinating examples of style and design will undoubtedly serve as models for those working in the next century towards greater durability, visual significance and aesthetic worth.

Kevin Edge

Architecture 1

ARCHITECTURE HAS BEEN PROFOUNDLY INFLUENCED BY MANY OF THE CENTURY'S IMPORTANT ARTISTIC MOVEMENTS, SUCH AS CUBISM, ART DECO AND MODERNISM. MANY STRIKING BUILDINGS, FOR EXAMPLE NEW YORK'S CHRYSLER BUILDING, HAVE BEEN THE RESULT. THE FASCINATING DEVELOPMENT OF ARCHITECTURE DURING THE CENTURY CAN BE SEEN IN A WIDE RANGE OF BUILDINGS.

Josef Hoffmann
Stoclet Palace, Brussels, Belgium

Antonio Gaudí
Casa Milà, Barcelona, Spain

1905 This impressive mansion was designed for the Belgian businessman Adolphe Stoclet, who knew of Hoffmann's work through living in Vienna. Hoffmann (1870–1956) was a key member of the Vienna School and a student of Otto Wagner. His work accordingly shows a reaction against Art Nouveau in favour of classical symmetry and proportions. The Stoclet Palace was a great opportunity for him to experiment with these ideas, as his client wanted a building which was a shrine to the arts as well as a place to live. Hoffmann responded to this brief by creating a rationalist but decadent mansion, with murals by the painter Gustav Klimt. Key architectural features are the asymmetrical yet balanced façade and a stepped stair-tower.

1905–10 The Casa Milà is one of Gaudí's (1852–1926) most eccentric buildings, looking more like a natural rock formation than a man-made structure. The Quarry, as it is known locally, was designed in 1905–6, but only completed in 1910 under the supervision of Gaudí's assistant. The building is remarkable in plan, section and elevation for its almost complete lack of straight lines. Later in his career, Gaudí said that the straight line belonged to human beings and the curved one to God. As a spiritual person, he developed an architectural vocabulary which evoked natural forms and forces in a worshipful way. At the Casa Milà, this is evident in the shape and texture of the stonework, which is designed to resemble a product of gradual erosion. The swirling curves

Overleaf: the spectacular Opera House which greets visitors to Sydney Harbour (see page 31).

Left: this grand residence was created for Adolphe Stoclet, a businessman. The interior features murals painted by the famous Viennese Secessionist Gustav Klimt.

Right: the local name for Gaudí's Casa Mila is 'La Pedrera' or 'the Quarry', due to its striking resemblence to a natural rock formation.

of the façade remind one of a cliff face, and the wrought-ironwork on the balconies suggests strange, twisted plants. But despite the references to natural forces, the structure of the Casa Milà, as with all Gaudí's buildings, is based on sophisticated structural principles. The entire weight is supported between the external elevations and the columns which surround the patio. This ability to reconcile expressionistic forms with a scientific approach to structure was one of Gaudí's greatest contributions to twentieth-century architecture.

Otto Wagner
Post Office Savings Bank, Vienna, Austria

1906 Wagner (1841–1918) played a similar role in Austria to that of Louis Sullivan in the USA. In 1903, Wagner won a competition for the Post Office, a building which was to reflect his view that 'new purposes must give birth to new methods of construction and by this reasoning to new forms'. With its structure of glass and metal, the building heralded a new age of industrialism and engineering. Wagner's belief that architecture should be for the people comes across strongly in the translucent central hall, reminiscent of a glazed railway shed. Light floods in from above, while the floor is made of clear glass bricks, suggesting that people should be able to see through to the bank vaults below.

Adolf Loos
Kärntner Bar, Vienna, Austria

1907 Loos (1870–1933) was one of the first modern architects to react against the decorative trends of Art Nouveau. Following architecture school, he lived in the USA for three years and studied the work of the Chicago School. Returning to Vienna in 1896, he wrote a series of articles condemning ornament in favour of functionalism. Houses he designed were built of concrete and had flat roofs, planar walls and strict symmetry. By Viennese standards, the Kärntner Bar was minimally decorated. The main feature was a marble ceiling with classical coffering. Strategic positioning of mirrors at a high level dramatically increased the sense of space.

 ## Charles Rennie Mackintosh
Glasgow School of Art, Scotland

1897–1909 The designs for the School of Art were begun in 1897, when Mackintosh (1868–1928) won a competition for an extension to existing buildings. At the time, they were condemned for their radical Art Nouveau style, but ironically the school is now revered as the best early Modern-Movement building in Britain. At the Glasgow School of Art, Mackintosh did not reproduce Art Nouveau wholesale, but adapted

Wagner's innovative design for Vienna's Post Office Savings Bank allowed the maximum of light into the building, by clever use of glass in its construction.

it in a unique way, using traditional Gaelic and Celtic patterns. The commission was to build several studios, a lecture theatre, a library and private rooms for the director. The site was an impossibly steep hill, with the north side and entrance on Renfrew Street. In plan, the School of Art is masterful, juxtaposing rooms of different shapes and sizes. Mackintosh also paid an enormous amount of attention to detail: every railing, window, chimney and steel bracket is beautifully designed. The elaborate craftsmanship of the library wing contrasts starkly with the spartan Scottish style of the rest of the building. The library reading room is elegantly ordered, with the expressed structure of horizontal beams and rectangular pillars supporting galleries above. Windows rise through the space to a height of 8.5 m (28 ft), creating a highly dramatic effect on the west façade, where the building perches on the hillside.

Henry van de Velde
Model Theatre, Werkbund Exhibition, Cologne, Germany

1914 The Werkbund Exhibition of 1914 involved a number of designers and architects, including van de Velde (1863–1957), Bruno Taut and Walter Gropius. All were grappling with the apparent contradiction between mass production and individual expression. Van de Velde's design for the theatre expressed his admiration for the Machine Age combined with his view that craftsmen should ultimately be in control. The Model Theatre, which is no longer standing, incorporated innovations in theatre design, such as an auditorium shaped like an amphitheatre and a three-part stage. As a socialist, van de Velde attempted to make this a communal building, celebrating democratic values through industrial production. Ironically, it remained the property of the cultivated middle classes.

Mackintosh fought off fierce competition to gain the contract to build the Glasgow School of Art. Today it is considered an icon of Modernist architecture.

Max Berg
Centennial Hall, Breslau, Germany (now Poland)

1913 The Centennial Hall was one of the most daring reinforced concrete structures of its time, taking advantage of the material's ability to span vast distances. This was the one major work by Berg (1870–1947), who was the Breslau city architect at the time he designed it. The Centennial Hall, essentially a huge dome built to commemorate the centenary of the rising against Napoleon in 1813, was the largest of its kind anywhere in the world. At that time, a system of glazing had not been developed that would follow the curves of the dome, so rings of windows were constructed at varying intervals, with a lantern skylight at the top. Inside, banks of seats rose in tiers under vast supporting arches.

Eric Mendelsohn
Einstein Tower, Potsdam, Germany

1921 The Einstein Tower was one of Mendelsohn's first buildings and had a tremendous impact, leading to dozens of other commissions during the 1920s. Built to symbolize the genius of Albert Einstein, the tower also had a practical purpose, namely to accommodate the scientist's astronomical laboratory. Mendelsohn (1887–1953) was one of the first architects to experiment with the creative possibilities of new materials like reinforced concrete, but in fact much of the structure of the tower is brick, due to a post-war shortage of materials. The brick was rendered with cement to make it look like a single sculptural form. In the 1930s, Mendelsohn left Germany to work for several years in England, completing the De la Warr Pavilion in Bexhill on Sea in 1934 with Serge Chermayeff.

Auguste Perret

Notre Dame du Raincy, Le Raincy, France

1922 Perret (1874–1954) left the Paris School of Fine Arts before sitting his finals and went to work for his family's building firm, which specialized in reinforced-concrete construction. His first building dates from 1890. It is no coincidence that Perret made this material his hallmark, developing an influential architectural language of beams and columns. Notre Dame du Raincy, probably the most famous modern church, expresses the traditional layout of nave and aisles in modern materials. The elegance of the interior results from amazingly slim columns, 12 m (40 ft) tall and no more than 35 cm (14 in) in circumference. Exterior walls were replaced by delicate concrete grills patterned with geometric shapes.

The Einstein Tower was built as a symbol of the greatness of Albert Einstein. The building made Mendelsohn's name as an architect, leading to many further commissions.

Schröder House is an excellent example of De Stijl architecture. The artist Piet Mondrian was also a member of the De Stijl movement.

Gerrit Thomas Rietveld
Schröder House, Utrecht, Netherlands

1924 In 1918, Rietveld (1888–1964) joined the De Stijl group of artists and designers based in the Netherlands. Rejecting nineteenth-century ideas, they wanted to express contemporary reality through geometrical forms, grids and planes. The Schröder House is the best example of the ideas of this movement, which were at first only applied to painting. The building is situated at the end of a row of houses in suburban Utrecht. Contrasting strongly with the brick construction of its neighbours, it features intersecting planar walls, with certain elements painted in bright primary colours. The Schröder House is asymmetrical, but its overall composition is perfectly balanced, like paintings by Piet Mondrian, also a member of De Stijl.

Walter Gropius
Bauhaus, Dessau, Germany

1926 In 1915, during the First World War, Gropius (1883–1969) was appointed director of two schools of art and design, which, because of his belief in the unity of the disciplines, he combined under the name 'Bauhaus' in 1919. The school was based at Weimar until 1925, when a new site was found at Dessau, and the opportunity arose for Gropius to design a building consistent with his philosophy. His business partner, Adolf Meyer, assisted with the design, and students were given the opportunity to participate in the creation of the decoration and furnishings. The complex consisted of five main elements: a glazed, three-storey workshop block; a teaching block; social areas; a five-storey dormitory block; and offices spanning a roadway. The forms of these elements were derived from their different functions, but together they made a coherent composition. The general public took a great interest in what went on at the Bauhaus, condemning it for decadent and subversive tendencies. During the 1920s, artists such as Paul Klee and Wassily Kandinsky were Bauhaus teachers and published books on their controversial theories. Gropius's design for the school was as much an expression of Bauhaus theory as these texts, representing the first coherent work of the International Style. In 1928, Gropius resigned as director to concentrate on architecture.

Gunnar Asplund
City Library, Stockholm, Sweden

1928 Asplund (1885–1940) was one of the most important Swedish architects of the twentieth century, since his work shows the transition from the traditional to the modern. The City Library expresses this particularly well, in its abstraction of classical forms. The reading room is housed in a central cylinder which pokes up out of a rectangular box. This strong form is a reference to nineteenth-century architecture, but the stripped-down details are unmistakably twentieth-century. The original plan was to top the cylinder with a dome, but this was abandoned in favour of a flat roof. Had the dome been built, it would have symbolized the human cranium, reinforcing the metaphor of the reading room as a chamber for reading and thinking.

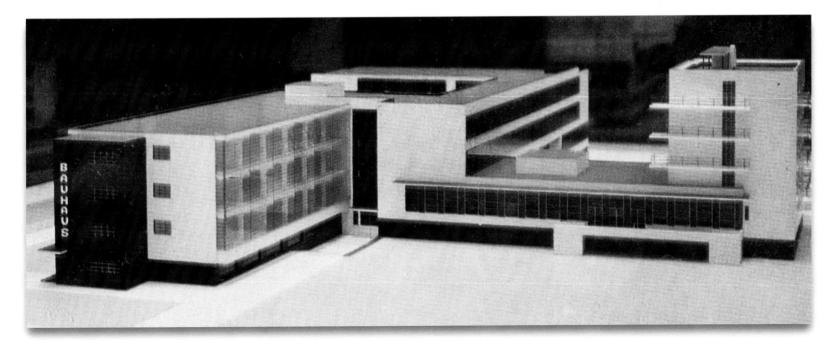

This model shows Walter Gropius's designs for a new Bauhaus building. The school moved from Weimar to Desau in 1925.

Ludwig Mies van der Rohe
German Pavilion, International Exhibition, Barcelona, Spain

1928–29 The Barcelona German Pavilion was built by Mies (1886–1969) as a temporary structure for the International Exhibition of 1929 to represent the cultural values of the Weimar Republic. It expressed perfectly 'clarity, simplicity and honesty', the brief stated by the commissar general of the German Reich, Georg von Schnitzler. In plan, the pavilion is a work of abstract art, with the walls as lines of different thicknesses in a balanced composition. Set on a podium, its structure is a frame of cruciform, chrome-plated columns supporting a delicately thin, concrete roof slab. Other more luxuriant materials – marble and onyx walls, reflective glass and stainless steel – distance the building from the International Style's aesthetic of industrial standardization. Intersecting walls placed at right angles lead one through a sequence of spaces which are neither entirely internal or external, but which form a continuity of partially enclosed rooms and courts. Two rectangular pools add to the atmosphere of calm reflection and act as reflectors for the planar marble walls. The smaller of the pools is enclosed on three sides by travertine walls, and the sculpture of a female figure by Georg Kolbe rises out of the water. Shortly after the exhibition, the pavilion was dismantled, but it was rebuilt in the 1980s following the original plans, although with new materials.

Konstantin Melnikov
Rusakov Workers' Club, Moscow, USSR (now Russia)

1929 In the Soviet Union during the late 1920s, social ideas were translated into architecture. Melnikov (1890–1974), a member of the Association of New Architects (ASNOVA), attempted to create new building types for new social functions. He believed that architecture could be a political force. Another group of architects, the Union of Contemporary Architects (OSA), condemned this idea as bourgeois idealism. The Workers' Club was designed to be a place where workers could go to relax, read books and discuss politics. It was a multipurpose building housing a theatre, library and lounge. The shape of the exterior was dictated by the three sections of the auditoria, which hung out over the back of the building to create a dramatic sculptural form.

Le Corbusier
Villa Savoye, Poissy sur Seine, France

1929–31 The Villa Savoye marked a turning point in the career of Le Corbusier (1887–1965), one of the twentieth century's most influential architects. Located 32 km (20 miles) from Paris, the two-storey house was a weekend retreat for the well-to-do Savoye family. In plan, the house is based on a square grid of 25 slender columns. Set within this are curved volumes enclosing rooms and internal courtyards. At ground level, the landscape enters the undercroft of the house, supported on the grid of columns. The first storey emphasizes the building's overall horizontality, with a row of windows where the floor becomes a gallery open to the sky. A ramp connects the space in three dimensions.

Top: the Rusakov Workers' Club was designed by Konstantin Melnikov as a place where workers could meet and relax. The building housed a theatre, library and lounge.

Bottom: the German Pavilion as seen here is a 1980s reconstruction of a temporary 1920s building. The original was built to house an exhibition.

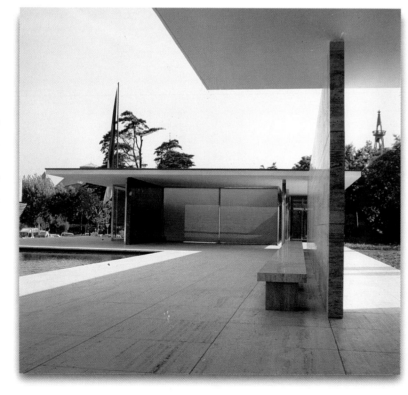

William van Alen
Chrysler Building, New York, New York, USA

1930 In complete contrast to contemporary socialist projects being built in Europe, the Chrysler Building, designed by van Alen (1888–1954) stands as a monument to capitalism. Very much a product of pre-Depression America, it was a celebration of the success of its client and of the free market. Until the early 1930s, the Chrysler Building was the tallest in the world at 259 m (850 ft). But even now that it is dwarfed by the Empire State Building and the twin towers of the World Trade Centre, it remains one of the most elegant skyscrapers on the Manhattan skyline. Tapering off as it reaches its zenith, its height is emphasized by a silvery reflective skin of grey bricks and windows, which rise in vertical shafts. The most distinctive feature is a stylized metal sunburst at the top, with the chevron patterns of the Chrysler logo. Other corporate symbols incorporated as decorations are metal radiator caps with wings, positioned at the corners of the 40th floor, and, alongside, a frieze of abstracted car wheels. Inside, luxuriant materials were intended to give visitors a sense of the wealth of the Chrysler company. The entrance lobby is clad in expensive marbles and red-tinted metals, with dramatic lighting to reinforce the effect, while the lifts are lined with wood and decorated with Chrysler logos.

Sir Edwin Landseer Lutyens
Viceroy's House, New Delhi, India

1930 Larger than Versailles, the Viceroy's House, designed by Lutyens (1869–1944), was the jewel in the crown of the urban master plan for New Delhi. Following some debate about the appropriate architectural expression for the new capital of the Raj, Lutyens's design was chosen as a hybrid of Western classicism and Indian forms from different periods. As such, it was a great success in terms of diplomacy as well as architecure. Architectural references were made not only to Indian culture but also to local climate. So, for example, traditional wide stone ledges were used to shade internal spaces. Warm-coloured sandstone was also in keeping with tradition, although here it formed porticos which associated the building with classical imperialism.

Before the Empire State Building and the World Trade Centre were built, the Chrysler Building was the tallest in the world. Today it is a powerful monument to a bygone era.

in 1932 in the Rockefeller Centre in New York City. Its grand six-storey foyer is perhaps the finest surviving Art Deco space in the world, with two massive cylindrical chandeliers of Lalique glass reflected in floor-to-ceiling mirrors on the walls. A majestic staircase fills the end wall, and the smoking lounge beneath the foyer is decorated in black glass and silver trim.

Alvar Aalto
Municipal Library, Viipuri, Finland

1935 The Viipuri Municipal Library was Aalto's (1898–1976) first major public building commission, won in a competition in 1927. It is one of the most important buildings in the history of Finnish architecture. There were three phases to the library project, which reveal Aalto's transition from Neoclassicism to Functionalism. Aalto did not use the Classical orders as such, but adopted Classical typologies such as proportions and layout of columns. Some of the forms used in the library's last phase – for example, the curved and textured wooden roof – suggest the more 'naturalistic' style Aalto was to adopt later on. In later years, his work was even more heavily influenced by the Finnish climate and local materials, such as timber.

Willem Dudok
Town Hall, Hilversum, Netherlands

1931 Dudok (1884–1974) designed the Town Hall in Hilversum after having been the town's municipal architect for some 15 years. He was strongly influenced by the horizontals and verticals of De Stijl, but his buildings, particularly those in brick like this one, were more massive in form than the architecture of Gerrit Rietveld or Theo van Doesburg. The main feature of the Town Hall was a tall, imposing tower counterbalanced by a darkly shadowed, horizontal row of windows on the ground floor. In the same year, Dudok built the Bijenkorf department store (now demolished) in Rotterdam, which was, by contrast, virtually all glass. Dudok has been criticized for being a Modern-Movement architect who adopted the International Style without understanding its meaning.

Top: Hilversum's impressive town hall was designed by Willem Dudok in a style which owes its origins to the De Stijl movement.

Bottom: Radio City Music Hall could seat 6000 people and was the world's largest indoor theatre. The view here is of its magnificent Art Deco staircase.

Donald Deskey
Radio City Music Hall, Rockefeller Centre, New York, New York, USA

1932 Deskey (1894–1989), a New Yorker, was an important exponent of the modern style. Like many of his successful industrial-design contemporaries, he came from the world of commercial art. In collaboration with other architects, Deskey designed Radio City Music Hall, with 6000 seats the world's largest indoor theatre, which opened

Berthold Lubetkin and Tecton
Highpoint I, London, England

1935 Tecton (founded in 1932), under Lubetkin (1901–1990), was one of the first modern architectural practices in Britain. Lubetkin grew up in Russia during the Revolution and was strongly influenced by Soviet ideas regarding design. After moving to Britain in 1930, he received a commission for the Penguin Pool at London Zoo, which became an icon of modernism. The Highpoint Flats, his next major commission, were built in two stages. Highpoint II was completed in 1938; the earlier Highpoint I expresses most clearly Lubetkin's commitment to modern principles. The eight-storey block was raised on slender columns, with curved elements swinging in and out of the grid. This approach to housing was applied on a broad scale after the Second World War.

Frank Lloyd Wright
Falling Water, Bear Run, Pennsylvania, USA

1937 Falling Water, a country house built by Wright (1869–1959) for the millionaire Edgar Kaufman, would have been impossible without twentieth-century materials and engineering skills. The site, above a waterfall, demanded a radical approach to take advantage of the view and dramatic forces of nature. Wright's solution was to cantilever a series of horizontal concrete trays from a core which seems to merge with an outcrop of rocks above the waterfall. Falling Water has the low horizontality of Wright's earlier Prairie-Style houses, such as the Robie House in Chicago (1910). But that style is given a new meaning and function here. The horizontal layers both act as shelter and allow the walls to take the form of almost invisible glass screens, set back from the edge. The balconies also form a backdrop against which the surrounding birch trees cast their shadows. The chimney, in roughly hewn local stone, contrasts with the smooth finish of the concrete balconies, reflecting the contrast between human and natural forms. Wright thought that modern architecture could bring about the close relationship with nature which he believed was the key to freedom. Inside the house, nature is again ever-present. Shafts of sunlight strike the rooms, and flanks of rock appear to penetrate the floor around the stone chimney.

Frank Lloyd Wright
Johnson Wax Administration Centre, Racine, Wisconsin, USA

1939 Here, Wright (1869–1959) attempted to achieve something entirely different from Falling Water. Instead of working with nature, an ugly urban setting required a whole new approach. Johnson Wax's corporate philosophy imagined the firm as an extended family. Wright's response was to design an inward-looking, windowless building which attempted to bring people together. The administration building was lit

Left: this block of flats in London was one of Britain's first residential buildings in the Modernist style. A sister block, Highpoint II, was built a few years later.

Right: Falling Water, a private house built in the beautiful countryside of Pennsylvania, affords spectacular views over its waterfall.

Frank Lloyd Wright spent the last five years of his life designing and building the Solomon R. Guggenheim Museum. Sadly, he missed its opening – which took place five months after his death.

from above through a glazed ceiling. A grid of slender mushroom columns divided the main space, above which trays were suspended inwards, accommodating the senior management, who could look down on the workers below. From the outside, rounded brick corners gave the building the quality of a fortress, but also echo 1930s design of household objects.

Frank Lloyd Wright
Solomon R. Guggenheim Museum, New York, New York, USA

1943–46, 1956–59 The Guggenheim Museum, which preoccupied Wright (1869–1959) during the last years of his life, eventually opened five months after his death. The design, which was at first extremely controversial, was based on an organic spiral form and realized in in-situ concrete. A metaphor for nature, the spiral is expressed both internally (as a cantilevered ramp) and on the façade as white, outwardly sloping walls. The building, which houses a collection of modern art, has been criticized on the grounds that it does not provide neutral, flat walls on which to hang paintings. On the other hand, the inspirational space created by the spiral forms makes it equal as a work of art to any of the paintings and sculptures housed within it.

Le Corbusier
Unité d'Habitation, Marseilles, France

1947–52 The Unité d'Habitation became a prototype for collective housing which was used by dozens of architects following Le Corbusier (1887–1966). It was also the culmination of years of experimention by this French architect into ways in which architecture could respond to modern society. One issue was how to combine high-density living with light, space and landscape. Le Corbusier thought mass production could provide good-quality housing on a large scale. Within the Unité, there are 23 apartment types to accommodate the varying needs of individuals and families. Each apartment was factory-produced, using different combinations of standardized elements, and was slotted in to the lattice of the structural frame. Inside, spacious, double-height living rooms give good views over Marseilles. An internal glazed street half-way up contains shops, a restaurant and a hotel, while a gym and crèche are expressed as sculptural shapes on the roof. This was seen as an important communal space – a new ground level in the air – featuring a swimming pool and running track. The entire building is raised off the ground on pilotis. Le Corbusier's broader idea (never implemented) was that a series of Unités should be placed around the city, leaving the ground free for greenery and traffic and breaking down traditional distinctions between town and countryside.

Pier Luigi Nervi
Exhibition Halls, Turin, Italy

1949 Nervi (1891–1979), who believed in the unity of art and engineering, based his work on the adage 'Form follows function'. He studied engineering rather than architecture at Bologna and lectured in structural engineering at Rome's School of Architecture. Nervi developed a thesis that the beauty of a structure was as much the outcome of intuition as of calculation. His characteristic material was reinforced concrete, which he mastered creatively and technologically. During the 1940s and '50s, Nervi carried out research on prefabricated concrete using moulds which made complex rib structures possible. The

Le Corbusier's designs became the definitive in collective housing; Unité d'Habitation was one of his foremost designs.

great hall of the exhibition building in Turin spanned 80 m (262 ft) and was made up of prefabricated units which had been moulded in diamond-shaped pans.

Ludwig Mies van der Rohe
Farnsworth House, Plano, Ilinois, USA

1950 This – Mies's (1886–1969) first privately commissioned house in the USA – summed up his expression 'less is more'. In plan, it is elegantly minimal, consisting of two rectangles placed side by side. The smaller one forms a platform connected to the larger living space by a wide flight of steps. This was a practical measure, since the site, on the banks of the River Fox, is liable to flooding. The living space consists of one glass room, shaded by silk curtains and divided by a service core. The structural steel frame is coated with zinc and finished with polished white enamel paint. Absolutely free from fussy details, the beauty of the house lies in its organizing structure, use of materials and proportions.

Le Corbusier
Pilgrimage Chapel of Notre Dame du Haut, Ronchamp, France

1950–54 This chapel was a radical departure from the machine aesthetic of earlier work by Le Corbusier (1887–1966). Irregular in plan, the building is dominated by a curved, concrete roof shaped like the hull of a boat. This is supported on a concrete frame which, from the outside, is concealed within white concrete walls. Inside, it becomes obvious that the walls do not support the roof, since a small gap runs just below the latter, letting in a sharp, bright slit of light. The curved east wall is monumentally thick and pierced by deep-set, coloured-glass windows. This wall extends to a point at the edge of the roof and forms a shelter on the other side for outdoor services.

Skidmore Owings and Merrill
Lever House, New York, New York, USA

1952 Skidmore, Owings and Merrill was founded in 1935, but only became influential after the Second World War, with the completion of the Lever Building. Gordon Bunshaft, who was chief designer, had joined the firm in 1937. This office building represents the commercialization of Mies van der Rohe's glass and metal geometry. Following the Lever House, SOM designed variations on the same theme in Chicago, San Francisco and Portland, and by the end of the 1950s there were imitation office blocks by other architects all round the world. The most distinctive features of the Lever House are the elegant, clean lines of the main vertical supports. These are set back from the outer glass skin to make the main slab look weightless.

Alison and Peter Smithson
Secondary Modern School, Hunstanton, England

1954 Hunstanton school is notable for being the first major commission for the Smithsons (1928–; 1923–), who won it in a competition fresh out of architecture school. It was also the first Brutalist building in Britain. This term referred not to the rough or brutal quality of concrete, as is often assumed, but to the architects' social realism and uncompromising dislike for the English élite. The building was strongly influenced by Mies van der Rohe's Illinois Institute of Technology (1944) and had an expressed steel frame welded on site. It was asymmetrical in plan, with the main two-storey block enclosing two open courtyards. A gymnasium stood alongside in a building of its own, and services, such as a water-tower, were exposed.

Marcel Breuer
UNESCO Headquarters, Paris, France

1958 During the 1920s, Breuer (1902–1981) studied at the Bauhaus, becoming director of the furniture department in 1924. His interest in standardized units led him to look at interior design and, eventually, architecture. After emigrating to the USA during the Second World War, he set up in practice with Walter Gropius and lectured in architecture at Harvard University in Boston, Massachusetts. Breuer's work is distinguished by the clear separation of architectural elements representing the various functions of the building. This approach is evident at the Paris headquarters of UNESCO, where he was selected as one of three architects (the other two were Pier Luigi Nervi and Bernard Louis Zehrfuss). The building consists of an eight-storey, Y-shaped block with a *brise-soleil* and tapered columns.

Opposite: the minimalist design of Ludwig Mies van der Rohe's Farnsworth House echoes the architect's famous axiom: 'less is more'.

Below: the Palais de l'UNESCO was built by three architects: Breuer, Nervi and Zehrfuss. Of these the most famous today is Marcel Breuer.

Ludwig Mies van der Rohe and Philip Johnson

House of Seagram,
New York, New York, USA

1954–58 Built for the gin manufacturers Seagram, this was Mies's (1886–1969) first building in New York City. At the time, it was the largest of its type anywhere in the world, and it soon triggered a phase of skyscraper-building based on the vertical slab. At ground level, a plaza flanked by two symmetrical pools pulls visitors off the street to the entrance, which is marked by a portico and over-hanging slab. The building is raised two storeys above the ground on stilts behind which sit elevator shafts. Materials such as travertine and green marble, rust-coloured bronze and tinted glass added to the prestige of the project. As at Mies's Lake Shore Drive Apartments in Chicago (1951), vertical mullions emphasize the building's height and elegance.

Gio Ponti and Pier Luigi Nervi

Pirelli Centre, Milan, Italy

1959 The finely tapered Pirelli Centre dominates the skyline and street plan around Milan's railway station. The company wanted a technologically advanced building to represent its aspirations for innovation. Engineer Nervi (1891–1979) came up with a double vertebrate structure of spines which gradually taper to a point at the top. Hexagonal in plan, this structure's base only takes up one-seventh of

This building was the creation of two eminent architects: Philip Johnson and Ludwig Mies van der Rohe. It was Mies van der Rohe's first New York building.

the site, being surrounded by an irregularly shaped base at ground level. On the outside, the building is finished in a light-toned metal cladding. The Pirelli building was unusual in not deriving its form from the Miesian glass-and-steel box towers which were rapidly going up in cities around the world at the time.

Louis Kahn
Richards Medical Research Laboratories,
University of Pennsylvania, Philadelphia, USA

1960 Kahn (1901–1974) became a major architectural figure fairly late in his career, in the mid-1950s. The influence of Le Corbusier can be seen in many of his buildings, with their use of monumental forms. At the Richards Medical Research Laboratories, service and stair-towers are expressed as separate sculptural objects in brick, while the interiors are left flexible. In plan, the building is a series of linked boxes, creating a highly modulated façade surrounded by semi-courtyards. Kahn used brick and concrete together to get away from the idea of the building as an impersonal box. The structure is of precast concrete, with joints and fixings emphasized as if to reflect the technical nature of the work going on inside.

Eero Saarinen and Associates
TWA Terminal Building,
Kennedy International Airport,
New York, New York, USA

1961 Eero Saarinen (1910–1961) began his career in partnership with his father, Eliel. In 1947, he won a competition to build the Jefferson National Expansion Memorial at St Louis, Missouri. His design was a monument 192 m (631 ft) high made of stainless steel. The expressive curve and aviation technology evoked in this work are also clear at the TWA Terminal. With its free-flowing concrete forms, it shows how technology can create dynamic, fluid spaces expressing the excitement and grace of flight. The

roof is made up of four intersecting barrel vaults supported on Y-shaped buttresses. Inside, features such as staircases and information boards are consistent with the shape of the roof, taking on forms which are almost science fiction-like.

Kenzo Tange
Olympic Sports Halls, Tokyo, Japan

1964 These two sports halls by Tange (1913–), which together seat 19,000 people, were designed for the 1964 Tokyo Olympiad and are probably the architect's most exciting works. The shapes are geometric, the smaller one being based on a circle and the larger an ellipse in plan. Both have concave suspension roofs which form great swooping curves and are suspended from cables anchored in concrete. A vast sloping walkway links the two buildings. Light enters the main sports hall through an elliptical opening in the roof ridge. Although the structure is technologically sophisticated, it echoes traditional Japanese architecture in its detailing. For example, the forked arms of the concrete masts allude to the crossed rafters of traditional Shinto shrines.

The two buildings in the centre here were designed for Japan's 1964 Olympics. They are linked by a walkway and can accommodate 19,000 people between them.

R. Buckminster Fuller
US Pavilion, EXPO 67, Montreal, Canada

This impressive dome was part of Canada's World Fair, held in Montreal in May 1967. Fuller's design was an important leap forward in environmental architecture.

1967 This 65-m (200-ft)-high geodesic dome was Fuller's (1895–1983) great contribution to the 1967 world exhibition and to modern architecture. The dome was a prototype for what he called an 'environmental valve', enclosing an entire community in a controlled atmosphere. The structure consisted of triangular elements on the outside, connected to an inner layer of hexagonal elements. A transparent skin of plastic was wrapped around the outside. The dome was one of the world's first 'green' buildings and expressed Fuller's aspiration to use technology to minimize resource use and protect the environment. Once the structure had been patented in 1954, 300,000 geodesic domes were built around the world over the next 30 years, accommodating a huge range of functions, from sports arenas to housing. Like Pier Luigi Nervi, Fuller did not train as an architect, although his ideas had a profound effect on architectural practice. His other highly influential work was the Dymaxion House (1929), an early example of prefabricated housing based on the principle that by reducing the weight of a house, you could lower its cost. Again a prototype, the house was featured widely in the press as the dwelling of the future. During the Second World War, Fuller was enlisted by the US government to develop lightweight, temporary steel housing to accommodate aircrew.

James Stirling
History Faculty Library, University of Cambridge, England

Jørn Utzon
Opera House, Sydney, Australia

1968 The History Faculty Library commission at Cambridge University was won by Stirling (1926–1992) as the result of a limited competition. The library reading room is housed in a fan-shaped room, covered by a conservatory-like glass roof, which leans on an L-shaped block housing teaching rooms and offices. This radial plan suggests that the space can be surveyed from a single, central point. The roof above the reading room consists of a system of elegant steel trusses supporting a double layer of factory patent glazing as protection from heat and cold. Stirling, who thought that glass buildings were 'appropriate to the English climate', designed a similar sloping glass wall at the Florey Building, student residences at Queen's College, Oxford (1971).

1973 Utzon's Sydney Opera House was the product of a competition won in 1956, nearly 20 years before the building was actually completed. Despite Utzon (1918–) resigning as architect before completion, it remains one of the world's most dramatic, beautiful buildings. Born in Denmark, Utzon worked for Gunnar Asplund and Alvar Aalto before travelling the world and winning the opera-house competition, his first major commission. His design is distinguished by the roof, a series of interlocking shells which stand on a podium surrounded by Sydney Harbour. Each of these segments is generated from a single sphere, an approach which Utzon described as 'additive architecture'. The shells are made from cast-in-situ and prefabricated concrete. The ribs of the

The spectacular Opera House which greets visitors to Sydney Harbour was designed to create the illusion of breaking waves, a fitting complement to its surroundings.

fan vaulting, also concrete, are clad in ceramic tiles, which are positioned to emphasize the roof curves and shimmer with reflected light. The main concert hall seats 2900, with a separate opera house accommodating another 1547. Instead of being lowered from fly towers, the scenery is raised from beneath the main stage, which means that the usual bulk is avoided. When Utzon resigned from the project in 1966, many of the interior details had not been decided, and it is likely that his own resolution of those aspects of the design would have been very different.

Aldo Rossi

Gallaratese apartment block,
Milan, Italy

1976 The Gallaratese apartment block stands in contrast to many housing schemes of the 1970s, a time when a backlash against modernism made the vernacular popular. Cottage-style hipped roofs were thought to be what people wanted, but Rossi's (1931–1997) solution for urban housing could not have been more different. This apartment block consists of a stark, linear white block raised off the ground on a gallery of columns. Square windows, the same width as the spaces between the columns, run in a continuous grid along the length of the block. Often described as a 'neo-rationalist', Rossi explains his designs in his book *L'Architettura della citta* (1966), where he sets out the case for a set of urban architectural types.

Paris's world-famous Pompidou Centre opened in 1977. In its first year, it attracted six million visitors.

Renzo Piano and Richard Rogers
Pompidou Centre, Paris, France

1977 Surrounded by historic buildings in Paris's Beauborg district, the Pompidou Centre designed by Piano (1937–) and Rogers (1933–) provoked outrage but also admiration when it was built: it was visited by six million people in its first year. The building is famous for being 'inside-out', with its services revealed and emphasized in bright colours on its exterior. This was also a practical measure, since it left the interior space free and open. Circulation routes were pushed to the outside, with escalators contained in an enormous transparent glass tube stepping up diagonally along the building's length. The main structure is a steel frame set back from the façade to give a feeling of lightness, emphasized by diagonal steel tie-rods for cross-bracing.

Aldo van Eyck
Hubertus House, Amsterdam, Netherlands

1980 Van Eyck (1918–) attempted to introduce human scale into the social utopianism of pre-war architecture. His design for an orphanage near Amsterdam (1962) scaled down the conventional idea of institutional building by breaking the space up into clusters of small pavilions combined with private courtyards. His later home for single parents and their children, Hubertus House, uses colour and transparency to create what he described as a small-scale 'kaleidescope' city. On the façade, the metal frame is brightly painted to indicate the different functions, while internally, coloured surfaces are painted to contrast and activate the space. Hubertus House shows the influence of De Stijl, but also breaks away from it by using unconventional colours such as orange and purple.

Michael Graves
Public Service Building, Portland, Oregon, USA

1983 Post-modernism was a significant, though now discredited, trend in architecture which emerged in the 1970s and '80s. The Portland building, designed by Graves (1934–), shows how Post-modernism coincided with a surge in the construction of commercial architecture which used Classical motifs almost as a marketing ploy to attract clients. This building is essentially a box with a curtain wall (where the façade is not structural, but is suspended from a frame). An enormous coloured keystone was rendered on to the stone cladding, and rustication was stencilled on to the blocks around the base. This Classical language was intended to evoke civic values, but in reality it became a convenient decorative device which was used superficially on dozens of commercial office developments during the boom of the 1980s.

Foster Associates
Hong Kong and Shanghai Bank, Hong Kong

1986 The work of Norman Foster (1935–), in particular this building, demonstrates how architecture has completely embraced technology and engineering during the twentieth century, a style known as high-tech. The structure of the Hong Kong and Shanghai Bank is revealed for all to see, with its distinctive 'coat-hanger' trusses from which eight storeys of offices are suspended. The trusses hang off vertical mast towers of which there are also eight, positioned in a grid. Internally, a 12-storey atrium is flooded with natural light from a glazed end wall, and escalators fan out diagonally from the ground floor, reinforcing the sense of movement and dynamism. The offices were planned to give the maximum number of occupants views and to keep the space open and transparent.

The Hong Kong and Shanghai Bank in Hong Kong was built in 1986. Its design adhered strongly to Feng Shui specifications and principles.

London's Lloyds Building is a celebration of industrial aesthetic architecture. Its design, with a steel structure and many floors, was created to look like a complicated machine.

Richard Rogers and Partners
Lloyds Building, London, England

1986 Another example of high-tech architecture is the Lloyds Building, designed by Rogers (1933–) and his firm, which looks more like a complicated machine than a building. This is a celebration of the industrial aesthetic, with its service ducts and lift shafts exposed on the outside in shiny stainless steel. Blue cranes, which are used for cleaning, are poised on the roof, making the building look almost as if it were still under construction. Cellular rooms clad in steel are 'clipped' on to the side, with port holes stamped out of the cladding. In the centre is a tall atrium topped with an arch made from a steel framework. This casts light down into the centre of the building where escalators connect the floors through a single space.

Tadao Ando
Church-on-the-water, Tomamu, Japan

1988 The architecture of Ando (1941–) provides a spiritual escape from what the architect saw as the materialism and consumerism of late twentieth-century society. The Church-on-the-water uses simple, cheap materials like polished concrete, but in such a way as to make them seem expensive. For Ando, nature is as important a building element as actual materials. As he put it, 'Architecture differentiates nature, and also integrates nature'. At the church, water and the surrounding hillsides enter the building visually through the structural frame, which is open on one side. Ando developed this approach on a later project, the Chikatsu-Asuka Historical Museum at Minami-Kawachi near Osaka (1994), where ascending platforms form an extension of the hillside.

I. M. Pei
Glass Pyramid, The Louvre, Paris, France

1989 The Glass Pyramid at the Louvre designed by Pei (1917–) was one of a series of 'grands projects' commissioned by François Mitterrand, former president of France. This programme of state-financed buildings contrasted greatly with the privatization of culture underway in Britain and the USA at the time. Completion of the Glass Pyramid coincided with the Bicentennial of the French Revolution and formed a new starting

Completion of the Louvre's Glass Pyramid coincided with the Bicentennial of the French Revolution of 1789.

point for the grand axis of the Champs Elysées, Arc de Triomphe and Grande Arche de la Défense (also completed in 1989). With its bold geometry and glass details, the pyramid was a controversial addition to the Louvre, but is now seen as a successful example of how modern buildings can be fused with historic ones.

Renzo Piano
Kansai International Airport Terminal, Osaka, Japan

1994 Kansai International Airport Terminal, along with the Great Wall of China, is one of two man-made structures which are discernible from space. A collaboration between engineer Peter Rice and architect Piano (1937–), it is built on an artificial island and connected to the mainland by a 5-km (3-mile) bridge. Three mountains had to be flattened to provide enough material to dump in Osaka Bay to build up the island. The terminal building is 1.6 km (1 mile) long and took at least 10,000 workers three years to build. However, it is not simply a feat of modern engineering; it is a most elegant structure which expresses the movement and weightlessness of flying. The most distinctive feature of the building is its curved roof, made up of 90,000 stainless-steel panels. Being located in a typhoon zone, the roof and its supporting structure have to allow for wind and thermal movement. Computers control hydraulics,

Kansai International Airport Terminal, together with the Great Wall of China, are the only two man-made structures discernible from space.

which continually adjust the position of the 900 supporting columns; expansion joints between the outer skin and structure allow for additional movement. A linear plan makes efficient use of runway and taxiing space, and huge areas of glazing give the interior space natural light, which helps passengers find their way around.

Frank Gehry
Guggenheim Museum, Bilbao, Spain

1997 The Guggenheim Museum in Bilbao, designed by Gehry (1929–), is the most developed of his 'cubist' buildings. It uses interpenetrating forms similar to those at his Disney Concert Hall in Los Angeles (1989) and Vitra Design Museum in Germany (1987), but on a far more impressive scale. The computer programme used to design Mirage jets mapped the building's curved walls and provided detailed construction plans. Titanium cladding was employed on the exterior, appropriately reflecting Bilbao's gritty industrial past, but also glistening beautifully in both sunlight and rain. Inside, the central feature comprises an atrium and three floors of galleries. The Guggenheim was the centrepiece of a regeneration programme for Bilbao that included projects by Foster, Santiago Calatrava and Cesar Pelli.

Richard Meier
The Getty Centre, Los Angeles, California, USA

1997 The Getty Centre houses a museum, four research institutes, several restaurants, a bookshop, a 450-seat auditorium and a 750,000-volume library. This huge, billion-dollar complex towers above the smog of Los Angeles in the Santa Monica Mountains. The overall effect of the secluded site and sensitive landscaping makes the centre a place of escape from the city and provides a sense of calm that is reinforced by Meier's (1934–) design for the complex. In characteristic style, he used white steel cladding and the neutral tones of travertine marble to reinforce the monumentality of the place. A state-of-the-art lift resembling a white tram takes visitors up to the site, on its way providing breathtaking views of the city below.

Interior design

2

THE INTERIOR OF A BUILDING SHOULD COMPLEMENT ITS EXTERIOR AND MANY FAMOUS ARCHITECTS, SUCH AS CHARLES RENNIE MACKINTOSH, HECTOR GUIMARD AND WALTER GROPIUS, INSISTED ON OVERSEEING BOTH ASPECTS. EXAMPLES OF INTERIORS BY THESE DESIGNERS AND OTHERS SHOW HOW THE CAREFUL USE OF LIGHT, COLOUR, SPACE AND TEXTURE CAN ENHANCE THE EXPERIENCE OF THE INSIDE OF A BUILDING.

Carlo Bugatti
Snail Room, Turin Exhibition, Italy

1902 Bugatti (1855–1940), an Italian furniture designer, was one of the chief exponents of Art Nouveau. Although trained as an architect, he soon turned to furniture design and interiors, exhibiting his first pieces at the 1888 Italian Exhibition in London. Bugatti's interpretation of Art Nouveau was unique, drawing on a mix of Hispano-Moresque architectural influences and painted with Japanese motifs and other exotic details. Bugatti's Snail Room showcased his striking modernity; the furniture designs were characterized by an unbroken sweep from their pierced, circular back-rests downwards and by their short legs and flat, circular seats. The pale beige vellum covering resembled plastic, a material which would only become popular 50 years later. Throughout his interior design work, Bugatti used rich materials such as ivory, mother-of-pearl and metal inlays and trim. Simultaneously, he used such primitive elements as rawhide thongs and rough geometric carving.

Henry van de Velde
Folkwang Museum, Hagen, Germany

1902 The Belgian Henry van de Velde (1863–1957) began his career as a painter, but in 1895 turned to decorative arts, design and architecture. Van de Velde's early decorative work in Germany, where he moved in 1899, brought some of the extravagance of Belgian Art Nouveau to that country, but by 1902, in his interiors for the Folkwang Museum, the style's biomorphic forms had solidified and become monumental. Van de Velde castigated the eclecticism of nineteenth-century interiors in his *Formule d'une esthetique moderne*, placing the emphasis on the interplay of curved lines and empty spaces. His works have an almost medieval logic and solidity, despite their flowing lines. Van de Velde produced chairs upholstered in tapestry to his own design, stained-glass screens and windows, tables, bookcases, desks, divans, furnishing fabrics and decorative metalwork, all of which show a graceful blending of contemporary influences.

Overleaf: Charles Rennie Mackintosh designed the interiors for Kate Cranston's Willow Tea Rooms in Scotland (see page 41).

Right: Bugatti was renowned for his ornate pieces which used materials such as ivory, mother of pearl and metal inlays and trims.

Opposite: these beautifully wrought panels in the Willow Tea Rooms show Charles Rennie Mackintosh's characteristic use of organic motifs, such as flowers.

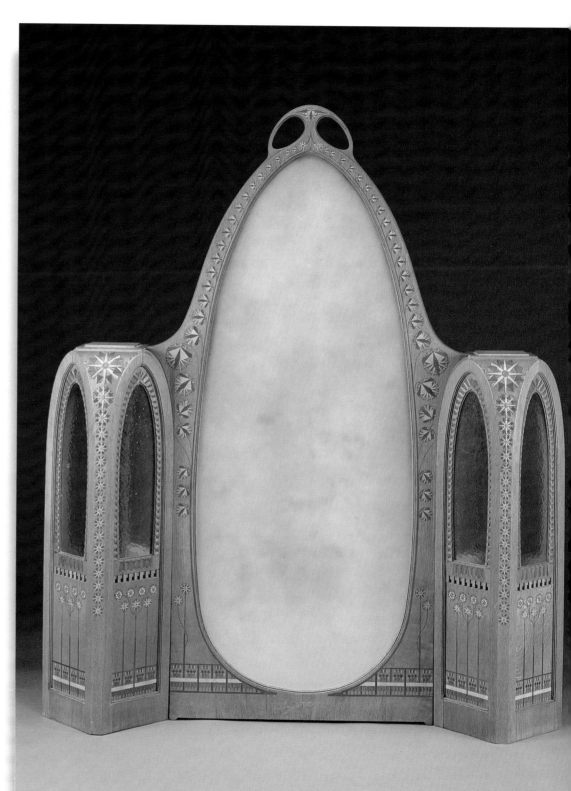

Charles Rennie Mackintosh
Hill House

1902–3 Hill House gave Mackintosh (1868–1928) the opportunity to create an integrated external and internal design; its interiors are, even today, a remarkable achievement. He used stencils throughout in order to establish a harmonious scheme within the interior, and this scheme was repeated around the room and echoed in the patterning of the window-seat upholstery and the gesso panel and embroidered decoration created by his wife, Margaret Macdonald. In the hallway of Hill House, Mackintosh's chequerboard squares are softened by curves and tendrils which are repeated in the carpets. The ensemble was completed by specially designed furniture, wallpapers, carpets and glassware, all of which worked together to present the ultimate manifestation of his artistic vision.

Charles Rennie Mackintosh
Willow Tea Rooms, Glasgow, Scotland

1903–4 The Willow Tea Rooms became the showpiece for Mackintosh's (1868–1928) considerable design talent. The interior, from the signboards and menus to the furniture and light fittings, was designed as a complete work of art. Mackintosh designed the wall decorations, the furniture and the carpets and even decided upon the appropriate cutlery and dress for staff. An exquisite chandelier in the form of a hanging basket of flowers lit up the centre of the main dining room. For the ground floor, Mackintosh designed the 'Willow Tea Room chair'; essentially a stylized interpretation of a willow tree, which was to act both as a chair and as a space divider. Resplendent stained-glass doors were set in the entrance, and the walls were decorated with Mackintosh's familiar rose motif and other natural forms.

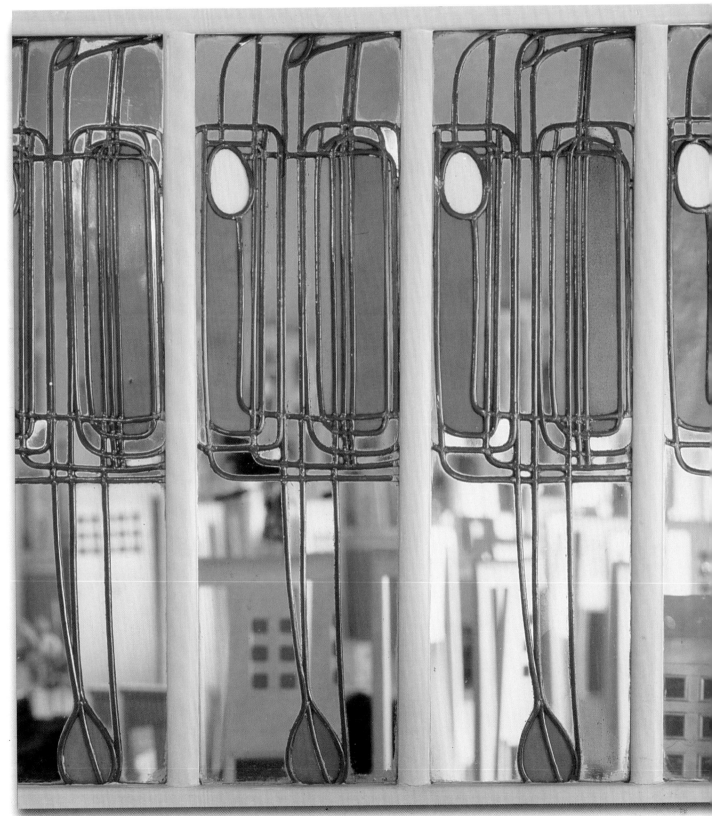

Louis Comfort Tiffany
leaded glass and bronze chandelier

1904 Tiffany (1848–1933) was the most notable American exponent of Art Nouveau. Although he is renowned for his stained and iridescent glass, his accomplishments ranged from painting, architecture and interior design to work in mosaic and jewellery. Tiffany's interest in the Arts-and-Crafts Movement led him to found the decorating firm of Louis C. Tiffany and Associated Artists in 1881; within a year, the company had become enormously successful. Tiffany designed interiors for the White House (1882–83) and for New York City theatres, clubs and private homes. In 1904, he built a palatial summer home, Laurelton Hall, on Long Island. Its style was Islamic-inspired Art Nouveau, with motifs gathered from Tiffany's 1868 journey to North Africa, a trip which had a lasting influence on his work. The villa's steel-frame construction and glass-panelled walls were architectural and stylistic innovations.

Hector Guimard
cast iron fireplace surround

c. 1904 Guimard (1867–1942) was the foremost French Art Nouveau architect and designer. He believed that a work of architecture should synthesize many arts and achieve a unity of external appearance and interior

This leaded glass and bronze chandelier, titled 'Alamander', was created in the studios of Louis Comfort Tiffany, perhaps the most famous of all Art Nouveau artists.

design. His work was often described as 'abstract naturalism', drawing its inspiration from organic forms without reproducing them faithfully, as can be seen to great effect in the fireplace surround illustrated here. Starting with the Castel Beranger apartment building in Paris (1894–95), he designed, constructed and furnished a series of projects that constitute his finest work. These also include the Humbert de Romans concert hall (1897–1901), the Jassede apartments (1903–5) and, finally, his own house (1909–10). One of Guimard's most spectacular designs is the Ville Flore (1909), an exclusive block of flats in Paris, representative of an integrated interior and exterior, infused with the bulbous and swelling character of a natural growth, modelled brick surfaces and iron details.

McKim, Mead and White
club interiors, New York, USA

1918 The firm of McKim, Mead and White was one of the largest and most influential American architectural firms around the turn of the twentieth century. Charles Follen McKim (1847–1909), William Rutherford Mead (1846–1928) and Stanford White (1853–1906) went into partnership in New York City in 1879, first designing houses and then, at the end of the 1880s, developing an elegant and historically precise classical style, which they complemented with sumptuous interior decoration. Their first work in this style was the Boston Public Library (1887–92), followed by such notable works as the University Club (1899–1900) and the Pierpont Morgan Library (1906) in New York City, all variations on Renaissance themes. In 1918, the firm designed the palace-like Racquet Club in New York. Every detail of the interior design was carefully considered in relation to the whole, and, as was the firm's trademark, no expense was spared.

Armand-Albert Rateau
interiors for Jeanne Lanvin, Paris, Francis

1920s The French furniture and interior designer Rateau (1882–1938) developed a traditional but distinctly personal style which both personified the Art Deco era and led to new developments in style and design in the 1920s and '30s. Among his most important commissions were the Blumethal family residences in Paris, Grasse and Passy, and Jeanne Lanvin's apartment in the rue Barbet-de-Jouy. There, Rateau decorated the bathroom and bedroom in Lanvin-blue silk embroidered with yellow and white roses, animals,

Guimard believed that architecture should be complemented by its interiors. His work has been described as 'abstract naturalism'.

pheasants and palm trees, themes he reproduced as mounts in the furniture. Rateau participated in the 1925 Paris Exhibition and, the following year, in a retrospective which toured eight American museums. In the second half of the 1920s, he completed interiors for the Duchess of Alba and Baron Eugène de Rothschild. Rateau's style was distinctive, with pheasants, butterflies and acanthus used as recurring themes.

Walter Gropius
Director's Office, Bauhaus, Weimar, Germany

1923 Gropius (1883–1969) was one of the pioneers of modern design in architecture. His ideas were furthered by his own work and through the famous Bauhaus design school, which he founded at Weimar in 1919. Gropius's most significant belief was that all design should be approached without reference to previous forms or styles. At the Bauhaus, he aimed to introduce a radical form of design education that would equip students with the skills and insight necessary for life in the new industrial society, and every aspect of the Bauhaus itself achieved these aims. Gropius's own office is perhaps the best example of early Bauhaus ideology, with light fittings inspired by industrial models and simple, geometric furniture suitable for mass production. The floorboards were bare except for rugs made by students, and the whole appearance was one of functional, almost technological elegance.

Gerrit Thomas Rietveld
Schröder House, Utrecht, Netherlands

1923–24 A leading member of De Stijl and a contributor to the group's magazine, Rietveld (1888–1964) created his principal work in the area of architecture and interior design. The Schröder House's interpenetrating white, grey and coloured planes formed a virtual three-dimensional translation of the paintings of Piet Mondrian. The interiors continued the same aesthetic themes, with details like the light fixtures or the glass stair-casing integrated with the building's overall style and proportions. Considerable attention was given to small touches such as ledges, stairs, shelves and window mullions. Details inside and out were themselves like small models of the whole and were fashioned to reveal the underlying form. The Schröder House was a total work of art, in which fixtures and overall form were consistent expressions of the same idea, and in which painting, sculpture, architecture and applied arts were all fused.

Ruhlmann designed furniture pieces, such as these, in his own workshop. He was one of the original exponents of Art Deco.

André Groult
Woman's Bedroom, Paris Exhibition, France

1925 Groult (1884–1967) is widely recognized as a key exponent of Art Deco. His reputation rests mainly on the Woman's Bedroom which he exhibited in the French Ambassador pavilion at the 1925 Paris Exhibition. Its *bombé* chest of drawers, veneered in *galuchat* with ivory banding, became one of the talking points of the Exhibition. The other furniture, created from *galuchat*, ebony and velour upholstery, imparted a sense of both elegance and femininity. The room established Groult as a successful interior designer, and he became known for his luxuriant wall coverings, draperies and upholstery materials in printed silk, cotton, damask, brocade and brocatelle, which, together with his rugs and lamps, complemented his lavish interiors so outstandingly.

Paul Poiret and Martine
barges at the Quai de la Seine, Paris, France

1925 Poiret (1879–1944), the leading Paris couturier from 1908 to 1925, entered the field of interior design with his Martine School and was inspired by Léon Bakst in particular, creating a wide range of designs for textiles – carpets, wallpapers and upholstery fabrics – which were spectacular and widely copied. In the 1920s, he went on to create, through his Martine Studio, pianos, lampshades, cushions, vitrines and

lacquered and marquestry tables. For the 1925 Paris Exhibition, Poiret captured the limelight with his three barges – *Amrous, Délices* and *Orgues* – moored in front of the Quai de la Seine. They were fitted with plush interiors and, in *Orgues*, 14 steam-dyed wall-hangings executed by Raoul Dufy, who had worked exclusively for the Martine Studio until 1912. By 1925, Poiret's heyday had passed, but his designs for the Exhibition provided testimony to his brilliance.

Jacques-Emile Ruhlmann
furniture

c. 1925 Ruhlmann (1879–1933) was among the most famous of the French Art Deco designers, producing sumptuous interiors throughout the 1920s and '30s. He designed carpets, furniture and textiles in his own workshop, using the modified Classicism which came to be known as Art Deco. One of his designs, for the Grand Salon of a Collector, was acclaimed at the Decorative Arts Exhibition in 1925 in Paris. Working within a palette of rich and expensive materials, he achieved his effects by the use of traditional craft techniques. The luxurious interior is focused around a salon with a bedroom, boudoir and dining room. The furniture was produced from rare woods, such as walnut and ebony.

Alvar Aalto
plywood reclining armchair

1929–33 Born in Finland, Hugo Alvar Henrik Aalto (1898–1976) was one of the major architects of the twentieth century. Aalto's greatest contribution was his considerable gift for humanizing the tenets of the Bauhaus and other exponents of the International Style. Aalto won international fame through his design of a tuberculosis sanatorium in Paimio. The six-storey convalescent buildings are screened from the staff quarters and sited so that maximum sunlight falls on the balconies. Aalto designed this famous plywood reclining armchair as part of the scheme; the pitch of the chair was calculated to assist breathing and maximize the sunlight which fell on patients' bodies. Inside the building, Aalto used natural materials which reflected his interest in the need for a humane aesthetic. These interiors were meant to reject the mechanical slickness which was then in vogue in the USA in favour of more lasting natural or 'human' themes.

Aalto designed this chair as an aid to tuberculosis sufferers: to ease breathing and help the patient obtain maximum sunlight from the seated position.

René Lalique
interiors for SS Normandie

1931–35 Lalique's (1860–1945) sleek, stylized formulations exerted a profound influence on his contemporaries, and his ideas were to affect glass design for many years. His innovative lighting fixtures were particularly influential in interior decoration. In his wall and ceiling lights, angular pieces of etched and frosted glass concealed the sources of illumination, and chandeliers were decorated with plant and animal forms or designed to suggest fountains and jets of water. Lalique's most famous single commission was the palatial first-class dining salon of the SS *Normandie*, the flagship of the French transatlantic passenger fleet. For this project, he designed decorative panels, light fixtures, illuminated ceilings and a wealth of other accessories, all made of glass and inlaid to present a sense of overwhelming opulence. Among Lalique's other well-known commissions was a dining room created in glass for Sèvres in France.

Frank Lloyd Wright
Johnson Wax Administration Centre, Racine, Wisconsin, USA

1936–39 Wright (1867–1959) was one of the most innovative figures in modern architecture. In his radical designs, as in his writings, he championed the virtues of what he termed organic architecture, a building style based on natural forms. Wright emphasized that spaces within buildings should be animated by natural light allowed to travel across textured surfaces as the incidence of sunlight and moonlight changed. His Johnson Wax Administrative Centre was a prime example of his unique modern approach to interiors. Wright employed a variety of themes, including an intimate interior enclosed by a skin-like wall, and made great use of curves in a streamlined, rolling design. Distinctive mushroom-shaped columns supported the glass ceiling. The walls were periodically broken by narrow seams of Pyrex glass, bringing natural light into the interior. As with most of his previous projects, Wright was responsible for all the interior fixtures and fittings.

As well as being the architect of the Johnson Wax Building, Frank Lloyd Wright also designed all the internal fixtures and fittings.

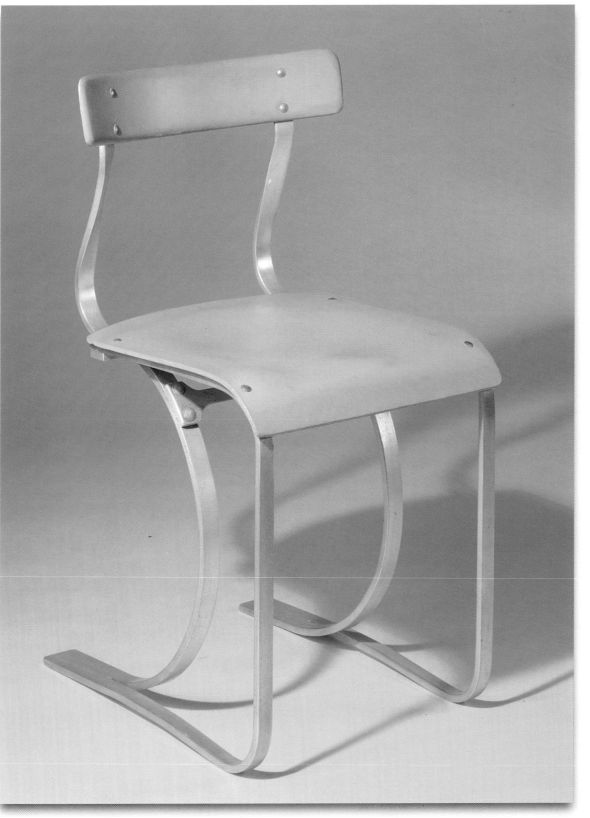

Marcel Breuer
S-shaped chair

1937 The Hungarian Marcel Lajos Breuer (1902–1981) was among the most important figures in twentieth-century architecture and design. Breuer became a student at the newly established Bauhaus in Germany in 1920, but left in 1928 to establish an independent architectural practice in Berlin, later working closely with Walter Gropius at Harvard University in Cambridge, Massachusetts. The overwhelming characteristic of his designs was the development of sculptural concrete forms and walls emphasizing solidity, pattern and the play of sunlight and shadow; he also built furniture to complement his architectural designs, such as this S-shaped chair. His own house, built and decorated in a contemporary New England style, combined ideas derived from collective experiments of the 1920s with curious rustic intrusions like a wall of local rubble. Compared with the taut Machine-Age designs of a decade earlier, there was a considerable mellowness, in both the use of colour and the manipulation of natural light.

Carlo Mollino
Casa Devalle

1939–40 The Italian designer Carlo Mollino (1905–1973) was inspired by Antonio Gaudí and Alvar Aalto, and his designs for buildings, interiors and furniture continue to be influential. Mollino based his artistic vision on the modernist idea

This S-shaped chair was designed by Marcel Breuer, one of the most famous of the Bauhaus designers. It was manufactured by the Embru company.

of opening up the interior space of a home, but unlike his contemporaries, he did not use objects as sculpture or for their geometrical forms. Instead, he filled his spaces with curving, luxurious textures and surfaces in the form of curtains, cushions, screens and padded furniture. Casa Devalle is one of Mollino's most important commissions, and the bedroom in particular was designed to provide the ultimate sensual experience: industrial doors and walls combine with sensual textures, flowing fabrics and mirrors. His interiors extend the theme of the body, for which Mollino had an overwhelming fascination, exploring open, curving space and the idea of organic movement.

Charles Eames
Eames House, Venice, California, USA

1949 The versatile American architect and designer Charles Eames (1907–1978) was best known for his utilitarian, mass-produced furniture and a range of other design projects. Eames began his career as an architect in St Louis, Missouri, and later taught at the Cranbrook Academy of Art in Bloomfield Hills, Michigan. In 1941, he won first prize in a furniture design competition at the Museum of Modern Art in New York City, with designs using plywood shells moulded in multiple curves; this innovation enhanced the furniture's sculptural qualities while greatly increasing its strength. Eames's own house and studio near Los Angeles was an important post-war architectural and interior design landmark. Inexpensive, mass-produced materials – in particular, prefabricated factory components – were used throughout in a remarkably restrained and simple design. The overall style recalled Japanese domestic architecture but avoided the severity of the International Style.

Henri Matisse
Dominican Chapel of the Rosary, Vence, France

1950s Matisse (1869–1954) ranks amongst the greatest painters of the twentieth century, also excelling at sculpture, illustration, graphics and set design. He developed a radical new approach to colour, using it in a structural rather than a descriptive way. After flirting with Fauvism, Matisse never again belonged to any identifiable school or movement. His final masterpiece, completed when he was more than 80 years old, was the decoration of the Dominican Chapel of the Rosary in Vence, near Nice in southern France, a picturesque little town where the artist had owned a villa from 1943 to 1948. Matisse began the project by agreeing to do some stained-glass windows. He then went on to do murals and ended up by designing nearly everything inside and out, including vestments and liturgical objects. Today, the chapel is one of the main tourist attractions near the Riviera.

setting for Warhol's infamous parties. The fundamental concept of the Factory was to serve the Pop lifestyle of the 1960s, pioneering the reclamation of industrial space and the idea of interior design as art installation. Name, who documented, organized and contributed ideas for the Factory, was particularly known for the 'cow' wallpaper he designed. He covered the walls of the Factory in silver foil, a feature celebrated by Warhol, who believed in the concept of 'anti-design', meant to contradict the lavish interiors for which New York was then famous. The silver interior of the Factory has become synonymous with the spirit of Pop design.

Arne Jacobsen
Danish National Bank, Copenhagen, Denmark

1971 The Danish architect Arne Jacobsen produced some of the most elegant and meticulous buildings in modern Scandinavia. Initially influenced by Gunnar Asplund, Jacobsen began as an architect of private houses and later turned to public commissions. The tradition of Scandinavian craftsmanship evident in the details of his buildings is also apparent in his designs for furniture and household articles. Jacobsen's Danish National Bank interior is one of his last works; completed seven years after his death, it is emblematic of his mature genius. The building is enclosed by two glass façades stretched between two gables. The lobby, which is 25 m (82 ft) high, extends through all six storeys, and the walls and floor are covered in Norwegian Porsgrunn marble. The style reflects Jacobsen's unique blend of Danish vernacular and Continental modernism.

Ludwig Mies van der Rohe
interiors for the Seagram Building, New York, New York, USA

1956–58 The German architect Ludwig Mies van der Rohe (1886–1969), one of the principal founders of modern architecture and design, created a number of starkly beautiful glass and steel buildings which have made his name synonymous with the functionalist aesthetic of twentieth-century design. Perhaps the most spectacular of all Mies's high-rise structures is the Seagram Building in New York City, a 38-storey tower clad in bronze and bronze-tinted glass, which he designed in collaboration with the distinguished American architect Philip Johnson. The Seagram Building is recognized as a masterpiece of American corporate architecture and design. The interiors were designed to complete the overall vision, with the external features repeated in the glass and bronze furnishings and decorative scheme.

Tadao Ando
Kidosaki House, Tokyo, Japan

1982–86 One of the foremost architects and designers in Japan, Ando (1941–) was the 18th winner of the Pritzker Prize, the highest honour accorded to the world's architect. Ando is self-taught, and most of his buildings have been built in Japan. His favourite construction material is a smoothly finished concrete, which he uses to produce simple and starkly geometric forms. The austerity of his work results in structures which seem to be imbued with a grace and spirituality felt most strongly in the many religious buildings he has designed. Ando's Kidosaki House, which provides space for three families, is a typical example of his philosophy. The interior uses light to articulate form, reflecting both modern design and the traditional Japanese way of life. One of the key themes in Ando's interiors is a rejection of the chaos of modern living to create haven-like interiors, often hidden away by walls.

Billy Name
The Factory, New York, New York, USA

1964 Billy Name (Billy Linich; 1940–) was a fringe figure at the Factory, Andy Warhol's famous New York studio. This converted Manhattan warehouse served as both film set and studio, as well as providing the

Opposite: this is the house of the noted architect-designer Charles Eames. He was best known for his utilitarian, mass-produced furniture.

Left: the celebrated twentieth-century artist Henri Matisse decorated the Dominican Chapel of the Rosary, in southern France, as his last great work.

Garden
& Urban
Landscape
3
design

FROM THE DYNAMIC URBAN LANDSCAPING OF
ANTONIO GAUDI TO THE ELEGANT GARDEN
DESIGNS OF SIR EDWIN LUTYENS, THE WORLD
OF LANDSCAPE PLANNING AND GARDEN DESIGN
IS ONE RICH IN POSSIBILITIES AND HISTORY.
THIS CHAPTER LOOKS AT CAREFULLY PLANNED
TOWN SCHEMES AS WELL AS SOME OF THE
WORLD'S MOST BEAUTIFUL GARDENS.

William Robinson
Gravetye Manor, Sussex, England

1885–1935 Robinson became a gardener at an early age, working at the Royal Botanic Gardens in Regents Park, London, from 1861. His work expressed a reaction against Victorian garden practice in favour of 'wild gardening', in which natural woodland, mixed borders and naturalized bulbs replaced neat ornamental rows of flowers. In 1871, a significant turning point in his career came when Robinson founded the weekly publication *The Garden*, which became the most widely read gardening journal of the period. His most significant work was the 400-ha (1,000-acre) garden at his own house, Gravetye Manor, which he purchased in 1885. He worked on this garden continually until his death, incorporating areas of woodland and a meadow of Alpine bulbs sloping down to a lake.

Sir Edwin Landseer Lutyens
Deanery Garden, Berkshire, England

1895 The business partnership of Gertrude Jekyll and Lutyens helped to establish the principle of unifying house and garden, and hence architecture and nature in harmony Jekyll met Lutyens when she was middle-aged and he was in his twenties shortly after he set up in architectural practice. Their partnership coincided with the growth in interest shown by the upper middle classes in improving their homes and gardens. At Munstead Wood, their first project, Lutyens first designed a cottage for Miss Jekyll and later an early arts and crafts house. The garden was the testing ground for ideas that Jekyll repeated in later projects. She tried out new colour schemes and plants, recording all the results meticulously. Another fine example of garden design can be found in the Deanery Garden in Berkshire.

Overleaf: the splendid gardens of Sissinghurst Castle, the home of the Sackville-West family (see page 55).

Right: Gertrude Jekyll and Sir Edward Lutyens adopted a principle of unifying nature and architecture and designed beautiful houses and gardens.

Antonio Gaudí
Guell Park, Barcelona, Spain

1900–14 Guell Park was commissioned by a Barcelona industrialist and patron of the arts as a garden city. The site was a 20-ha (50-acre) field on the southern side of the Montana Pelada. Gaudí's (1852–1926) plan was to enclose the site with a 2-m (6-ft)-high wall behind which the park would be laid out in triangular plots. Access was through a gatehouse from which drives would make concentric circles around a raised central area accommodating a market and performance space. In financial terms, the plan was a failure, and in 1914 the local council bought the land and turned it into a municipal park, scrapping Gaudí's further plans for houses, schools, community centres and a church.

George Kessler
The Paseo, Sunken Gardens, Kansas City, Missouri, USA

1910 Kessler's (1862–1923) system of open spaces and avenues for Kansas City combined naturalistic parks with smaller, more controlled squares. As part of the City Beautiful Movement, the basis of which was the notion that attractive urban spaces would improve society morally, he created a new type of park. 'Social space' was symbolized by its clear organizing principles and the influence of architectural forms and spatial geometry. Walks, planted areas and trees all

Guell Park was commissioned by a patron of the arts, to be turned into a garden city. Sadly the plans were abandoned and the local council turned it into a municipal park.

George Kessler devised a system of open spaces and avenues for Kansas City; he combined naturalistic parks with smaller squares of more cultivated land.

conformed with a linear plan and incorporated Classical pergolas and ornately patterned flower beds. At the time, improved public transport was beginning to give city-dwellers easy access to the countryside, so parks like these did not need to emphasize rural qualities to the extent that they had in the past.

Antonio Sant'Elia
New City

1914 The New City was a visionary design for a utopian city of the future. In 1914, the sketches and designs were exhibited by the Association of Lombard Architects in Milan. Although this imaginary metropolis was never built, Sant'Elia's ideas about circulation and movement through urban spaces were highly influential and were adapted for later urban plans. Detached lift shafts, pedestrian bridges and walkways criss-crossing at different levels all anticipated later methods of dealing with circulation and three-dimensional space. The basic unit of the New City was the New House, a set-back high-rise building with a separate tower for lifts. Usually, two of these set-back skyscrapers were positioned back-to-back and connected by means of parabolic arches, creating an inner street between them.

Clarence Stein and Henry Wright
Sunnyside Gardens, Queens, New York, USA

1928 Sunnyside Gardens was an urban housing project created out of 31 ha (77 acres) of barren land by the City Housing Corporation. Architects Stein and Wright used a pre-existing street grid and arranged housing to face both the street and interior garden spaces. Umbrellas of plane trees lined the paths of each block, and instead of private yards the landscape completely surrounded the rows of two- and four-storey houses, even on the street side. When it was completed in 1928, Sunnyside housed 1,231 families. The density was up to five times lower than other contemporary housing projects. The resulting increased costs were offset by the simplification of the building forms, which were reduced to strict rows to minimize construction costs.

Vita Sackville-West
Sissinghurst Gardens, Kent, England

1930–62 The garden at Sissinghurst Castle is considered by most historians to be the quintessential twentieth-century English garden. Created from a derelict site after Sackville-West's family moved to the castle in 1930, it consists of compartmentalized areas, each with a different character, and a water-filled moat. A dilapidated tower is the centrepiece, with a courtyard on one side and a lawn on the other. While her husband, Harold Nicolson, worked out an ordered plan, Sackville-West took responsibility for planting the garden and creating the right atmosphere of romance and nostalgia. The emphasis was on climbing roses and subtle shades of lilies, irises and flowering shrubs. The garden took nearly 20 years to develop, but by the 1950s its reputation was well established.

Thomas Church
El Novillero, California, USA

1947 Although Church (1902–1978) did all of his landscape design work in California, as a pioneer of Modernism, his ideas spread around the world. His main contribution was to design gardens to be extensions of houses. Rather than using them as decoration to be enjoyed visually, he saw them as outdoor rooms to be lived in. Plants and boundaries in concrete or stone became the defining edges, and intricate detailing was used to create spatial illusions. The house and garden of El Novillero are set in salt marshes and enclosed by oak trees. The main feature is a

The splendid gardens of Sissinghurst Castle owe their beauty to Vita Sackville-West and her husband Harold Nicolson, who restored the once-derelict site.

Lucio Costa
master plan for Brasilia, Brazil

1957–60 Costa's city plan for Brasilia was intended to create an alternative capital city to Rio de Janiero. The idea was to build an inland city which looked towards the vast hinterland of Brazil rather than towards Europe. It was intended to reshape Brazilian national identity and symbolize the country's industrialization and modernization. Wide-open spaces were complemented by reflective pools, ramps and changes of levels. In simple terms, the plan consisted of two axes intersecting to form a cross, an idea which recast a traditional symbol as a modern device. Costa's plan provided the perfect framework for monumental state buildings designed by Oscar Neimeyer, the focal point being the Plaza of the Three Powers containing the Presidential Palace, the Supreme Court and the Congress.

Left: Hemel Hempstead was intended to be the town of the future and has been a model for town planners since it was constructed in 1947. Its population then numbered 60,000.

Right: Brasilia's Congress centre, with the Presidential Palace (left background) and the Chamber of Deputies (the bowl to the right). To the left is the dome-shaped Senate.

kidney-shaped pool set into a formal ground of linear concrete and redwood decking. Beyond the pool, the garden seems never to end, flowing into a rocky landscape and, eventually, mountains.

Geoffrey Jellicoe
Hemel Hempstead town plan and Water Gardens, Hertfordshire, England

1947 The plan for Hemel Hempstead new town was made in 1947 for a population of 60,000. Its design was a logical development of Ebenezer Howard's vision spelt out in *Garden Cities of the Future*. The first areas to be constructed were the neighbourhoods, which were followed by the town centre and civic buildings. Ten years after planning the town, Jellicoe (1900–) was commissioned to design the Water Gardens, which gave the community its special character. They occupied a narrow strip of land along the River Gade, following a design intended to evoke the Serpentine in London's Hyde Park. Upstream, the canal emerged from the natural river, while downstream it culminated in a lake with pedestrian bridges.

José Luis Sert
Charles River Campus, Boston University, Massachusetts, USA

1965 Sert (1902–1983) trained as an architect in Barcelona and, early in his career, worked with Le Corbusier in Paris. In 1939, he moved to the USA and began to concentrate on town planning. The challenge at Boston University was to make the most of the urban site, using the expensive city-centre land intensively and turning the campus to address the river. On this project, Sert worked with a group of architects who were commissioned to design new buildings while he concentrated on the intervening spaces: a series of quadrangles with one large square between the existing and new buildings. Sert's approach was to treat the campus like a mini-city, considering the relationships between the volumes, textures and shapes of the buildings.

Luis Barrágan
Folke Egerstrom House, Mexico City, Mexico

1968 Barrágan (1902–1988), trained as an engineer, was a self-taught architect. His work in Mexico City, where he lived and worked from 1936, treated landscape and architecture as one discipline. A use of water to reflect the geometric forms and colours of his buildings was particularly characteristic. The Folke Egerstrom House was built for a family of horse-lovers. The plan of the house, stable and surrounding grounds was intended to reflect this interest, with the animals' presence apparent all around. The area Barrágan constructed for the horses themselves is dominated by strong pink and blue and a screen of green vegetation surrounding the site. A fountain is picked out in red against the stark white of the house.

Boston University was designed by José Luis Sert, an architect who had worked with Corbusier before moving to America at the start of the Second World War.

Household goods

4

THROUGHOUT THE CENTURY, DESIGNERS HAVE MET THE CHALLENGE OF MAKING EVERYDAY HOUSEHOLD OBJECTS – CUTLERY, KETTLES AND EVEN VACUUM CLEANERS – BOTH FUNCTIONAL AND STYLISH. A RANGE OF SUCH ITEMS, INCLUDING ETHEREALLY BEAUTIFUL TIFFANY TABLE LAMPS AND THE MOST UP-TO-THE-MINUTE SAFETY RAZORS, DEMONSTRATE HOW PRACTICALITY AND BEAUTY CAN BE SUCCESSFULLY COMBINED.

Mrs Curtis Freschel
'Wisteria' lamp for Tiffany Studios, USA

1900 Louis Comfort Tiffany, an American with a highly developed taste for the exotic, was widely regarded as the person who introduced unabashed luxury into twentieth-century life. Although glassware formed only a small part of his vast decorative schemes, it is for glassware that he remains famous. His 'Favrile' glass, made by hand, is amongst the most sought-after glass today. Perhaps the most beautiful objects made under his name, however, are the table lamps which received international acclaim in 1900 when Mrs Curtis Freschel designed the famous 'Wisteria' lamp. The leaded-glass shades were not an innovation of the Tiffany Studios, but their designs were far superior to any other similar product. The famous 'Wisteria' lamp, with its dripping blue-green tendrils and solid base, became an enduring favourite.

Jan Eisenloeffel
tea service

1900–3 The Russian designer Jan Eisenloeffel (1846–1920) was a renowned goldsmith and silversmith noted mainly for his dedicated and innovative application of the Arts-and-Crafts tradition. Keeping decoration to a minimum, with a simple pattern of three engraved parallel lines, his tea set was, uniquely, made of brass, with rattan and ebony accents. The handle of the tea kettle is wrapped in rattan, with details of craftsmanship, including the handle's unique ability to swivel, left exposed to view. The shape is strongly geometric, anticipating the Art Deco fascination with silhouette, and each item is constructed of broad, plain surfaces. A similar set was exhibited to wide acclaim at the first Arts-and-Crafts exhibition, held in Turin in 1902.

Overleaf: Earl Tupper's invention of Tupperware has become one of the best-known household designs of all time (see page 65).

Right: this leaded glass and bronze table lamp, entitled 'Wisteria', was created for the Tiffany studios by Mrs Curtis Freschel.

Frederick Carder
*'Three Bronze Nudes' lamp for Steuben
Glass, USA*

1920 The work of the English glassmaker
Frederick Carder (1863–1963), who was the
chief designer of Steuben Glass in the USA
from its beginning in 1903 until 1934, was
influenced largely by Art Nouveau. Among
Carder's creations were aurene (an
iridescent glass in blue and gold lustre),
coloured opalines (in light rose, jade green,
translucent white and shades of blue), clear
glass combined with colours, and pressed
glass. Carder's 'Three Bronze Nudes' lamp is
clearly from the Art Nouveau period, when
bronze typically was used for both hanging
and table lamps. The lamp is a glorious
celebration of organic styling, with the
curving, undulating bodies reaching up to
grasp the opulent glass fixture. It was
produced by Steuben, who became market
leaders in one-off design creations and who
were renowned for the quality of their
design and manufacture.

Wilhelm Wagenfeld
lamp

1923–24 Wagenfeld is noted for his
distinctive lamp designs. One of the most
simple and successful to emerge from the
Bauhaus studios was the Bauhaus table
lamp, created in the metal workshop, then
under the direction of László Maholy-Nagy.
Designed by the student Wagenfeld and his
collaborator Karl Jucker, the lamp generated
enormous interest, particularly when it was
shown at the Leipzig Trade Fair in 1924. It
was modern and industrial in feeling, with a
rounded glass shade and a steel tube
forming the central stem, designed to
conceal the wiring. Representing a move
away from Art Nouveau, the Bauhaus table
lamp was produced by hand.

*This classic design was
created for the Bauhaus
school by Wilhelm
Wagenfeld. The lamp is
made from glass and
metal.*

Pierre Cartier
clock

1925 The Parisian jeweller Pierre Cartier (1878–1964) was responsible for designing the first wristwatch (for French aviator Santos Duman). His work was recognized and sought after early in his career; he created 27 diamond tiaras for the coronation of King Edward VII, and his watches and clocks became collector's items. Cartier's clocks represented the height of Art Deco style and drew on many influences, including Cubism, the Bauhaus and Orientalism. His use of precious stones and metals was unusual and reflected his belief that clocks and other time-keeping pieces should be 'jewellery for the home', their overwhelming stylistic feature being ostentatious display rather than innovative design. In the 1940s, Cartier's clocks were made in gold, silver, rock crystal and diamonds, and became essential household accessories for the upper echelons of society. The Cartier clock has now achieved icon status.

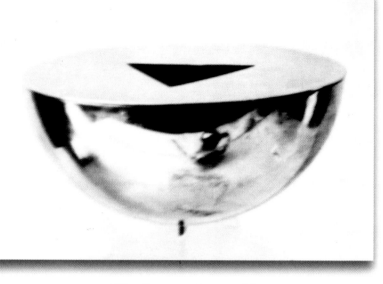

Marianne Brandt
ashtray

1926 Brandt (1893–1983) joined the Bauhaus in 1923, working in the metal workshop under the direction of László Moholy -Nagy. She then moved to Berlin to work as a designer in the studio of Walter Gropius, chiefly on mass-produced single-piece furniture and the interior decoration of some of the houses for the Building Exhibition at Karlsruhe-Dammerstock. All of Brandt's designs for domestic ware were craft prototypes, with uncompromising geometric purity, marking an aesthetic which would come to be widely employed by other manufacturers and designers. Her exquisitely simply ashtray, which had become a must-have household accessory in the 1920s, was re-edited by the firm Alessi in 1985 and had a second successful life.

Top: Marianne Brandt worked in the metal workshop of the Bauhaus. Her purity of design and geometric lines have made classics of her household items, such as this ashtray.

Bottom: Cartier's clocks were considered the pinnacle of the Art Deco movement, and became highly sought-after collectors' pieces.

Jean Puiforcat
tea service

1928 Puiforcat (1897–1945), one of the most important designers of the twentieth century, produced some of the most elegant and influential silverware of the late 1920s and early '30s, crystallizing the high Art Deco style. His silverwork is often compared to the precious jewellery sold by Tiffany and Cartier, and fetched prices which were nearly equal to those of the high-class jewellers. Produced in his native France, Puiforcat's silver tea services are characterized by their simple geometry and pure, clean lines, often contrasted with a rich, rare wood, like walnut, or inlaid with glass. Puiforcat was fascinated by the mathematical principle known as the 'Golden Section', which provided a system of pleasing proportion for his work.

This silver tea service was made by Jean E. Puiforcat, one of the most important and influential designers of the twentieth century.

George Carwardine
'Anglepoise' lamp

1934 The Anglepoise lamp, designed in 1933 by the British designer George Carwardine, is the century's most successful and innovative desk lamp. Carwardine, an automobile designer, employed his engineering skills to produce a lamp which used hinges to mimic the elbow joint of the human arm. The hinge system, which allowed the lamp to hold any position and provided a wide range of possible adjustments over an extensive arc, was widely copied throughout the industry. The original Anglepoise, which was put into production by Herbert Terry & Sons in 1934, was chic, flexible and balanced, and the design is still produced today, by Anglepoise Ltd of Redditch, with only slight variations. The Anglepoise reflected the utilitarian and functional approach to office and domestic appliance design which characterized the late 1920s and early '30s.

Left: the Anglepoise lamp was created by George Carwardine, a car designer. The lamp was designed to mimic the action of the human elbow.

Right: Tupperware was created by Earl Tuppe, an American designer. Since its invention in the 1940s, Tupperware has become one of the best-known household designs of all time.

Raymond Loewy
'Coldspot' refrigerator for Sears Roebuck, USA

1935 Loewy (1893–1986) emigrated to the USA after serving in the First World War, establishing himself as an illustrator and display designer. He soon became known for the visual simplification of industrial design, the highlight of which was his Coldspot refrigerator, designed for the American firm of Sears Roebuck. The refrigerator was encased in plain white enamel, with chrome hardware used to create a jewel-like effect. The interior was carefully designed to accommodate containers of different sizes and shapes, with a semi-automatic defroster, instant-release ice-cube trays and a glass rolling-pin which could be filled with ice-cubes to make perfect pastry. The model set a new trend in refrigerator design, and Loewy dramatically proved the impact of design on sales: the Coldspot refrigerator sold more than 275,000 units in five years.

Tupperware
plastic containers

1945 The name Tupperware, developed in 1945 by the American Earl Tupper, has become synonymous with plastic storage containers of every description. Designed from polyethylene, with air-tight seals to keep contents fresh for long periods of time, Tupperware revolutionized the storage of food in the home. The functional Tupperware design was produced in a variety of forms and translucent colours which are being constantly updated. Tupperware was flexible but durable; in 1947, the range was featured in an article in the American magazine *House Beautiful* under the title 'Fine Art for 39 cents'. Part of the commercial success of Tupperware was due to the unique ploy of home-party selling, which was introduced in the USA in 1946 and in the UK and Europe in 1960. The range now includes kitchen storage and utensils, as well as cooking, table- and picnic ware.

Dieter Rams
Braun Electric Shaver for Braun AG, Germany

1951 Rams (1932–) became head of design at Braun AG in the mid-1950s and was one of the most influential designers of the century. Under his direction, Braun consumer appliances exhibited a restrained elegance in line with his belief that they should appear so neutral as to be invisible. His Braun Electric Shaver made it possible to dispense with shaving creams and soap. Company founder Max Braun himself had pioneered the electric razor in 1938, but the Second World War had delayed production until 1951, when the prototype was launched, using a simple outer case and an oscillating motor run on rechargeable batteries. The white colour was unusual for the time, since most products for men were produced in black, grey or silver, but it was in keeping with Ram's approach: every Braun product had to reveal their trademark of simplicity and function, in either black or white.

David Mellor
tea service

1954 In 1954, the UK designer David Mellor (1930–) designed 'Pride' cutlery, probably still the best design for cutlery to have emerged from the UK since 1945. Achieving both commercial and aesthetic success, the 'Pride' range was produced in silver-plated metal; the knives had white/cream-striped celluloid handles. The 'Pride' range set the standard for good-quality, middle-market table manufacture, combining precious and non-precious materials in a unique combination which was both beautiful and functional. The design was elegant, clean and modern, with its roots in eighteenth-century English silverware. Although not truly modern, the range's combination of stylistic features and materials broke new ground in twentieth-century household design. Mellor was also noted for design of other tableware, such as the tea service illustrated.

Marcello Nizzoli
'Mirella' sewing machine for Necchi, Pavia, Italy

1956 Nizzoli (1895–1969) was best known for his association with typewriter and office-equipment specialist Olivetti, but over the course of his career he worked across most of the main design disciplines. In response to the economic boom in Italy in the 1950s, the demand for

David Mellor's silver-plated tea service is part of his now-famous Pride range. Pride was an elegant design, with its roots in eighteenth-century English silverware.

electrical household appliances soared, and the country's steel industry underwent huge growth and technological development. Die-casting, which enabled the production of sophisticated outer casings, was developed and applied successfully to home appliances. One of the most important of these appliances was Nizzoli's 'Mirella' sewing machine, produced for the Italian manufacturing company Necchi. The 'Mirella' design concentrated on strongly organic outlines which disguised the machinery within a solid, practical form. The controls for the machine were carefully placed for optimum function and yet managed to contribute to a chic overall appearance.

Gerd Alfred Muller
KM3 Multi-purpose Kitchen Machine for Braun AG, Germany

1957 The German electrical company Braun were one of the first to use design as the foundation of a corporate identity programme. In 1951, after their father, Max's, death, Artur and Erwin Braun took over the firm and took their interest in modern design to its logical high point. With Fritz Eichler as head of design, Braun began to pursue a policy of uncompromising modernity for products aimed at the top of the market; Dieter Rams took over the job in the mid-1950s. The first Braun designs aroused widespread attention, in particular the KM3 Multi-purpose Kitchen Machine designed by Muller (1932–), with its solid, stable appearance and clean lines. Every element of the design was balanced and unified, and every unnecessary detail was eliminated, with the emphasis on the ordering of essential elements.

Sigurd Persson
'Jet Line' cutlery

1959 Persson (1914–), a well-known, innovative Swedish designer, produced the 'Jet Line' cutlery range for use on Scandinavian Airlines. This range, the first truly modern cutlery design to emerge from Scandinavia, was created with the idea that everyday things should

be beautiful. Persson's cutlery was made from stainless steel, and the knives were created as a single unit, making them cheap to manufacture. The design was sculptural – the knife blades, fork prongs and spoons were generously sized, with squat handles. The design was considered to be radical for mainstream taste in the rest of Europe and North America, but its sophistication soon encouraged a range of copy-cat designs which went on to take free-flowing organic styling to its extreme.

W. M. Russell
K3 Kettle for Russell Hobbs, UK

1959 Designed in 1959 by W. M. Russell of Russell Hobbs in the UK, the K2 Kettle was an improvement on the design of the K1 Kettle, produced in 1954, part of a range which Russell Hobbs called 'Forgettable', because they included an automatic cut-off switch. The K2 was available in a variety of finishes, including stainless steel and copper and chrome, and has remained in fashion over the years, even with the advent of the plastic jug kettle. The design included a smooth, practical exterior, with a knob-and-handle lid which remained cool despite the high heat of the body. The model contained a powerful heating element which claimed

The K3 was the descendant of Russell Hobbs's celebrated K1 kettle, designed in 1959 by W. M. Russell.

to bring water to the boil in just seconds, and an indicator level in the handle which automatically snapped back when it was turned off. The huge success of the K2 led to a variety of other designs, including additions to the 'Forgettable' or 'Forgettle Kettle' range, including a popular model launched in 1973. The next version, K3, is illustrated.

Marco Zanuso
'Black 12' television for Brionvega

1962 Milan-born Zanuso (1916–) studied architecture at Milan Polytechnic and established a practice with which he worked on such projects as Olivetti's headquarters in São Paulo. He was editor of the magazine *Casabella*, but after working with Pirelli on furniture design in 1948, moved increasingly towards design projects, employing a minimalist, sculptured approach. Zanuso designed Broletti's 1957 sewing machine, and in 1964, he produced the innovative TS 502 radio. He worked with Richard Sapper from the late 1950s to the early 1970s, and their 'Black 12' television for Brionvega won several awards for its high-tech styling. The television marked a trend in Italian design, countering the cold precision of Bauhaus modernism and the warm biomorphic forms and textures of Scandinavian design by playfully celebrating the artificial. Zanuso also created brash electrical appliances and furniture out of plastics and chrome.

Ettore Sottsass
'Astroide' lamp

1968 Sottsass (1917–), one of the most important designers of the century, studied architecture in Turin and organized the first international show of abstract art in Milan in 1946. He combined the rectilinear approach of Rationalism with more organic shapes, putting himself at the forefront of Italian design consciousness by combining technical and aesthetic interests and using plywood, plastics and metal rods. In 1957, he collaborated with Olivetti to introduce technological advances while applying his sense of style in order to raise the profile of the product. Sottsass enjoyed creating new readings of familiar items, eventually pioneering Post-modernism. One of his most unusual and exciting creations for the

home was the 'Astroide' plastic and metal model lamp. Pink on one side and blue on the other, the lamp makes innovative use of plastic, in the 1960s the 'new' material for lighting.

Enzo Mari
3089 ABC graduating table bowls for Danese, Milan, Italy

1969 In 1964, Mari (1932–), who worked for the Italian company Danese in Milan from 1957, designed a series of objects, including desk accessories and housewares, which helped to define the company's product image and provide it with a reputation for stylish products in plastics. Plastic had had, until the 1960s, a rather cheap image, but the designers of the Pop age saw it as a wonderful medium in which to explore strong colours and durable designs. Mari was one of the most intellectual of the Pop designers, pursuing design as a linguistic system. His ABC table bowls, produced in melamine, formed a series of perfect cylinders, with holes on the side. The bowls were light and practical, but also ingeniously stylish, leading to their inclusion in the seminal exhibition of Italian design at the Museum of Modern Art in New York in 1972.

Sheaffer
'Pen for Men'

1970s The most successful pen ever designed, Walter A. Sheaffer's 1907 'snorkel' or lever-filled pen, was produced in 1907, using a thin tube which emerged from the underside of the hooded nib when the user turned the knob at the end of the barrel. The tube was then tipped into the ink and by extending and pulling back the plunger, the ink was drawn into the rubber sack while the nib remained dry. This pen, widely used for the next 40 years, inspired the designs of some of the most successful pens ever marketed, including a model produced by designer Walter Dorwin Teague. In the 1970s, Sheaffer launched their 'Pen for Men', using the snorkel system and designed with a barrel meant to appeal for the 'traditional' male. The pen could be filled without submerging the nib in ink and had an elegant yet solid form. The commercial success of the 'Pen for Men' encouraged a variety of manufacturers to produce copy-cat designs.

Give her the fashion pen of the year!

Sheaffer's PFM II, $15.00

HE'S WRITING WITH THE BOLD NEW

Sheaffer's PFM. *Pen For Men*

THE NEWEST GIFT YOU CAN CHOOSE FOR A MAN! New bold styling; balanced heft and a man-sized grip. Newly designed, inlaid points ...14 kt. gold or palladium-silver. New loss-proof clip. New massive capacity. Famous Snorkel Pen filling action. Five *Sheaffer's PFM* Fountain Pen models from $10.00 to $25.00. Matching Pencils from $4.95 to $10.00. Gift Sets from $14.95 to $35.00. Choose *his* today!

Just say, "PFM... Pen For Men!" **SHEAFFER'S**

See Jimmy Durante in Sheaffer's spectacular holiday show, "Give My Regards to Broadway," NBC-TV, Dec. 8

Sheaffer's 'Pen for Men' was launched in the 1970s. Its distinctive wide-barrelled design spawned many copies from less-successful manufacturers.

Bang and Olufsen
'Beogram' 4000 Record Player

1972 The best examples of slimline domestic electronic products were produced by Bang and Olufsen, a Danish company, who accomplished in the late 1960s and '70s what Braun of Germany had begun in the 1950s – the creation of a corporate identity for their products. Bang and Olufsen stereos came in beautifully worked, slim boxes, with neat graphic detail, doing away with knobs and replacing them with buttons and sliding switches. The look was produced by Jakob Jenson, who designed the 'Beogram' stereo units and turntables between 1969 and 1973. The combination of dark-grained wood veneer, satin aluminium and stainless steel provided an exquisite balance between art, technology and nature. The 'Beogram' 4000 turntable featured the tangential pick-up arm pioneered by Bang and Olufsen and much emulated.

Massimo and Lella Vignelli
MAX 1 stacking dinnerware for Heller Design

1972 During the 1970s, French, Scandinavian, Italian, German and North American designers were working with melamine, polyethylene and ABS plastics to create containers, dinner services and picnic ware. The best example of design which looked great and made a superb use of space was the melamine MAX 1 stacking dinner service, designed by Lella and Massimo Vignelli for Heller Design. This line showed that plastics could look good alone and within an integrated 'alphabet' of shapes. The designers invested the form and function of this dinner set with a sense of high quality, thus raising the status of melamine commercially. The simple design formed smooth cylinders of white melamine, which fitted neatly on a small tray, with a moulded lid topping each cylindrical 'tower' – an exquisitely functional yet trend-setting design which influenced dinnerware design for years to come.

Kenneth Grange
'Protector' razor for Wilkinson Sword

1992 British designer Kenneth Grange's 'Protector' razor for Wilkinson Sword combined all of the successful features of previous razors, including a swivel head, a lubricating strip and twin blades. However, its chief commercial advantage came in the form of 'wire bars', which stopped the blades from nicking the skin. Although 'safety' razors had been available since the turn of the century, no designer had come up with a concept which would actually prevent the razor from accidentally cutting the skin. Grange's design also included a unique biomorphic handle, which was designed to fit snugly in the hand. Produced in fiery red, the razor was both light and solid, conveying an impression of stylish elegance, with trend-setting design features.

James Dyson
Dyson 'Dual Cyclone' vacuum cleaner for Dyson Appliances UK

1993 The Dyson 'Dual Cyclone', designed by the owner of Dyson Appliances UK, James Dyson, heralded a new age of vacuum cleaners with the most innovative design and technology since the first Hoover had been produced nearly a century earlier. The 'Cyclone' eliminated the dustbag, using G-force technology to collect dirt in the cylindrical body. The product claimed 100-per-cent suction, even when the cleaner was almost full, because the centrifugal spin ensured there was no restriction to the airflow through the vacuum. The machine sucked up and revolved air at high speed through two chambers until the dirt dropped to the cylinder base. The styling was both sleek and unconventional, with a cylindrical body providing a high-tech, almost space-age appearance.

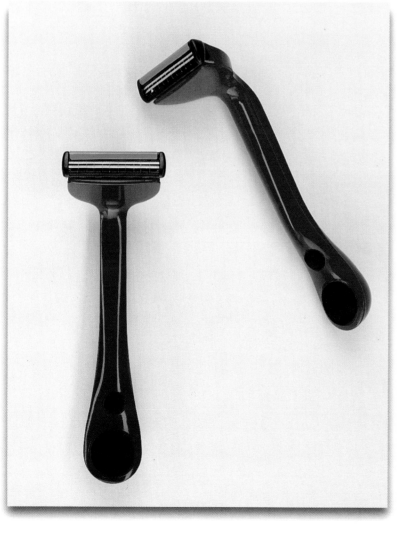

Kenneth Grange's Protector razor was a breakthrough – it was the first razor that could actually prevent accidental cutting of the skin.

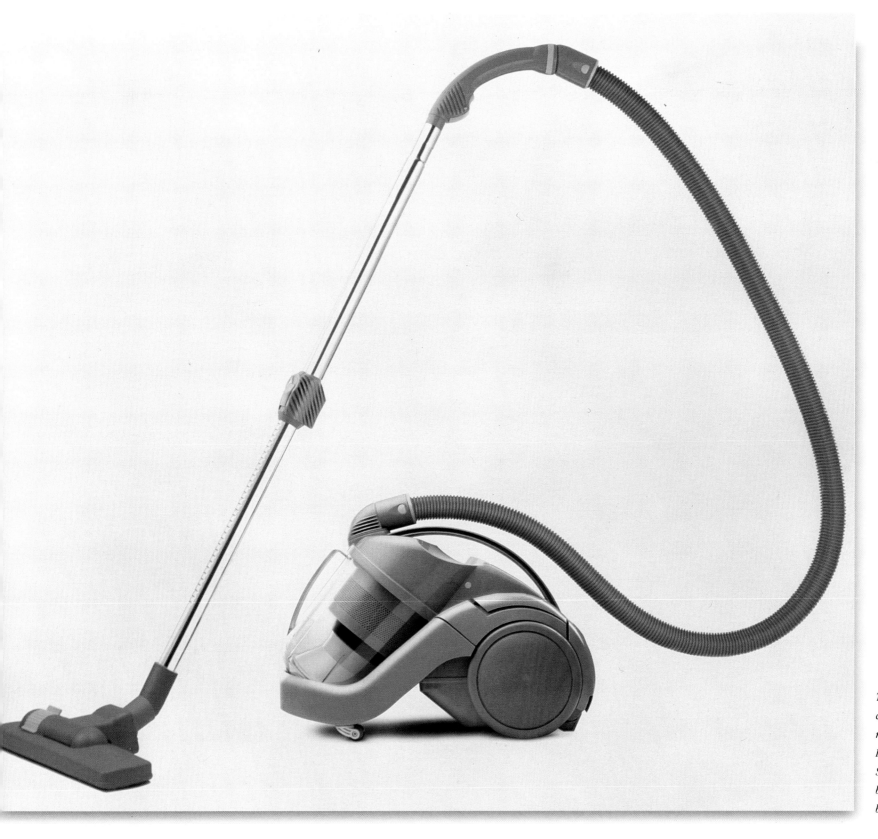

The Dyson Dual Cyclone cleaner has generated as much interest as the first Hoover vacuum cleaner. Since its launch, it has become a maintained best-seller.

Decorative Arts, Ceramics & Glassware

THE ART NOUVEAU, ART DECO, SURREALIST AND BAUHAUS MOVEMENTS FIND SOME OF THEIR RICHEST EXPRESSION IN THE DIVERSITY OF COLOUR, FORM AND MATERIALS IN TWENTIETH-CENTURY DECORATIVE ART. FROM ANCIENT DEPICTIONS OF LIFE AND MYTHS ON EVERYDAY OBJECTS HAVE COME TRADITIONS OF DECORATION THAT HAVE DEVELOPED INTO THE EXTRAVAGANCE OF THIS CENTURY'S POTTERY, PORCELAIN AND GLASSWARE.

Emile Gallé
vase and jug

1900 The work of Gallé (1846–1904), in both glass and furniture, dominated the decorative arts at the 1900 Paris Exhibition. Gallé founded the School of Nancy, where he worked, and became the leading glass maker of his time in France. There were two strands to his work: mass-produced cameo vases, and one-off or limited-edition wares which turned glassware into a sculptural art. Gallé's exotic jugs and vases were inspired by nature, but also showed a strong Japanese influence. He treated glass surfaces with acid to create different textures and also applied coloured and shaped glass to already sculpted surfaces. For the Exhibition, he created a series of wares as a retrospective of his career.

Louis Comfort Tiffany
'Zinnia' leaded glass, mosaic 'Favrile' glass and bronze table lamp

1900–5 Tiffany (1848–1933), the son of a prominent New York jeweller, studied in Paris, and on his return to America in 1878 founded an interior decorating firm. The company designed a number of rooms in an elaborate late nineteenth-century style, anticipating Art Nouveau. In 1885, Tiffany founded his glass company and began to produce elaborate and unique stained-glass panels and lampshades, usually employing bold, colourful floral motifs. In 1894, he patented his much-imitated 'Favrile' range of iridescent glass. Tiffany's 'Favrile' punchbowl exhibited at the 1900 Paris Exhibition was probably one of the few works in glass to rival that of the French master glass craftsman Emile Gallé.

Overleaf: this frosted glass, table lamp by René Lalique, depicts a dome of autumn leaves. The piece was titled Feuilles de Murier *(see page 74).*

Right: Exquisite glassware such as this helped Emile Gallé win international recognition at the Paris Exhibition of 1900.

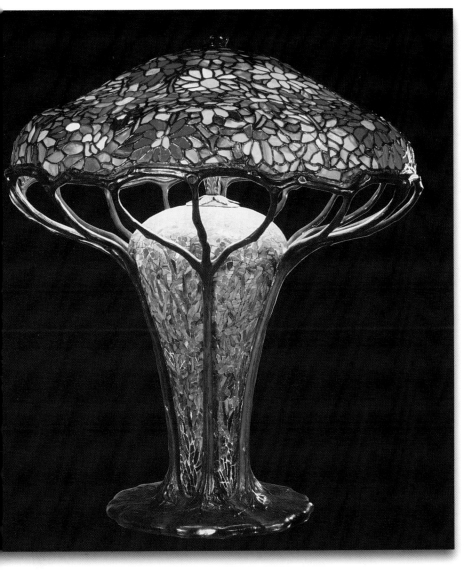

Carlo Bugatti
vase

1900–10 Bugatti (1856–1940) is perhaps best known for his architecture and furniture designs of the last quarter of the nineteenth century. Italian-born, he spent much of his later life in Paris. The small decorative objects he produced there, in silver and other metals, show him moving away from his early Moorish influences to a style more sinuous and florid, now known as Art Nouveau. Unlike his French contemporary Hector Guimard, Bugatti employed stylized animal forms in his designs, so his work has a generally more eccentric and exotic appearance. His son Ettore, and grandson, Jean, became well-known automotive designers.

Daum brothers
vase

1900–30 The Daum brothers were glass makers working in Nancy who, together with Emile Gallé, co-founded the team of artists and designers known collectively as the School of Nancy. Strongly influenced by nature, japonism and the Baroque architecture of their native town, the Daum glassworks produced a varied output. Moving from etched and enamelled glass in the 1890s and early 1900s, through *pâte-de-verre* and cameo glass in the 1910s and '20s, they modified their work to keep pace with prevailing fashion. In the 1930s, their thick-walled glass vases were deeply acid-etched with geometric designs. The factory continues today, unlike the majority of its contemporaries.

Left: *pieces such as this 'Zinnia' table lamp made Tiffany's name. It is created from leaded glass, mosaic favrile glass and bronze.*

Right: *Carlo Bugatti's silverware was among the first works executed in the style that has now become known as French Art Nouveau.*

Maurice de Vlaminck
vase and plate

This table lamp, created by René Lalique from frosted glass, depicts a dome of autumn leaves. The piece was titled Feuilles de murier.

c. 1907 De Vlaminck (1876–1958) was a Fauve artist who exhibited paintings at the 1905 Paris Salon and 1925 Paris Exhibition. His ceramics exhibited at the 1907 Autumn Salon were a result of his association with the French potter André Métthey. Métthey considered surface decoration to be of prime importance in ceramics, and he produced vases and plates decorated by a number of leading contemporary artists, including Edouard Vuillard, Henri Matisse and de Vlaminck. All of these wares were radically different from traditional French art pottery. Exemplifying the Art Deco style, they were to have an important influence on the ceramics of the 1920s produced by factories such as Sèvres and Boch frères.

Frederick Carder
Art Nouveau glass

c. 1910 Living to 100 years of age, Carder (1863–1963) effectively had two careers, the first as a glass designer and engraver in Stourbridge, England, in the 1880s and '90s, and the second after he moved to the USA and co-founded the Steuben Glass Works in Corning, New York, in 1903. Between 1903 and 1932, under his direction, the Corning factory produced a huge amount of decorative glassware, ranging from scent bottles to lamp shades, which were retailed through major department stores. The 'Aurene' range, with its iridescent surface in blue or gold, is perhaps the best known. Other ranges included 'Tyrian', 'Cintra' and 'Intarsia', and complex one-off pieces were also made to special commission.

Koloman Moser
dish

c. 1910 Moser (1868–1918) studied at the Vienna Academy for Visual Arts and become a leading member of the Vienna Secession. In 1903, he founded the Wiener Werkstätte, which were based on the English Arts-and-Crafts ideal of a group of artists, craftspeople and designers working in a range of media. By 1905, over a hundred craftsmen were employed in the workshops. Moser himself designed furniture, metalwork, glass and bookbindings for the Werkstätte. Many younger artists were influenced by his rectilinear style, which owed much to the work of Charles Rennie Mackintosh. The Werkstätte continued after Moser's death, being dissolved only in 1932.

René Lalique
table lamp

1910s–'20s Lalique (1860–1945) trained as a designer of jewellery; he did not begin to make commercially the glassware for which he is so famous today until 1910. After initial experiments with lost-wax techniques of casting based on the use of complex piece-moulds, he moved on to industrial-scale, factory-produced glassware, bringing his stunning, colourful designs within the price range of ordinary people. Lalique exploited the possibilities of glass in the modern era, making electric light fittings, lamps, car mascots and even furniture and interior panelling. He had many imitators, particularly in England and France, but the quality of his design and production techniques ensured that his factory led the field, even after his death in 1945. The factory still flourishes, one of the few industrial-scale artistic glass companies of the modern day.

Simon Gate and Edward Hald
Orrefors 1917 collection

1917 The glass factory of Orrefors was one of the first in Sweden to employ artist-designers, breathing dramatic new life into their art and tableware ranges. Gate (1883–1945), an artist who had studied at the Stockholm Academy, and Hald (1883–1980), who had studied under Henri Matisse, both went to work at the factory in 1917. Their designs, exhibited that year at the 'Ideal Homes Exhibition' in Stockholm, were a great success. Engraved motifs dominated – and were to continue to dominate – Swedish glass production into the 1950s and '60s. Other techniques were also employed, including an entirely new cased technique developed by the two designers and known as 'Graal', in which a coloured design was sandwiched between two layers of clear glass.

Marcel Goupy
ceramics

1920s The ceramic factory of Boch frères, Keramis in Belgium produced some of the most innovative industrial and art ceramics of the first half of the twentieth century. Under its art director, Charles Catteau, between 1905 and 1945, Boch frères employed a number of outside decorators, Marcel Goupy (1886–1980) being one of the best known. Originally trained as an interior designer, Goupy designed tableware for Boch frères in a bold Art Deco style; typical motifs were bright, large-petalled flowers and stylized animals and butterflies. As house designer for the retailer George Rouard in Paris, he also designed glassware and ceramics for the manufactory at Sèvres, along with his contemporaries Paul Follot and Jean Luce.

Bernard Leach
Pilgrim Plate

1920s Born in Hong Kong and educated in England, Leach (1887–1979) went to the Slade School of Fine Art in London to study painting. In 1909, he returned to the Far East, becoming fascinated with the art of Japanese pottery. In 1920, he settled at St Ives in England, where he created his own pottery, combining what he had learned in Japan with the techniques of native English slip-decorated pottery. Leach believed that pottery, like other craft forms, should be an expression of the inner self, but also that it was essential to study and appreciate the good work of other skilled craftspeople. Considered by many to be the main pioneer of British studio pottery, his beliefs were published in his influential *A Potters Book* (1940).

Hall China Company
'Rhythm' teapot

1939 Streamlined design, also known as Machine-art Modern or American Modern, was the all-pervading design style in the USA in the 1930s, equivalent to Art Deco in France. Cars, locomotives and buildings were designed with bold, sweeping, excessively streamlined curves, as were the ceramics of the day. The Hall China Company of Ohio, makers of kitchenware and heavy-duty industrial pottery since 1903, produced in the late 1930s a limited but dramatic range of boldly coloured streamlined ceramics, including the 'Rhythm' teapot and the 'Streamline' jug. Simply made in two-part moulds, these types of wares were to have a huge influence in the 1950s on British ceramic designers, who in the austere post-war environment were looking to the perceived glamour of the USA for inspiration.

The Japanese pilgrim depicted on Bernard Leach's plate, clearly demonstrates its creator's wide-ranging artistic influences.

Pablo Picasso
ceramics

1947–69 Picasso (1881–1973), who needs no introduction as a painter, is less well known for his work in ceramics. In 1947, he visited the pottery-making centre of Vallauris in France and was captivated by the medium. Between 1947 and 1969, he produced a large range of plates and jugs at the Madoura Pottery there, at first painting in flat enamels or in low relief on simple, flat forms, and later modelling unique hollow shapes. Most of his ceramics were produced in limited editions of 100 to 600 pieces. Picasso's work consists of stylized animal and human forms, with the face a recurring subject. His pieces are unique; the notion of function, inherent in most ceramics, is entirely subordinated in them to his artistic invention.

Fernand Léger
La Pentecote

1950s Although well known as a painter of Machine-Age Cubism, Léger (1881–1955) was also a leading designer of decorative arts from the 1920s onwards. He was enthralled by machines and their products, and this is reflected in the clean, clear lines and bold blocks of colour in his work. He designed carpets for room settings at the major Paris exhibitions of the 1920s and '30s, and in the 1950s executed commissions for stained glass. His religious pieces, of which La Pentecote is one, also include *The Holy Tunic*, now in the Vatican collections. This much-celebrated work has a monumental power borne out of simplicity of line. Léger's influence on the decorative arts of the 1920s and later was immense, and he inspired many designers to move away from the rather florid designs of the early Art Deco period to bolder, simpler 'block' designs.

Fulvio Bianconi
vase

c. 1952 The tradition of glass-making in Venice is legendary, but in the late nineteenth and early twentieth centuries, very little innovative work was produced. Glassworks owner Paolo Venini was not himself a glass maker by trade, but he was an innovator and saw the value of employing designers to revitalize the struggling Venetian glass industry. In 1947, he appointed Fulvio Bianconi (1915–) as his artistic director. During the period immediately following the Second World War, Venini's company produced some of their most influential wares. Bianconi was one of a number of designers who used the 'Pezzato' technique of fusing segments of brightly coloured glass together. These wares were radical not only in colour but in shape, being typically asymmetrical.

Luigi Colani
'Drop' tea service

1971 The Rosenthal factory in Selb, Germany, was originally set up as a decorating studio in the late nineteenth century. Shortly afterwards, they began to manufacture fine white porcelain. Rosenthal became known for their tea and dinner services, in which shape was of equal importance to surface pattern. The factory always employed contemporary artists as designers, particularly in the period after the Second World War. Designers and their ranges included Raymond Loewy, 'Form 2000'; Tapio Wirkkala, 'Variation'; Timo Sarpaneva, 'Suomi'; and Luigi Colani, 'Drop'. Designed in 1971, 'Drop' is a tea service consisting of nine pieces. The teapot, jug and cup are of radical aerodynamic form (the jug is a simple elongated teardrop shape, lacking even a handle).

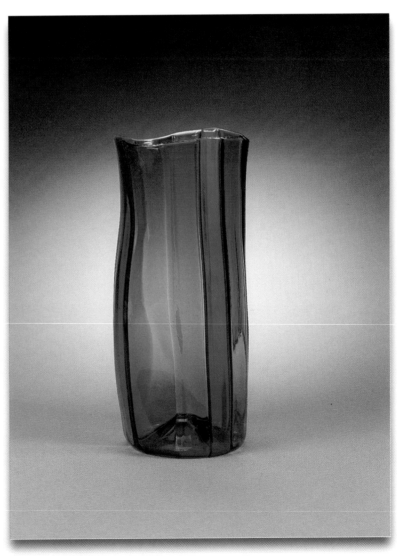

Opposite: most of Pablo Picasso's ceramics were limited editions, produced in batches of between 100 and 600 pieces.

Left: Léger's work was strongly affected by his love of machinery. He reflected this fascination in his pieces, using linear designs and bold blocks of colour.

Right: Bianconi experimented with a technique called 'Pezzato', combining and fusing segments of brightly coloured glass to create one shape.

6 Fashion & Accessories

THROUGHOUT THE CENTURY THE EXCITING WORLD OF FASHION AND ACCESSORIES HAS BEEN ONE OF CONSTANT CHANGE AND INNOVATION. FROM POIRET'S GLITTERING ACCESSORIES, VIA CHRISTIAN DIOR'S QUINTESSENTIALLY ELEGANT 'NEW LOOK', TO VIVIENNE WESTWOOD'S AGGRESSIVE 'BONDAGE' TROUSERS, FASHION REMAINS AS FASCINATING AND STARTLING AS EVER.

Karl Fabergé
eggs

Overleaf: examples of Emilio Pucci's brightly coloured sunglasses and scarves (see page 90).

Below: Fabergé's exquisite jewellery style and attention to detail can be seen in the decoration of his world famous eggs.

1897 This world-famous jewellery designer (1846–1920) made his name by creating a series of gem-studded eggs for the Russian monarchy. Extravagance and attention to detail are hallmarks of the Fabergé style, as is his love of coloured golds, translucent enamels, fine filigree work, and the unrestrained use of sapphires, rubies, emeralds and moonstones. One of his most famous pieces was a coronation egg presented to Alexandra Feodorovna by Nicholas II. Made of red gold, the egg contained a 13 cm (5 in) high, diamond-encrusted replica of the imperial coach, with platinum wheels, rock crystal windows, and a correctly-slung chassis. In addition to his work for royalty, Fabergé created many commercial pieces, produced for Europe's burgeoning merchant classes.

Charles de Bevoise
the first brassière

1902 De Bevoise created the first brassière – not the brassière as we know it today, but a sleeveless, low-necked corset cut high at the waist and tapered towards the front to push in the stomach. It supported the breasts and allowed wearers to move with greater ease than before in the loose-fitting fashions championed by Charles Worth and Paul Poiret. The brassière proper did not come into being until 1913, the brainchild of New York socialite Caresse Crosby, who manufactured it from two triangles of fabric held together with cross-over straps. Calling her creation a bra, Crosby patented it with high hopes of instant fame. A few women purchased bras, but most thought them obscene. Disillusioned, Crosby sold the idea for a pittance in 1914 to a then little-known company called Warners, which proceeded to become an international business.

Mariano Fortuny
'Delphos' dress

1909 Painter, inventor, alchemist and aristocrat, Fortuny (1871–1947) also designed some of the most exquisite textiles of the twentieth century and created a dress which influenced designers from Mme Grès to Issey Miyake. In 1909, Fortuny patented his now famous method of pleating, designing the 'Delphos' dress with Ionic creases (based on the Greek chiton), a loose overblouse, long sleeves and adjustable waist and shoulder cords to facilitate fit. These dresses could be rolled for storing and never lost their shape when unpacked. To increase their beauty, Fortuny created a range of semi-transparent vegetable dyes which shimmered and glistened like coated silk.

Madeleine Vionnet
bias-cut dress

1913 Vionnet (1876–1975) was the first designer to make the bias cut (fabric cut against the grain) her own, using it to drape, pleat, hang and sculpt fabric about the body in ways that gave garments a three-dimensional quality. Her use of structured materials, such as gaberdine, crêpe-de-chine and satin, helped her achieve this. A love of Greek dress, particularly the peplos, led Vionnet to experiment with the geometric symmetries and fluid shapes which became her hallmark. It is for her bias-cut dresses, however, that Vionnet is best remembered. Without hooks, plackets, eyes, boning or corsetry, these look dead on the hanger, but they slide on over the head to create the most sensual and articulate of shapes. Faggoting and diagonal seaming were used to further enhance this sensation. The real secret of Vionnet's success lay in her method of designing – she didn't sketch, but instead made up miniatures of her dresses, fitting them on 60-cm (2-ft)-high *poupées* to examine how they draped and moved in the 'round'. Her colours were neutral – whites, blacks and cool greys – but they were often livened up with lichen-, banana- and cactus-green. Vionnet always kept detail to a minimum, believing that her client's body was the only thing her dresses needed to make them live and breathe.

Paul Poiret
silver-trimmed bonnet

1914 Although Poiret (1877–1944) lived until he was 67, his fashion career lasted a mere six years, from 1908 to 1914. In that period, however, his energies were legion. He replaced corsets with long, loose skirts and introduced Turkish pants and lamp-shade dresses. Perversely, he also designed the 'Hobble' skirt, a tulip shape cut so tight on the ankle that it impeded movement. Poiret's designs were popular, a fine example

This cocktail dress, made in part from peach-coloured crepe, was one of Vionnet's classic designs. Bias-cut dresses, such as this one, made her name.

being his Silver-trimmed bonnet. He took much of his inspiration from Russia and the Ballets Russes and commissioned artists to create sumptuously illustrated books which were among the first fashion catalogues. He also used painters such as Raoul Dufy to design fabrics. After a visit to Josef Hoffmann's Wiener Werkstätte studios in 1911, Poiret established his own workshops in Paris, known as the Martine, where female apprentices produced fabrics, lacquered vases, and created furniture, cushions and wallpapers for sale to the public. In 1912, Poiret launched fashion's first commercial fragrance, 'Rosine'; the following year, he manufactured coloured nail varnishes. Even his bottles, shaped like apples, minarets and coiled snakes, were revolutionary. At the outbreak of the First World War, business suffered, and by 1925 Poiret was unemployed. He became a journeyman designer in Paris and London, but his health failed and his friends abandoned him. Shortly before his death in 1944, he was so poor that his clothes had to be made from old curtains.

This silver lamé bonnet was created in 1914 by Paul Poiret. It is trimmed with seven plumes of black horsehair.

Jean Desprès
modernist jewellery

1920 Desprès (1889–1980) is regarded as one of the key players in the history of modern jewellery. His Machine-Age shapes and stripped-down functionalism were as much a product of the ideologies he subscribed to – Bauhaus, the Glasgow School, the Vienna Secession – as they were a product of his aeronautic and engineering background. His materials were simple (silver, platinum, steel and brass), his shapes were cubistic, and many of his rings were constructed with sealed joints and knuckle welts to re-enforce their factory-floor origins. In 1929, Desprès co-founded the Union of Modern Artists (UAM) to further his ideas of functional sparseness or 'great nudity'. In 1930, he collaborated with the painter Etienne Cournault to produce his 'Bijoux Surréalistes' collection, and in 1934 he became the director of the highly influential Gallery of Art and Fashion.

Jeanne Lanvin
'L'Heure du Thé'

1920 In 1914, Lanvin (1867–1946) introduced a dress known as the '1830 frock', adapted from an eighteenth-century pannier; it was later reintroduced as a 'Pannier gown' and, finally, in the 1920s, as a 'Robe de style'. Familiar with Coco Chanel's *garçonne* look, journalists scoffed at Lanvin's full skirts, myriad pleats and frilly necklines, but the look endured, and she showed variations on her original for nearly 20 years. Lanvin's work was praised for its youthfulness and strong colour sense, inspired by French painters such as Auguste Renoir, Henri Fantin-Latour and Odilon Redon, a fine example being her 'L'Heure du Thé'. To duplicate their colours, she established her own dye-works, where she created the famous 'Lanvin Blue'.

Jean Patou
1929 collection

1929 Patou (1887–1936) invented the *garçonne* look which Coco Chanel then adapted and made so popular. Patou's clothes were mannish and tough, but slimline pure. He dressed female sports stars, aviators and dancers in the kind of clothes that reflected their individuality and financial freedom: V-neck sweaters, trousers and corsetless blouses. He opened the world's first female sports shops, gave us our first unisex scent and was the first designer to brand his clothes and sell off-the-peg, machine-made knits. In 1925, he launched the 'Princess' line, and in 1929, he introduced a silhouette which became the defining look for the next several years: ankle-length skirts rounded on the hip, natural waistlines and boned bodices which shaped the

This illustration of Lanvin's L'Heure du Thé appeared in a 1920 edition of Le Gazette-du-bon-bon. *The drawing is by Benito.*

breasts comfortably. A style innovator, Patou was also a gambler and *bon vivant*, two factors which led to his early death from a stroke, aged 49.

Raymond Templier
jewellery

1929 Templier (1891–1968) was one of a handful of twentieth-century designers who revolted against the rococo excesses of their fellow jewellers. Inspired by Le Corbusier and the Bauhaus, he looked to the future. Templier's obsessions were mechanical, his leanings were Cubist, and his bracelet designs, like those of his fellow designer Jean Desprès, were drawn from abstracts based on aeroplanes, trains, machines and motorcars. Templier's finishes, however, had an Art Deco warmth – dull golds, sanded lacquers, soft silvers – so the effect, although austere, was never hard or uncompromising. He was one of the founding members of the Union of Modern Artists (UAM), collaborated with Cassandre and Marcel Percheron, and founded the Group of Five with Pierre Chareau, Dominique, Pierre Legrain and Jean Puiforcat.

Top: the 'Minaudière' toiletries case was created from gold and precious stones. It measures just 3.6 cm x 9.4 cm x 4.5 cm.

Bottom: this beautifully worked brooch in silver and black enamel is by Raymond Templier. It is now housed in the Musée des Arts Decoratifs in Paris.

Van Cleef and Arpels
minaudière

1930 In 1930, Louis Arpels created the *minaudière*, a small, hard, tubular purse with a shoulder chain for the American heiress Florence J. Gould to keep her toiletries in. The purse, copied by Boucheron and Cartier, became the most popular accessory of the 1940s and '50s. In 1935, the firm of Van Cleef and Arpels triumphed again, this time with a brooch for Wallis Simpson which used a series of fine metal rods to secure diamonds edge to edge, eliminating the need for a clasp. The effect was extraordinary: rivals copied the design immediately, and it has since become one of the most popular and widely used methods for setting stones in the history of jewellery design.

Gilbert Adrian
'Letty Lynton' sleeves and designs for Greta Garbo

1932 Adrian (1903–1959) was Hollywood's most renowned designer. His white organdy 'Letty Lynton' dress, with ruffled sleeves, sold over half a million copies when retailed through the American department store Macy's in 1932, and the looks he created for actress Greta Garbo (crêpe coats, pillbox hats, slinky satin dinner gowns) became overnight sensations. In 1941, he set up Adrian Ltd. With Joan Crawford as his inspiration, he created a tailored two-piece with padded shoulders which defined American fashion for the 1940s. Adrian's patterns were bold, his fabrics were sumptuous, and his shapes were sharp; animal prints and bold geometrics were his signature, especially in his daywear. It was in Adrian's slinky, smouldering eveningwear that he gave the fullest acknowledgement to his screen-idol muses.

Charles James
'Spiral drape' dress

1934 The Spanish designer Cristobal Balenciaga called him the world's greatest couturier, yet the Chicago-born James (1906–1978) is hardly known outside the fashion industry, despite the fact that his 'Shamrock-leaf' ballgowns and 'Spiral drape' dresses are design classics. These could take weeks to make, many evolving from an interchangeable kit of parts whose sleeves, bodices, armpits and trains could be mixed and matched to produce new lines, almost like designing new automobiles. The results were breathtaking: soft sculptural gowns with formal collars, strict

backs and fabric skins which worked in concert to create rippling, flowing panniers. So great were James's efforts that Picasso hailed him as the world's first soft sculptor, while women like Elizabeth Arden were happy to wait weeks or sometimes months for one of his dresses.

Elsa Schiaparelli
Surrealistic clothing

1935 The ethos of Schiaparelli (1890–1973) was to astound and amuse. This she certainly achieved, with help from creative legends such as Salvador Dalí, Louis Aragon and Jean Cocteau. With Dalí, she produced hats which resembled shoes, and bags with telephone-handles; with Aragon, 'aspirin' necklaces; with Cocteau, trompe-l'oeil jackets containing women's faces and hair cascading down necks to form sleeves. In her 1938 'Circus' collection, models sported ice-cream-cone hats and balloon handbags and wore jackets sprinkled with prancing horses and buttons resembling free-falling acrobats. In Schiaparelli's accessory lines, there were hats which mimicked lamb cutlets, buttons like padlocks and music-playing handbags. When critics condemned her for her excesses, she printed their views on fabric and sold them off as dresses and scarves. Behind all of Schiaparelli's apparent triteness was a razor-sharp businesswoman and a tailor of the first order – her Place Vendôme boutique in Paris continued selling beautifully cut jackets and exquisitely draped eveningwear. Her pagoda sleeves, padded sweaters, dyed furs, parachute dresses, sleek trouser suits – even the world's first male fragrance ('Snuff', introduced in 1939) – remind us that she was a designer well ahead of her age.

This 1940s design from Elsa Schiaparelli features an outsize leopard-skin muff to cover the whole arm, worn with a matching cap.

G. H. Bass & Co.
Bass 'Weejun' shoes

1936 Many consider Bass 'Weejuns' to be based on the moccasins worn by Native Americans; however, it is more likely that they were a development of shoes worn by Norwegian fishermen. Brought to the USA by Scandinavian immigrants, commercial versions were produced by G. H. Bass & Co. in the 1930s. These were designed with tassels and decorative straps stitched into the vamp. Schoolgirls in the 1940s wedged polished pennies between the straps, and by the 1950s the shoes had become known as 'penny loafers'. In the 1960s, the Italy firm of Gucci first produced a version which – worn without socks – became a jet-set perennial; the penny slot was replaced by a gold snaffle.

Claire McCardell
'Monastic gown'

1938 McCardell's (1906–1958) 'Monastic gown' was a bustless, dartless, wrapover dress with tie fronts – the first modern sportswear. Easy to manufacture, it was copied instantly, a fact which contributed to the closure of the company for which McCardell worked. However, encouraged by the popularity of her design, and using techniques learned from Mariono Fortuny, Madeleine Vionnet and Jean Patou during her student years in Paris, McCardell produced range after range of functional, easy-fit basics which have become womenswear classics: leotards, cropped sweaters, pedal pushers, leggings, dirndls, hooded tops and pumps. Her famous popover dress (1942) sold 40,000 copies when launched, and she was said to have one of her hostess gowns in every household in middle-class America. McCardell was among the first designers to produce a six-piece modular wardrobe and to sell separates for working women, so that they could mix and match clothes to suit their own needs rather than those of a designer or fashion editor. Her fabrics were easy-care durables – denim, seersucker, calico, mattress ticking and nylon – and her name is forever linked with the development of popper studs, drawstrings, double stitching, rivets, patch pockets and welted seams for use in everyday fashion. McCardell's output was prolific, and when she died in 1958 from cancer, she was rightly hailed as the first designer to have made ready-to-wear clothes a viable concept.

Mainbocher
Armed Services uniforms

1943 With their fitted jackets, taut waists, built-up shoulders and pencil-line skirts, the uniforms designed by Mainbocher (1890–1976) arguably did more for recruitment figures in Britain than the posters they graced.

The look summed up the Mainbocher woman: confident, poised, elegant and slim. In addition to uniforms for the WAVES, he created looks for the women's marine corps, the American Red Cross, and the American girl scouts, who continue to wear his designs today. Mainbocher pioneered the first strapless evening dress (1934), and, 17 years before Christian Dior's 'New Look', he previewed full skirts, wasp waists and boned jackets to an aghast audience. Originally an illustrator, Mainbocher was editor-in-chief of *Vogue* in Paris before leaving to design clothes in 1929.

Louis Raerd
bikini swimsuit

1946 Although Raerd, a Swiss designer and engineer working out of Paris, is credited with giving the bikini its name, the look itself was created by the French couturier Jacques Heim. Because of its brevity, Heim named it the *atome*, but three weeks later, when Raerd unveiled his version, he called it a bikini, referring to the Pacific atoll on which the USA had just tested the first atomic bomb. Raerd's designs, which were shorter and sheerer than Heim's, became the new measure for poolside daring.

Christian Dior
'New Look'

1947 Although Dior (1905–1957) did not open his own couture house until he was 42, his first collection was a runaway success. Dubbed the 'New Look' by US journalists, it offered women a fabulous alternative to the butch 'make-do-and-mend' fashions of the fabric-starved war years. Rounded shoulders, raised busts and cinched waists abounded, while below-the-knee skirts were cut so wide that up to 37 m (40 yds) of fabric were used in their construction. Boning too was re-introduced, as well as padding at the shoulders and the waist to give the figure a deliberately exaggerated sense of femininity. All this came from Dior's love of French Belle-Epoque styling and his memories of his early years as a sketch artist for old-world houses like Piquet and Lelong. His 'New Look' clothes were highly controversial, and resulted in a wave of criticism about their extravagence and style. Dior, however, persevered in the face of this hostility, and with backing from textiles millionaire Marcel Boussac, followed his revolutionary line with a series of experimental silhouettes: the 'A-line', the 'H-line', the 'Y-line', the 'Arrow line' and – in response to Coco Chanel's return to the catwalk with her softly tailored suits in 1954 – his 'Lily of the Valley' line, a look he continued to refine until his death in 1957. The 'New Look' was a turning point in post-war fashion.

Norman Norell
'divided skirts'

1950 The 'divided skirts' designed by Norell (1900–1972) demonstrated his preoccupation that clothes should, above all, be functional. He based these skirts on men's trousers, cutting them to move like 'legs'. Norell's signature chemises, peacoats, turtlenecks and wrap coats all came with hand-stitched buttonholes, correct interlinings and tailored darts to keep garments structured and sharp. Necklines were low, collars rounded and sleeves cigarette-shaped. A true creative genius, Norell anticipated Yves St Laurent's seminal safari jackets. In 1960, when American women wanted smart, easy outfits to go to work in, Norell designed pant suits and belt-over jumpsuits, modelled on air-force overalls, which became shopping staples. His short, sharp ice-skater skirts were copied by Paris, while his all-over sequined sheaths were, and still are, copied by department stores in Britain and the USA.

Yves St Laurent
'Trapeze' line

1958 The debut collection by St Laurent (1936–) for Dior was a triumph: a full-vented silhouette, with skirts which swept down to the knee, but with an elevated bust to create an upbeat mood. His streetwise beatnik collection of 1960 was less popular; cashmere turtlenecks and mink-trimmed leather jackets were deemed too tacky and inappropriate for the house's *grand-dame* clientele. However, St Laurent was already a legend. Leaving Dior, he went on to create some of the century's most memorable looks: pea jackets (1962); smock tops, thigh boots (1963); see-though blouses (1968); and his seminal 'le Smoking' (1966), a tuxedo jacket worn with trousers in the softest wools. Like Coco Chanel, he used the male wardrobe for inspiration, but also ideas from the paintings of Piet Mondrian, the Ballets Russes, De Stijl, the work of Picasso and, for his eveningwear, the fantasy dresses of women in Marcel Proust's novels. In 1965, St Laurent was the first couturier to launch a cheap ready-to-wear line, 'Rive Gauche', and in the 1970s he became one of Paris's most respected costume designers. In 1983, in recognition of his artistry, the Metropolitan Museum of Art in New York City held an exhibition of his work.

Cristobal Balenciaga
evening dresses

1958 Women adored the work of Balenciaga (1895–1972), since 'it made the old beautiful, the young dignified'. His melon-shaped evening gowns (1952) and three-tiered 'wedding cake' dresses (1954) are works of art in their own right and were also flattering to the figure. To create

The yards of fabric used in Dior's 'New Look' were a reaction to wartime rationing. This red wool coat has large pockets and several pleats at the back.

This luxurious gown by Cristobel Balenciaga is made from blue taffetta. The snug-fitting bodice and enormous skirt were the height of fashion in 1958.

them, he used stiffened fabrics like gazar, corduroy and double-faced wool, but also incorporated pleats, drapes and invisible darts to reduce the number of seams. Balenciaga's gowns are slightly reminiscent of those in paintings by Diego Velásquez and Francesco Goya, yet they were also inspired by the Cubist planes and subtle colour sense of Georges Braque and Picasso. His early designs were austere – tailored suits and black, hip-draped jersey dresses which 'fitted the figure like a wet glove' (1938). During the Second World War, Balenciaga's mastery of cut and colour – often inspired by the torrid reds and melon oranges of his Basque-country youth – blossomed, and the 1950s became his defining period. It was then that he designed his gravity-defying coats, stand-away collars, three-quarter-length sleeves, baby-doll dresses and elegant evening gowns. In the 1960s, his influence waned, and the slim-fit fashions of former pupils made his cowl shapes seem dated. In 1968, Balenciaga pronounced couture dead and retired to his native Spain.

Ⓜ Gabrielle 'Coco' Chanel
Chanel suit

1959 Although the Chanel suit had been around since the 1920s, it was not until the designer's return to fashion in 1954 that it became the suit we recognize today: a three-piece uniform of soft tweeds, collarless cardigan jackets and weighted pockets and blouses made to match the inner lining of the jackets themselves; skirts were always below the knee. Chanel's (1883–1971) tailoring was always masterful and masculine. Like Jean Patou, her arch rival, many of Chanel's best ideas came from the male wardrobe, but also from the coastlines of Brittany and the boardwalks of Biarritz and Deauville, where she began life as a

milliner working from her lover's apartment. Her heyday was the 1920s, her associations with names like Picasso and Le Corbusier putting her in touch with a 'less is more' aesthetic she made her own. Chanel adopted beige as her favourite colour, borrowed from the functionality of sportswear to put her women in trousers and designed skirts with 'walking pleats' to facilitate greater movement. She also gave us the fashion beret, the cloche hat, costume jewellery as an acceptable accessory, and the strapless, backless, bias-cut evening dress. In 1939, accused of aiding the Nazis, Chanel retreated to Switzerland, but in 1954 she returned to the rue Cambon in Paris to run her couture house, where she continued to design and refine her look until her death.

André Courrèges
'Hipsters'

1964 Courrèges (1923–) created 'Hipsters' as 'machines for lounging' in much the same way as his idol, Le Corbusier, created houses as 'machines for living'. 'Hipsters' were clean, functional and sparse, with the designer's engineering background encouraging him to dispense with pleats, darts, cuffs and plackets in favour of an aerodynamically smooth look. Trained by Cristobal Balenciaga, Courrèges used only the most ascetic of materials – wool, gaberdine, cotton, plastic and leather – and shades of white to keep his clothes striking and minimal. Detail came in the form of appliquéd daisies, chevron stitching, bib yokes and keyhole necklines. His 'fashion moment' (1964–68) was short-lived, but his 'space-age' wardrobe of knitted catsuits, mini-dresses, trapeze skirts, goggle hats and white go-go boots are now the stuff of 1960s legend.

This classic suit dates from 1959 – the heyday of Chanel's fashion career. The suit is made from oatmeal-coloured wool trimmed with navy.

Barbara Hulanicki
'Dolly' dresses

1964 The 'Biba look' was launched by Hulanicki (1936–) from her first London boutique in 1961. It consisted of smock-style dresses, sometimes with frills, reminiscent of the short-sleeved, flouncy frocks worn by Victorian children, as well as shifts, T-shirts, straw hats and feather boas. All the clothes were dyed in Biba's trademark colours – 'Auntie' colours, as she called them – of blueberry, rust, plum and bruised purple. Some clothes were new, many were second-hand, but all were surrounded in the boutique by objects inspired by Art Nouveau or Art Deco. The huge Biba emporium opened in the former Derry and Tom department store in London in 1972; it was one of the first youth-orientated lifestyle boutiques of its kind, selling everything from food to wallpaper, music, cosmetics and art.

Emilio Pucci
accessories

1965 Like his clothes, accessories designed by Pucci (1914–1990) are now collectors' items. His shoes, hats and handbags are distinguished by the bold, brash prints in which they are covered: psychedelic colour fields broken by zigzags, circles and exploding flower shapes, all in shades of blue, purple, red and fuchsia pink inspired by his beloved Capri and trips to Bali and Tanzania. Pucci also created large scarves, worn as shawls, wraps or sarongs or knotted together to create one of his 'Chute' dresses (1960). An Olympic skier, Pucci designed male and female sportswear, 'Capsula' jumpsuits, stretch unitards (1959), body stockings (1968) and a fabric called 'Emilioform'. He also created a range of colours: 'Pucci Pink', 'Emilio Blue' and 'Punchy Purple'.

Left: two distinctive Emilio Pucci designs: brightly coloured plastic sunglasses, stamped with the Pucci name, and contrasting scarves.

Right: this pair of bright red, see-through plastic boots are shown here with their original Mary Quant plastic carrier bag, bearing the logo 'quant afoot'.

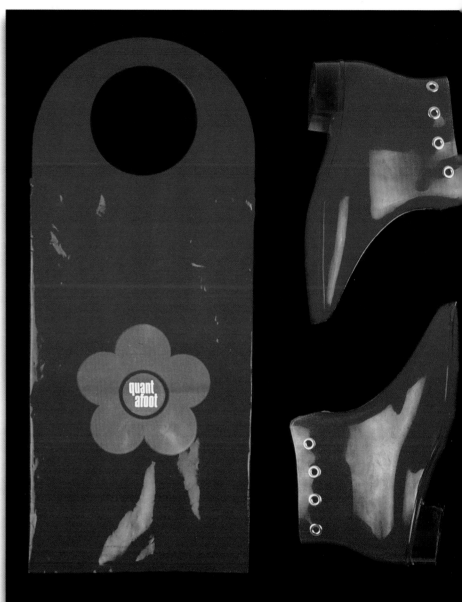

Mary Quant
the 'Mini'

1965 Did she or didn't she invent the 'Mini'? Whatever the truth of the matter, it is generally agreed that Quant (1934–) popularized the look, along with the 'kooky' styles we now associate with the Swinging '60s: black stockings, hot pants, tall boots, tight polo-necks, sleeveless shifts and pinafore dresses. Quant, who began making clothes in her bedsit, went on to open one of Britain's first concept boutiques, Bazaar, in 1955.

Stephen Burrows
'lettuce' hems

1967 An Afro-American designer who rose to fame during the disco years of the 1970s, Burrows (1943–) created fluid, flirty, hip-hugging creations which became the standard uniform of the Studio 54 set in Manhattan. His contemporaries Halston, Giorgio di Sant'Angelo and Calvin Klein all took direction from his sleek modernity and after-dark sophistication. Burrows's 'lettuce' hems, created by stitching the edges of a hem to make it pucker and curve, are period classics, and his colour sense – vibrant, flashy and supremely confident – are still aped by downtown sportswear designers today. Burrows continues to live and work in New York, designing custom-made clothes and body-sculpting eveningwear for a discerning and appreciative clientele.

Bill Blass
Mid-west modern

1970 Blass (1922–) is the man credited with making middle-American fashion modern and durable, marrying the simplicity of Coco Chanel with the hard-shouldered glamour of 1940s Hollywood. His eveningwear included hip-hugging dresses which shimmered like cinema signs and spaghetti-strapped sheaths evoking Greta Garbo and Marlene Dietrich. Blass's daywear became the prototype for 'ladies who lunch' everywhere: shirt-jackets, safari trouser suits, twin-sets, and mannish shirts in masculine combinations of checks and plaids. The colours were confident – tomato, emerald, black and dove grey – to reflect the mood of the women who wore them, while his fabrics – cotton, wool, linen and silk – evoked modern 'can-do New York' without being cold or austere.

Ralph Lauren
'Polo' logo

1971 Although the mallet-swinging polo player had existed in various guises since 1896, when the American Brooks brothers produced their first button-down polo shirts, it was not a recognized trademark until Lauren (1937–) used it to launch his womenswear line in 1971. The logo's appeal as a symbol of Ivy-League success was immediate, and it soon appeared on everything from Ralph Lauren menswear (launched in 1967) to diffusion lines like 'Chaps', 'Ralph', 'Double RL' and 'Polo Sport'. The trademark signifies Lauren's fascination with WASP America – his love of club ties (his company was founded on them), cricket sweaters, English tweeds and white button-down Oxford shirts – and sends out a message as timeless and old-world polite as the designer himself.

Here, customers could buy 'a bouillabaisse of clothes and accessories' under one roof. Other shops followed, as well as a mail-order service, an American line, cosmetics, toys, hats, scarves, mugs and even bed-linen. In the interim, Quant designed for Alligator rainwear, Kangol and Dupont and continued to exploit and develop London street looks: woolly tights (1958), sleeveless shifts (1959), coloured nail varnish (1966) and vinyl hot pants (1970). In 1966, she was awarded the OBE.

Mary Quant is widely credited with having invented the mini skirt. At the very least she was the designer who brought it to the streets and made it her own.

Manolo Blahnik
stiletto heels

1973 Few shoes rival those of Blahnik, with their hand-carved heels, tapered vamps, seductive fabrics, sliver-thin straps and a fit which hugs the foot like a lamé glove. So crafted are Blahnik's shoes that as many as 50 different production procedures are needed to make a single pair. He has chosen to opt for quality, rejecting the methods of mass production. As a result, his Italian factory can only produce 80 pairs per day – a mere trickle by competitor standards – but none can duplicate his soft leathers, subtle colours or soles sprung so light that they create an almost bouncing sensation in the wearer.

Halston
minimalist fashion

1973 Many have followed him, but Halston (1932–1990) was the first to push minimalism to its limits. The American designer's monochromatic sparseness was reminiscent of Greek walls and monastic settings. His favourite creations, lacking seams, pockets or lapels, hung from the shoulder in ancient Greek style. Fabrics were the softest he could find – silk, cashmere, double-faced wools and Ultrasuede, a synthetic which became his signature. Strapless column dresses were a staple, as were shirtdresses. Only at night did Halston deviate from his reductivist creed; in his eveningwear, glitter was permitted, in shimmering gossamer or silks which caressed the torso like errant butterfly wings.

Manolo Blahnik's shoes are internationally renowned for their superb quality and the fine production techniques employed at his factories.

Giorgio Armani
soft tailoring

1974 Soft tailoring, a technique developed by Armani (1934–) during his time as designer at Cerruti, proved an instant hit. It is flattering and unstructured, achieved by eliminating interfaces, linings and shoulder pads in jackets, and by making trousers and skirts without darts or pleats. When Armani launched his own label in 1974, he became the biggest-selling European designer ever in the USA. Even now, his silhouette seldom changes; this is the secret of his longevity. Seasonally, collections are refined – shoulders may be widened or slimmed, jackets are shown with two buttons or three, trousers are sent out flat-fronted or pleated – but the softness, consummate minimalism and use of high-quality fabrics (soft wools, rich suedes, light cashmeres and cool cottons) remain. Other labels include 'Emporio Armani', 'Mani', 'AX', 'Armani Exchange' and 'Giorgio Armani Calze'.

Elsa Peretti
heart jewellery for Tiffany

1974 A model in the 1960s, Peretti (1940–) began designing for Halston and Giorgio di Sant'Angelo before becoming Tiffany's 'star turn' in 1974. Her minimalism, like that of Halston, is absolute. However, unlike him, her inspiration came from nature, featuring a stylized heart in a range of necklaces, bracelets, rings and belts, mostly in silver. Other themes in her work are bones, snakes, scorpions and scuttling crabs. Like the British designer William Morris, Peretti works with a team of close-knit craftspeople, many of her pieces thus being a collective effort. Her jewellery is made from natural materials found locally or in her native Italy. Peretti's work is never elitist; for Tiffany, for example, she produced her much-lauded 'Diamonds-by-the-yard' in an attempt to make precious stones available to a greater number of purchasers.

 ### Vivienne Westwood
'Bondage' trousers

1976 Westwood (1941–) is one of fashion's great innovators. Her 1976 'Bondage' collection was a turning-point in her career. Westwood's ripped mohair sweaters, torn trousers with straps and tartan bondage suits were followed by kilts, bum flaps and the infamous 'Anarchy' T-shirts. These showed Queen Elizabeth with safety pins pushed through her nose, the figure of Christ from a Renaissance altarpiece upside-down, and cowboys flashing their genitals. Westwood was prosecuted for these efforts, but her creativity remained undimmed. In 1981, she anticipated trends like Neo-romanticism with her colourful 'Pirates' collection. In 1984, she moved towards deconstruction, with clothes containing

Vivienne Westwood's 'Bondage' trousers caused a fashion sensation, playing on the 1970s punk revolution and the trend for more aggressive fashion.

exposed seams, torn fabrics and jackets constructed inside-out. In 1985, she unveiled the 'Mini-crini' (remade corsets in the shape of corset dresses) and simultaneously gave us Harris-tweed suits and prim and proper twin-sets. Throughout, Westwood's references were wide-ranging – Marcel Proust, Bertrand Russell, the French socialite Mme Recamier and the Regency dandy – and tweeds and tartans were among her most recognizable fabrics. Westwood shows collections in Paris and London twice-yearly and has been awarded an OBE for her contribution to British fashion; characteristically, she arrived to accept this honour sporting a tartan micro-mini and no underwear.

Zandra Rhodes
'Conceptual Chic'

1977 In 1977, Rhodes (1940–) produced a collection of T-shirts, ripped tops and asymmetrical dresses held together with diamanté safety pins that courted instant controversy. Few understood its origins (Elsa Schiaparelli's infamous 'Tear' dress), and most criticized Rhodes for using deluxe fabrics like silk jersey and chiffon to produce such a trashy aesthetic. Her punk wedding dresses were particularly reviled, and her delicately wrought spider-web stoles, now collectors' items, were laughed at, despite the fact that their 'holes'

Zandra Rhodes's 1977 collection is now considered a period classic. Its art studio origins have earned it the label of 'art' as well as that of 'fashion'.

were cleverly constructed openings which allowed them to be worn 17 different ways. Called 'Conceptual Chic', the 1977 collection is now viewed as a period classic. Given its origins in the studios of such artists as Allen Jones, Duggie Fields and Andrew Logan, it is perhaps better regarded as an art rather than a fashion happening.

Ⓜ Rei Kawakubo
grunge and deconstruction

1981 Although she had been designing in Japan since 1975, it was not until her 1981 Paris debut that Kawakubo (1941–), under the Commes des Garçons label, became an international name. The show was a direct attack on the prettified fashions of the previous decade, her distressed yarns, torn fabrics, fractured weaves, ill-fitting jackets and asymmetrical silhouettes challenging the idea that clothes should simply be something pretty to wear. In 1982, Kawakubo unveiled her infamous 'Holes' collection, and she has continued with this line of attack for over a decade: garments with slashes, jackets with seams on the outside, and coats which resemble the wrapover gowns of war-ravaged samurai warriors. Of late, lumps have appeared, eruptions on the surface of her fabrics that suggest disease and radiation poisoning. Kawakubo's monologue is extremely important: without her, there would be no deconstruction

The harsh punky lines of Rhodes's 1977 collection was a reaction to the gentle hippy and flower power fashions of the Sixties and early Seventies.

Left: Jean Paul Gaultier's fashion corsets reached new heights when worn on stage by the singer Madonna in one of her most publicized international tours.

Right: when Jean Paul Gaultier unveiled his corset dress in 1982, he wowed the fashion world and started a long-enduring trend for corseted items.

or grunge – or second-hand clothes – as a response to the blandness of the high street and the spiralling cost of designer labels.

Jean Paul Gaultier
'Corset' dress

1982 Trained at the couture houses of Cardin and Patou, Gaultier (1952–) is undoubtedly fashion's clown-prince of kitsch. In 1982, he produced the 'Corset' dress; in 1984, his spivvy pinstripes parodied 'City Man' tailoring, and he introduced conical bras; in 1985, in his notorious 'And God Created Man' collection, he shocked audiences by introducing skirts for men; in 1990, Madonna brought attention to his range of corsets and bras. Despite his anarchic approach, Gaultier never diverts from strict cut and a good finish. His choice of quality fabrics is also of utmost importance, combining his lust for the new – Tencel, Tactel, neoprene and coated rubbers – with more classic, old-time favourites.

John Galliano
Napoleon-style jackets and Empire-line dresses

1984 Four-time British Designer of the Year, St Martin's graduate Galliano (1960–) is justly deserving of such plaudits. From his graduate collection, 'Les Incroyables', to his current role as head of Dior, his work is mesmeric. Bias-cut gowns, frock coats, Napoleon-style jackets and Empire-line dresses all speak of a tailoring talent as fastidious as it is unique. Tricks have been borrowed from the archives of the Victoria and Albert Museum in London, including historic draping, layering and cutting techniques from Paris and China. Bias cutting, scooped backs, scissored fronts, slashed jackets, asymmetrical hems and fabrics such as gaberdine and silver lace give Galliano's clothes a contemporary look.

Donna Karan
business suits for women

1985 Sleek, black, minimal, shoulder-padded and very forgiving of a woman's figure, these suits designed by Karan (1948–) became a symbol of the 'no-nonsense' 1980s executive. Built around the stretch jersey body inspired by Martha Graham, Karan's suits were part of a foundation wardrobe which came in deluxe fabrics, such as cashmere, wool, alpaca and cotton, as well as simple, easy-care pieces. The look was trans-seasonal, the fabrics were light, and each module came with long and short skirts, tailored coats, masculine blouses and office-to-evening jackets. It was an instant hit, as was Karan's philosophy – 'You gotta accent your positive, delete your negative' – learned from the successes of Anne Klein, Claire McCardell, Norman Norell and Calvin Klein.

Donna Karan really made her name with the success of her business suits for women. The one featured here is from her Spring 1995 collection.

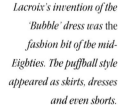

Lacroix's invention of the 'Bubble' dress was the fashion hit of the mid-Eighties. The puffball style appeared as skirts, dresses and even shorts.

Christian Lacroix
'Bubble' dress

1985 In his designers, museum curator-turned-couturier Lacroix (1951–) reveals his world of wild pastiche and high-octane drama. Fabrics are exotic – brocades, furs, psychedelic tweeds and jewel-trimmed *devorés* – and references are always breathtaking and broad – Picasso, Cecil Beaton, Biba, ancient Pompeii and punk. Like his colours, Lacroix's hemlines vary in every collection. In his trapeze-line look, which he created while working at Patou, pouf dresses were stuffed and tucked to give them extra shape and buoyancy. Other dresses swelled up and puffed out to balloon proportions. Lacroix took over Patou in 1982, leaving in 1987 to design under his own name. He is highly regarded for his contribution to couture of master tailoring and supreme wit.

Issey Miyake
concertina pleats

1987 Miyake's (1938–) pleats are triumphs of technology over fabric. Advanced synthetics and rubberized coatings allow him to create twists, eddies and origami folds which even Mariano Fortuny could not have achieved. While some of his clothes are austere and cowl-like (inspired by samurai warriors and Buddhist monks), Miyake's 'Pleats Please' label is a distinctly mischievous, child-like collection: dolly-mixture colours, kimono wraps, 'bouncing' dresses and shirts and T-shirts which fold up into tubes and squares. Miyake views this line as kinetic sculpture. His shows resemble happenings rather than the usual catwalk events; dancers, actors and even octogenarians are used as models, forcing us to re-examine the nature and meaning of fashion.

Philip Treacy
mad hattings

1995 A graduate of the Royal College of Art in London, Irish-born Treacy's style is instantly recognizable. Surreal, sculptural Post-modern-lite, his Mad Hatter's toppers sprout cock-feather monocles, while model Spanish galleons set sail on black tulle seas. Even Guardsmen's busby's receive the Treacy touch: instead of bearskin, he uses yellow ostrich feathers which shimmer and ripple like windswept grass. Treacy's unique palette – vivid reds, acidic yellows and imperial blues – as well as his mastery of balance and proportion have earned him the title of 'fashion's Rembrandt'. His influences are diverse (Martha Graham, Salvador Dalí, Renaissance painting), but his results are always breathtaking and modern. Treacy has received commissions from top names such as Valentino, Karl Lagerfeld, Rifat Ozbek and Oscar de la Renta.

Issey Miyake is famed for his mastery of the art of fabric pleating. This concertina dress was shown in his collection for Spring 1995.

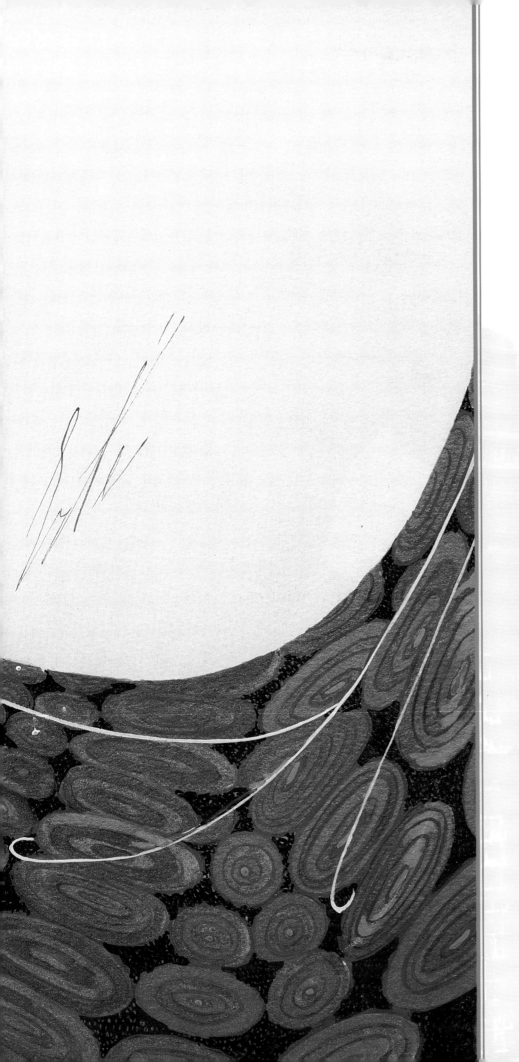

Costume & Set design

7

THE COSTUMES FROM THE BALLET *THE RITE OF SPRING*, WHICH CONTRIBUTED TO THE OUTBREAK OF A NEAR-RIOT ON THE OPENING NIGHT, AND THE SET DESIGN FOR THE SCIENCE FICTION FILM *2001: A SPACE ODYSSEY*, SHOW HOW COSTUME AND SET DESIGN CAN HAVE AN INFLUENCE IN WIDER SOCIETY. A RANGE OF OTHER WORKS DEMONSTRATE THE SHEER DIVERSITY OF DESIGN IN THE ENTERTAINMENT FIELD.

Aleksandre Benois
designs for the Imperial Theatre, St Petersburg, Russia

1900s Benois (1870–1950) was a painter, designer and art critic who played a leading role in Russian artistic life in the early twentieth century. A native of St Petersburg, he was a member of the group of young men who published *Mir Iskusstva*, a journal of the arts. Benois is best known for his costumes and set designs, created first for the Imperial Theatres in St Petersburg and later for Serge Diaghilev's Ballets Russes. In 1926, Benois emigrated to Paris. His designs for the Imperial Theatre influenced all of the performing arts, and as a close friend and collaborator of Diaghilev in both Russia and Paris, he designed *The Pavilion of Armide*, *Sylphides* and *Petrouchka* (1909–11). Benois' stage designs juxtaposed the tradition of Russian folk art with French Rococo elements.

Léon Bakst
Scheherazade ballet

1910 The Russian artist Léon Bakst (1866–1924) is known primarily for his association with Serge Diaghilev and his Ballets Russes. Bakst's sumptuous decors for such ballets as *Scheherazade* and *Afternoon of a Faun* (1912) contributed to the success of the company and launched a craze for exotic colours and patterns in fashion. His first sets were for a mime staged by Marius Petipa at the Hermitage court theatre in 1902. After his success with the Ballets Russes in Paris in the 1900s, Bakst returned to Russia, where he founded a school of painting. His last years were spent in Paris designing sets for plays, ballets and operas.

Scheherazade helped to transform ballet into a new form through a vivid combination of movement, sound, passion, fantasy and colour. Bakst concocted 'Oriental' sets and costumes in dazzling, barbaric colours; the resulting demand for exoticism in the fashion world was answered by the couturier Paul Poiret.

Overleaf: one of Erté's legendary stage costume designs (see page 104).

Right: Léon Bakst designed this watercolour in 1910, as one of the costumes for the Ballets Russes's production of Scheherazade.

Left: Bakst worked closely with Serge Diaghilev and Rimsky-Korsakov on Scheherazade, for which he designed this wonderful stage set.

Mikhail Fokine
Firebird ballet

1910 Fokine (1880–1942) ranks as one of the most important and influential choreographers of the century. He studied at the Imperial Ballet School in St Petersburg and became a notable soloist in the Maryinsky (now Kirov) Ballet. Fokine left the Maryinsky in 1909 to become chief choreographer for Serge Diaghilev's troupe of Russian dancers, which was to emerge as the Ballets Russes and change the course of Western ballet history. Fokine rejected the artificiality of conventional ballets for greater naturalism of movement and integration of story, music, choreography and scenic design. It was in these areas that he served Diaghilev's similar artistic vision. *Firebird*, with a score by Igor Stravinsky, is characteristic of Fokine's innovative work. He was able to portray the artistic essence of the characters in the dancing and conceived a unique overall design for the production, reflecting his mastery of plastic values and dance-mime effects.

V. E. Meyerhold
production of Don Juan, St Petersburg, Russia

1910 In a career spanning nearly 40 years as a director and producer in Russia, Vsevolod Emilievich Meyerhold (1874–1940) is generally acknowledged to have almost single-handedly revolutionized the modern theatre. His innovative career began at the Moscow Art Theatre, where he played the part of Treplev in Anton Chekhov's *The Seagull* and, later, at Konstantin Stanislavsky's invitation, staged Symbolist drama in the experimental studio. From 1908 to 1919, Meyerhold directed opera and drama at the Imperial Theatres in St Petersburg and also staged experimental productions based on improvization, clowning and acrobatics. Having dispensed with the use of a curtain in 1905, he turned auditorium and stage into a single, well-lighted area for his 1910 staging of Molière's *Don Juan*. A believer in total theatre, Meyerhold invited the collaboration of artists, musicians and poets in one of the most successful and innovative experiments of the twentieth century.

Edward Gordon Craig
production of Hamlet, Moscow Art Theatre, Russia

1911 Craig (1872–1966) was an English scene designer, producer, actor and writer about the theatre who exerted a pervasive influence on modern theatre with his stagecraft as well as his theories. Craig debuted as an actor, but soon abandoned the craft to concentrate on production and design. He attracted international attention with innovative stage designs which emphasized portable structural elements and the use of light to create atmosphere. In his best-known book, *The Art of the*

Tamara Karsavina as she appeared in Mikhail Fokine's production of L'Oiseau de Feu ('Firebird') in 1910.

Theatre (1905), he first set out his theories on the theatre of the future. Craig worked with Konstantin Stanislavsky for the Moscow Art Theatre's 1911 production of *Hamlet*, which featured an extraordinary moveable set with dramatic lights; to this day it is one of the most evocative and brooding productions of the play.

Nijinski
The Rite of Spring ballet

1913 Vaslav Fomich Nijinski (1888–1950) was one of the greatest male dancers in the history of ballet, entering the Imperial Ballet School in St Petersburg in 1898. In 1908, he met Serge Diaghilev, who was to become his mentor. Nijinski performed in Europe with the Ballets Russes, achieving success in such productions as *The Pavilion of Armide* (1909), *Sylphides* (1909) and *Scheherazade* (1910). Nijinski created two ballets in 1913, *Games* and *The Rite of Spring*; both were highly innovative, and the latter created a riot due to its heavy, asymmetrical, primeval choreography. The score was expressed through repetitive passages of walking, stamping and heavy jumping, and the audience at the premiere reacted violently to it. Many of his contemporaries considered Nijinski's experiments with style to be an artistic dead-end. Today, however, his ideas have won great respect.

Illustration from a scathing review of Nijinski's production of Stravinsky's The Rite Of Spring, *which premiered in 1913.*

Jean Cocteau
Parade ballet, Paris, France

1917 The French artist and writer Jean Cocteau (1889–1963) was both an inventor and a producer of art in many forms. Enormously prolific and extremely influential among the Parisian avant-garde for over four decades, Cocteau had a lasting effect on a distinguished coterie of painters, composers, dancers, theatrical designers and actors, and writers in every genre. His first volume of poetry was published in 1909, and his involvement with the Ballets Russes and Serge Diaghilev began the same year. After serving as an ambulance driver on the Belgian front during the First World War, Cocteau returned to Paris and in 1917 produced his ballet *Parade*, with music by the modernist Erik Satie and scenery by Picasso. The latter's drop curtain bore little relation to events on the stage, although Cocteau's fabulous conception of the play included acrobats, musicians and clowns, foreshadowing the ballet's fairground setting.

Robert Wiene
The Cabinet of Dr Caligari

1919 *The Cabinet of Dr Caligari*, a German silent horror film, is one of the most famous films of all time primarily because of its use of Expressionistic sets. The narrative, centring on a fairground magician who uses a somnambulist to commit murder, turns out to be the dream of a madman. The film raises questions about who is really sane, and the distorted sets are employed to lure the audience into a lunatic universe. The viewer sees what the madman sees – daggers of light; twisted, frightening perspectives; odd angles; brooding shadows creating an inexplicable and threatening world. Adapted from the stage, the use of stylized decor to augment plot and character development was a radical advance in film technology which influenced cinematic art direction in all countries. Director Robert Wiene undertook the experiment with the assistance of three Expressionist painters, Walter Rohrig, Hermann Warm and Walter Reimann.

Erté
Folies Bergères, Paris, France

c. 1919 Erté (Romain de Tirtoff; 1892–1990) took his name from the French pronunciation of his initials, RT. After studying at the Julian Academy in Paris, he was employed as a fashion designer by Paul Poiret. From 1915, he created drawings for the covers of *Harper's Bazaar*. Erté's inimitable style is charactized by his use of vivid colour and of floral, figurative and geometric motifs; his meticulous attention to detail and exquisite ornamentation have led to him being labelled as a

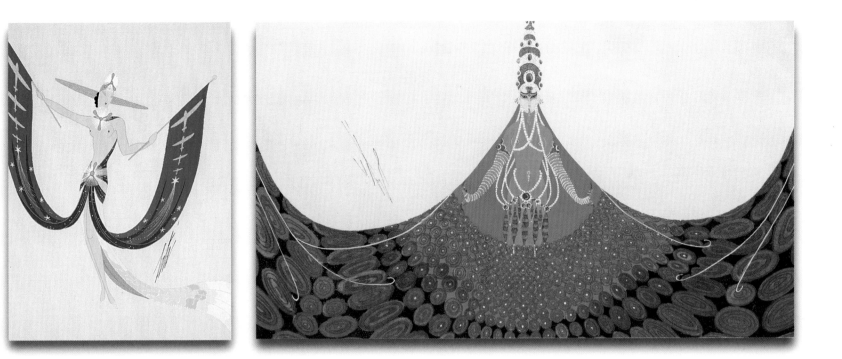

'decorative designer'. By the 1930s, Erté's theatrical designs were legend; he had produced designs for prestigious theatrical and cinematic productions around the world. For a decade, he designed the sets and costumes for the Folies Bergères almost exclusively. His lavishly colourful productions were the epitome of Art Deco design.

Henri Matisse
The Nightingale's Song ballet, Paris, France

1920 Some of Matisse's (1869–1954) most important and creative forays into theatre included costumes and sets designed for his good friend Serge Diaghilev, the brilliant impresario. In 1920, Matisse designed the Chinese set for *The Nightingale's Song*, proving a stage picture which was both simple and original. Against a mainly white background outlined in black, with touches of sky blue, the Chinese costumes stood out in the clear colours of Ming porcelain, green with pink as on a *famille-verte* vase; saffron yellow barred with orange and black. The grotesque soldiers, whose armour Matisse sketched from originals in the Cluny Museum, were sky blue and white. The overall effect was dramatic yet pure.

Pablo Picasso
Pulcinella ballet, Paris, France

1920 Another friend of Serge Diaghilev, Picasso (1881–1973) became involved with the Ballets Russes in the early 1920s, designing the set and curtains for *Mercury* at the Cigale Theatre and *The Blue Train* at the Champs-Elysées Theatre, both in Paris. One of his most important designs for the Ballets Russes was *Pulcinella*. His first idea, to design a contemporary setting for the Italian comedy, was rejected by Diaghilev. The final result – a Neapolitan street scene, conceived in Cubist terms and painted blue, grey, dark brown and white, with the houses framing a view of the bay with a boat, Mt Vesuvius and the full moon – is one of the most beautiful stage settings ever made. Picasso also designed a white floor-cloth, to give the effect of moonlight, which had to be repainted for each performance. No footlights were used. Paris was enraptured.

Norman Bel Geddes
The Miracle production, New York, New York, USA

1924 Bel Geddes (1893–1958) was one of the most visionary of American scene designers. Many of his designs comprised mood-evoking, multilevelled, abstract constructions which united the lighting techniques of Adolphe Appia with the grandeur of Edward Gordon Craig. Bel Geddes's most spectacular achievement was the transformation of New York's Century Theatre into a Gothic cathedral for Max Reinhardt's production of *The Miracle*, a set which brought him fame world-wide. His design for an adaptation and production of Dante's *Divine Comedy* comprised a crater of concentric levels whose appearance was altered by light. Envisioned for Madison Square Garden, it, like many of the designer's projects, was never realized.

Left: as well as designing for the stage, Erté also produced covers for Harpers Bazaar. This stunning sketch for a stage costume demonstrates his inimitable style.

Right: Erté's designs for stage costumes are legendary. He produced designs for some of the world's most prestigious companies.

Fritz Lang
Metropolis

1926 Lang (1890–1976) is one of the most famous and influential of the European film producers who fled Nazi Germany for Hollywood during the 1930s. Lang's early studies of painting and architecture clearly influenced the Expressionist style and grand scale of such films as *Destiny* (1921), the two-part *Nibelung Saga* (1924) and his celebrated depiction of a futuristic slave society, *Metropolis*. This silent film has long been considered a classic, but is now valued more for Lang's powerful, geometric Expressionist design than for its theme. In particular, the spectacular riot scenes are profoundly stimulating, with Lang choreographing blocks of humans as architectural elements. *Metropolis* has been reissued several times at varying lengths.

Luis Buñuel
The Golden Age

1930 Buñuel (1900–1983) was a Spanish film director whose works are characterized by mocking humour, a spirit of anarchy, irreverence and religious undertones. He was renowned for his ability to shock, instruct and entertain. *The Golden Age* created a scandal by depicting Christ and the Marquis de Sade together. The film was made in part in collaboration with Salvador Dalí, and it carries the essential hallucinatory elements of Surrealism, an aesthetic style much applauded by the European avant-garde and bewildering to everyone else. A turbulent career led to Buñuel settling in Mexico and then in France, and when he returned to Spain to make *Viridiana* (1961), the film was banned as anticlerical by the Franco regime. In January 1983, Buñuel was awarded Spain's highest civilian honour, the Grand Cross of Isabel, for work embodying an ideology that had resulted in almost 40 years of exile from his native country.

Martha Graham
Primitive Mysteries

1931 Graham (1894–1991) is universally acknowledged as the creator of modern dance, having designed and developed powerfully expressive dances based on angular, percussive gestures using the muscles of the lower torso. Dancers were encouraged to move on the floor and in space, using unconcealed tension and effort. Graham choreographed and designed *Primitive Mysteries* after a visit to the American Southwest, utilizing the region's unique blend of Spanish Christianity and native culture in a powerful re-enactment of a ritual in honour of the Virgin Mary. The simple staccato movements emphasized the dancers' connection to the earth. The scenes, costumes and choreography were deliberately austere, using black and white to highlight the stark primitiveness of Graham's subject. Graham herself played the Virgin, the only white-clad soloist.

Salvador Dalí
Sentimental Colloquy ballet

1944 The Spanish Surrealist Salvador Dalí (1904–1989) worked in several media, including jewellery, advertising, beer-bottle design and, in collaboration with Luis Buñuel, played in the film *An Andalusian Dog* (1928) and *The Golden Age* (1931). Dalí also designed the sets and costumes for several ballets, including *Sentimental Colloquy* and *Tristan Insane*. *Sentimental Colloquy* represents his serene classicism and uses dream pictures with photographic realism to create a dramatic, almost hallucinatory set. The draped costumes reflected the tranquil theme of the ballet, which was, however, disturbingly surreal.

Sir Cecil Beaton
costume designs for My Fair Lady

1958 The English designer and photographer Sir Cecil Beaton (1904–1980), best known for his photographs of such notables as Greta Garbo, Edith Sitwell and the British royal family, won a Tony Award for the period costumes in the stage production of *My Fair Lady* and an Academy Award for those in the film *Gigi*. He also designed for the

Comédie Française in Paris and for New York's Metropolitan Opera. *Gigi* is the best-known adaptation of Colette's novel, with innovative cinematography, art direction, set design and Beaton's gowns constituting an elegantly crafted confection. The designs for Audrey Hepburn in particular were stunning, inspiring many fashion designers of the day to produce copy-cat collections.

Jacques Tati
My Uncle

1958 The French film director Jacques Tati (1908–1982) began his career as a mime and established himself as an actor, writer and director with *Holiday* (1947). Subsequently, he created the comic figure of Mr Hulot, who appeared in *Mr Hulot's Holiday* (1953), *My Uncle* (1958) and *Traffic* (1971). *My Uncle*, one of Tati's most successful films, won the

Opposite: this still is from Fritz Lang's 1926 film Metropolis. *It is a silent film that has generated a cult following, as well as being considered a masterpiece of Expressionist design.*

Above: Sir Cecil Beaton won a Tony Award for his costumes used in the stage production of My Fair Lady *in 1957.*

Special Jury Prize at the Cannes Film Festival in 1958 and an Oscar for best foreign film in 1959. It combines a variety of images to portray the contrasting lifestyles of Mr Hulot and his nephew Gerard Arpel. Set designer Jacques Lagrange produced an extraordinary array of detail, referring directly to modern design classics. The Arpels' house is white, cubic and impractical, distinguished by the noise of modern appliances and harsh, vibrant colours. Mr Hulot's romantic attic apartment, in contrast, is characterized by warm colours and the gentle sounds of a Parisian suburb.

Stanley Kubrick
2001: A Space Odyssey

1968 Kubrick (1928–) is an American film writer, director and producer with a virtually legendary status. Early films include *Fear and Desire* (1953) and *Killer's Kiss* (1955). *The Killing* (1956) caused critics to take

Stanley Kubrick made 2001: A Space Odyssey *in 1968. Many aspects of his films have greatly influenced later film-makers, particularly his set designs.*

notice of his taut, brilliant style and bleakly cynical outlook, while *Paths of Glory* (1957) solidified his reputation as a film maker interested in depicting the individual at the mercy of a hostile world. *2001: A Space Odyssey* and *A Clockwork Orange* (1971), both made in England, where Kubrick has worked since 1961, engendered critical controversy, but the former has now become accepted as a landmark in modern cinema. It is a long film, obscurely symbolic, but intensely exciting from a visual point of view. The model-work is magnificent, and the Oscar-winning low-tech special effects, engineered by Douglas Trumbull, remain persuasive even in the age of computer-generated visuals.

Franco Zeffirelli
Romeo and Juliet

1968 The Italian producer, director and stage designer Franco Zeffirelli (1923–) is widely known for his sumptuous productions of classic plays and operas. After studying architecture at the University of Florence, Zeffirelli took up stage design and acting, establishing himself as a scenic designer for Luchino Visconti's operetta productions in the late 1940s. He was assistant director on several Visconti films. In the 1950s, Zeffirelli won acclaim for his own lavish opera and theatre productions, gaining a reputation for his vivid eroticism and opulent sets and costumes. From the late 1960s, he was known primarily as a film director, with credits including The *Taming of the Shrew* (1967), *Romeo and Juliet, Brother Sun and Sister Moon* (1972) and *Othello* (1968). *Romeo and Juliet*, which used teenage actors, is renowned as a lavish yet subtly stylish production, with a simmering eroticism running through both the design and the direction.

Halston
designs for Martha Graham's Acts of Light

1981 Roy Halston Frowick, known as Halston (1932–1990) was a New York fashion designer who also designed for the Martha Graham Ballet and the Dance Theatre of Harlem, among others, as well as producing the official non-competitive designs for the 1976 Montreal Olympics. In the 1970s, Halston took charge of the Graham company's wardrobe, redesigning or editing the aspect of very nearly all the ballets currently performed. The costumes became opulent, bolder and more glitzy. For *Acts of Light*, Halston dressed the performers in golden tissue which almost reduced the work to a cosmetic display. The male dancers throughout seemed more naked than before, and Halston's attention to the 'well-groomed

buttock' almost amounted to a fetish. His work with the Graham company transformed the idea of costume for modern dance, relying heavily on costuming effects to create stunning drama.

Lawrence G. Paull, Syd Mead and others
set design for Blade Runner

1982 The futuristic thriller *Blade Runner* is based on Philip K. Dick's novel *Do Androids Dream of Electric Sheep?*. It has become something of a cult film primarily because of its exceptional appearance. Both novel and movie are set in 2019 in Los Angeles, a post-apocalyptic megalopolis drenched by relentless rain. The set design is expensive, spectacular and utterly distinctive: swirling fog obscures the titanic infrastructure of the twenty-first-century city, creating a murky, congested atmosphere. The design was developed by director Ridley Scott, production designer Lawrence G. Paull, the visual futurist Syd Mead and many others, including special-effects superviser Douglas Trumbull and matte artist Matt Yuricich. It successfully evokes both past and future. Critics of the film claimed that the performances lacked the gritty, film-noir quality which would have matched the production values, but the set design and art direction earned Academy Award nominations nonetheless.

The expensive, spectacular set design for Ridley Scott's Bladerunner *has become an influential landmark in film culture.*

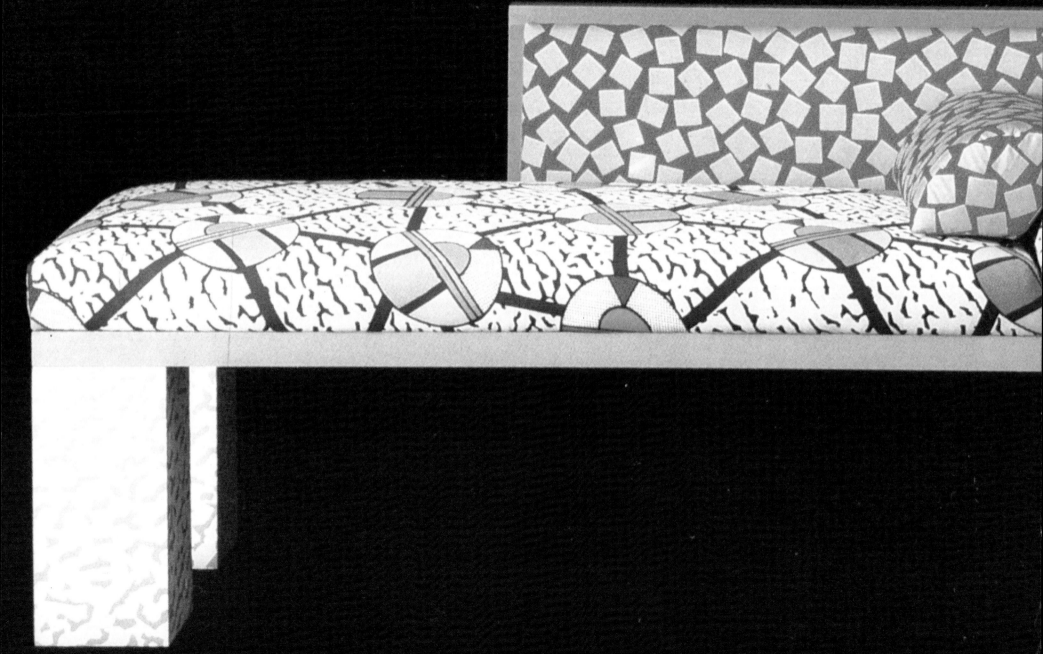

Furniture

8

PEOPLE'S BASIC REQUIREMENTS OF FURNITURE
MAY NOT HAVE CHANGED MUCH DURING THE
TWENTIETH CENTURY, BUT THE WAY IT LOOKS
HAS. FROM EMILE GALLÉ'S EXOTIC WOODEN
PIECES TO ROBIN DAY'S INJECTION-MOULDED
POLYPROPYLENE CHAIRS, THERE HAVE BEEN
ASTONISHING DEVELOPMENTS IN STYLES AND
MATERIALS USED BY FURNITURE DESIGNERS.

natural colours, alongside a more unusual use of mother-of-pearl. Gallé was inspired by nature, using plants and insects as subject-matter, his treatment owing much to the Japanese art which had been imported into France since the opening up of Japan in 1868. Symbolism and poetry were important to Gallé, and lines of poetry were inlaid in his furniture, often along with his distinctive signature. He was largely responsible for reviving the eighteenth-century art of marquetry, but took the technique a step further due to the complexity and irregularity of his designs, which were often pictorial. In 1901, Gallé founded the School of Nancy, a group of artist-craftsmen who worked along similar lines. In furniture design, however, none achieved the complexity of Gallé's work.

Charles Rennie Mackintosh
Ladderback Chair

1897 A trained and practising architect, Mackintosh was also a pioneering and highly versatile designer of textiles, wallpaper and metalwork, as well as a renowned watercolourist. The foundations for his style were laid with his first large commission – the Argyle Street Tea Room in 1897–99. The solid oak Ladderback Chair which he designed for the Tea Room, with its organic curving arms and elongated tapering proportions, was an important first step in the development of Mackintosh's style. The clarity which he brought to his designs was to have a profound influence, particularly on the development of the Vienna Secessionists in Austria.

Georges de Feure
chairs

1900 De Feure (1868–1943), born Georges Joseph van Sluiters, adopted a French name in 1890. A painter and a poet, he worked on the interior decoration of a cabaret run by Rudolph Salis. In 1900, de Feure produced furniture for the Art Nouveau House in the rue de Provence in Paris. This project was organized by Léon-Albert Jallot, at the head of a studio of artists, for the impresario Samuel Bing. With its gilding, coloured lacquer and organically inspired carved detail, de Feure's was some of the most exceptional Art Nouveau furniture. His work captured the spirit of that style in its rhythmic movement inspired by dance, its colour palette and its decoration.

Eugène Vallin
dining room

1900 Vallin (1856–1922) was a student of Emile Gallé. Vallin's furniture designs are most notable for being highly sculptural and heavily organic, almost to a point of excess, the fluidity of his decoration taking over the

Overleaf: Nathali du Pasquier's 'Royal' bed, shown at the 1983 Memphis exhibition (see page 123).

Above: this highly detailed example of Emile Gallé's work dates from around 1900. The elaborately carved cabinet is inlaid with marquetry.

Emile Gallé
carved and inlaid furniture

c. 1880–1900 Gallé (1846–1904), who achieved worldwide renown as a designer and maker of glass, was equally successful in his own time as a furniture designer, his works becoming the epitome of Art Nouveau. Gallé became interested in furniture in the 1880s, first exhibiting in 1889. His furniture was richly inlaid with a variety of exotic woods in bright,

functional aspect of his pieces. Around 1900, Vallin executed a complete room setting in the Museum of the School of Nancy, which, if nothing else, shows how overbearing a collection of his dramatic, emotional work can be in a confined space. As with all his fellow students at Gallé's school, it is, however, always noticeable how exquisitely crafted and produced such designs were.

Louis Majorelle
cabinet chair

c. 1900 Majorelle (1859–1926) trained as a painter in Paris from 1877, but stayed only two years before having to return home to Nancy to take over his father's cabinet-making and ceramics business. It was in that city during the 1890s that he became increasingly influenced by the work of Emile Gallé, whom he joined in 1901, becoming vice-president of the School of Nancy. Majorelle was one of the leading French Art Nouveau cabinetmakers, developing a strong, abstract, sculptural style and using materials as a virile expression of his craft. His furniture, much more commercial than that of Gallé, showed his evolving, personalized, organic style. His table and chair designs *aux orchidées* of 1905 incorporate rich, fluid forms carved in mahogany and embellished with gilt-bronze orchid mounts, reflecting eighteenth-century French furniture traditions.

Koloman Moser
armchair

1900–5 Moser (1868–1918) is remembered as an influential teacher and as one of the pioneers of modern furniture. As promoter of good design, he was a founder-member of the Vienna Secession in 1897, exhibiting his first furniture designs in the 1900 Secession exhibition. In 1903, he founded the highly influential Wiener Werkstätte together with Josef Hoffmann and the financier Fritz Wärndorfer. Moser was a prolific designer of furniture, jewellery, metalwork, bookbinding, leather goods and toys. This armchair exemplifies his designs: highly rectilinear constructions, often using contrasting coloured-wood veneers to create a chequered effect.

Liberty & Co
chairs and desks

1900–20 The famous Liberty store was established in 1875 in London by Sir Arthur Lasenby Liberty, and is still in business on the same site. The most significant contribution that Liberty & Co has made has been as a venue for independent designers to show their work, although there has been a catch: the designers have remained largely anonymous, their

This ladderback chair dates from 1903. It was built from rare ebonised oak and designed to be used in Kate Cranston's Willow Tea Rooms.

International Exhibition of Modern Decorative Art in Turin. The eccentric design of the 'Snail' room, which showed a strong Egyptian influence, was extensively commented upon. Worthy of mention, too, is Bugatti's design for the Waldorf-Astoria Hotel in New York (1893).

Josef Hoffmann
'Sitting Machine'

1908 Hoffmann (1870–1956) was an architect and designer who worked in Austria, designing plain, linear furniture and interiors for the Wiener Werkstätte. The 'complete furniture' designs of Charles Rennie Mackintosh exhibited at the 1900 Vienna Secession exhibition had a profound influence on Hoffmann and others at the Wiener Werkstätte, a guild of designers organized along the lines of the British Guild of Handicrafts, with students involved in all aspects of design related to textiles, graphics, furniture and metalwork. In 1908, Hoffmann designed the 'Sitting Machine', a reclining chair which sums up many of the principles and aims established at the Werkstätte, namely function with minimal ornament, utility, strength in good proportions and the correct use of materials. In the 1920s, Hoffmann turned to a more curvilinear style in his metalwork, in considerable contrast to his earlier rectilinear style.

Top: Carlo Bugatti's furniture was unique in its eccentricity. These examples of his work are made from richly inlaid wood, covered with parchment.

Bottom: Josef Hoffman designed this revolutionary reclining chair, made from stained beechwood, c. 1905. The Sitzmaschine was manufactured by J. J. Kohn.

work being commissioned and sold under the Liberty brand name. Liberty was also regarded as an important arbiter of good taste in furniture and furnishings, creating standards which other designers followed. In the main, the furniture made in the Liberty workshops, under the control of Leonard F. Wyburd, was based on rustic English forms made of solid oak in the Arts-and-Crafts manner or reflected the Glasgow style made in mahogany. Prominent designers of the early period whose work was sold in Liberty included William Birch, C. F. A. Voysey and George Walton of Glasgow.

Carlo Bugatti
chair

1901 Bugatti (1856–1940), born in Milan, came from a family of designers. He worked in various media, but it is for his furniture, mostly produced in the last two decades of the nineteenth century, that he is remembered. Bugatti's influences were Oriental and North African, and his eccentric furniture is constructed from an exotic combination of wood, copper discs, tassels, parchment and ivory. Unusually, he modelled his pieces in clay or plaster before production, perhaps in anticipation of his later sculptural work. In 1902, Bugatti received a special honorary diploma for four rooms he designed for the first

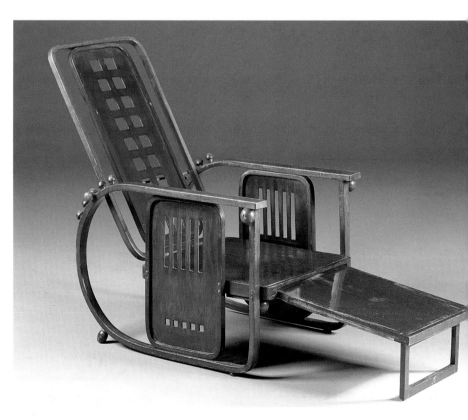

Gerrit Thomas Rietveld
chair

1917 In his search for the new, purer, mechanized furniture of the future, Rietveld (1888–1964) developed one of the most striking and far-reaching designs of the early twentieth century. Born in Utrecht, the son of a cabinet-maker, Rietveld started his own cabinet-making business in 1911, initially influenced by architectural drawings. In 1917, he started experimenting with design, producing the famous 'Red and Blue' chair (1917–18). The first prototype for this chair was constructed out of cheap wood and left unpainted. It was suggested to Rietveld that he might paint it, which he did using the simple primary colours of De Stijl. In so doing, he was able to emphasize the spatial characteristics of the chair, highlighting the ease of construction through standardized machined parts. Rietveld joined De Stijl following publication of an article about the chair in the group's magazine. The 'Red and Blue' chair came to epitomize in three dimensions the ideals of De Stijl and the two-dimensional work of its members, such as Piet Mondrian.

Emile-Jacques Ruhlmann
dining-room furniture

1925 Ruhlmann (1879–1933) was the most important French furniture maker of the early twentieth century, receiving international acclaim at the 1925 Paris International Exhibition of Decorative Arts. His first exhibition had been held in 1913 at the Paris Autumn Salon, but his style peaked at the 1925 Exhibition, for which he created a special room setting entitled 'Grand Salon of a Collector'. This scheme was highly praised by the critics and later acclaimed as the most important Art Deco room in the entire show. Ruhlmann's style unreservedly borrowed from the lavish and decorative styles of eighteenth-century France. His pieces are extremely luxurious and sumptuously decorated, using exotic wood veneers – Macassar ebony being a particular favourite – with shiny inlays and colourful lacquers.

Marcel Breuer
'Cesca' chair

1928 Marcel Lajos Breuer (1902–1981) was born in Pécs and at the age of 18 went to the Bauhaus in Weimar. From 1925 to 1928, he taught at the Bauhaus in Dessau, as head of the furniture workshop, where he initiated the first classic furniture of the twentieth century, namely the 'Wassily' (1925). From the very beginning, Breuer strove to produce simple furniture with a purity of form. The 'Wassily' chair developed out of his experiments with a material new to furniture: tubular steel, previously used only in bicycle frames. But it is the 'Cesca' chair which

Top: Emile-Jacques Ruhlmann was one of the most famous Art Deco furniture makers. This dining-room suite comprises a table and six chairs.

Bottom: Marcel Breuer designed this chromium-plated, tubular steel armchair in 1929. It was manufactured by Thonet in the 1930s.

Corbusier, together with his cousin Pierre Jeanneret and Charlotte Perriand, designed the 'Grand Comfort' for a villa in Ville d'Avray, France. When it was first exhibited at the Autumn Salon in Paris in 1929, it caused an outcry. It was the use of contrasting materials – metal and leather – together with the proportions based on the human form and the exposing of the normally hidden metal frame that made the design so unusual. The chair is probably one of the best-known furniture designs of the twentieth century and remains in production today. The 'Grand Comfort' has complete clarity of design and is a highly original solution which influenced many subsequent 'free-form' chairs.

Ⓜ Ludwig Mies van der Rohe
'Barcelona' chair

1929 Born in Aachen, Mies (1886–1969) was initially trained as a draughtsman before working in the offices of Peter Behrens in 1908. One of his most notable designs was the 'Barcelona' chair for the German Government pavilion at the Barcelona International Exhibition in 1929. This piece of furniture was the result of instructions to design a chair fit for a king, dictator or ambassador. It is both lavish and elegant; its visual impact is quite dramatic, especially when seen from a low angle. The quality of the materials and craftsmanship are outstanding. The amount of labour and number of components required are staggering: the upholstery alone consists of 40 separate square panels. Yet there is no

has come, through numerous reworkings, to represent the ideals of the avant-garde Modern Movement for a mass audience. The 'Cesca' chair, of cantilevered tubular-steel construction with cane seat and back, appears to defy gravity through the use of thin, resilient materials. It is lightweight yet stable. This design rejected historical precedent and was in tune with the architecture of the period. This is not surprising, as Breuer also designed several important interiors. Interestingly, although architecture and interior design have altered radically since the late 1920s, the 'Cesca' chair remains in production six decades later. Manufactured by Knoll International in New York, it is still a popular choice for the 'modern' interior.

Top: Mies van der Rohe designed this 'Barcelona' chair, with removable cushions fit to receive a king, a dictator or an ambassador.

Bottom: Alvar Aalto designed this wooden chair in 1930. Aalto usually used the wood of the nordic blond birch to create his furniture.

Ⓜ Le Corbusier
'Grand Comfort' 'chair'

1928 The Swiss architect Charles-Edouard Jeanneret (1887–1965) first proclaimed his controversial ideas on modern design in the magazine *L'Esprit nouveau* (1920–25), which he published in partnership with Amédée Ozenfant under the pseudonym Le Corbusier. His 'machines for living in', as they became known, initially received a great deal of criticism for being cold and impractical. However, Le Corbusier stuck to his aims of producing an uncluttered environment, reducing traditional furnishings – what he called 'equipment' – to a minimum and in the process revolutionizing attitudes to the home of the future. In 1928, Le

hint of this complexity in the chair's outward simplicity and lightness of design. The 'Barcelona' chair is one of the classic designs of the century due to its meticulous proportions and dynamic modernism.

Alvar Aalto
moulded and laminated wood furniture

1930s Aalto's (1898–1976) work first received international acclaim as a result of the pavilion he designed for the 1939 New York World's Fair. In 1927, Aalto designed his first piece of modern furniture, a wooden stacking chair, and it was from this design that his life's work of designing mass-produced wooden furniture using a minimum of parts developed. His first significant commission was for the building and interior design of the Paimio Sanatorium in Finland, which he won in 1928 and completed in 1933. For this building, he designed the 'Paimio' chair, which in many ways crystallized his aims and ideals. Consisting of only six components, the seat and back were made out of a single piece of bent plywood. The seat was curved to fit the human spine. Aalto was aware of the psychological importance of materials, especially within hospital and home environments, finding chrome- or nickel-plated tubular steel too harsh for hospitals and cold climates. He used native blond Nordic birch instead, as it was especially flexible and free from knots (the same wood is used in Finland to make skis). Although his influence reached far beyond the borders of his native country, Aalto's designs were born out a need to find solutions to the specific needs of that region.

Eugène Printz
cupboard

1930s Printz (1889–1948) was apprenticed in his father's cabinet-making firm in the Faubourg St-Antoine in Paris. Printz first exhibited his work at the 1925 Paris Exhibition, but it was at the 1926 Salon of Artist-Decorators that he began to be noticed. Printz's furniture was praised for its eccentricity and its bold, imaginative combinations of materials, as well as for its ingenuity. A cupboard he exhibited in 1933 is typical: the long drawer unit in exotic Brazilian jacaranda wood with patinated, gold-plated copper handles is supported on an elaborate metal-filigree pedestal, making the top appear to be floating in mid-air. Worthy of mention, too, is Printz's highly innovative device for folding doors or tables. He frequently collaborated with notable artists of the Art Deco period, including Jean Dunand.

Eugène Printz collaborated with Jean Serrieres to create this cupboard. The scenes at the top of the doors each depict a woman with a child.

Charles Eames
functional mass-produced furniture

1940s The most significant contribution made by Eames (1907–1978) to the history of furniture design was his unswerving desire to solve problems of mass production. In 1940, he collaborated with Eero Sarrinen to produce a series of chairs using plywood and new techniques of manufacture, including a method of bonding metal to a wooden shell with a rubber weld joint, for the Museum of Modern Art's 'Organic Design in Home Furnishings' competition. In 1948, at another MOMA competition, Eames won second prize for his designs for low-cost furniture with his proposal for a moulded fibreglass chair, which became the first piece of mass-produced furniture. Eames joined the firm of Herman Miller, one of the two largest and most innovative American furniture manufacturers, and this association brought both parties worldwide renown and acclaim. Many of the designs by Eames are now hailed as classics.

Carlo Mollino
roll-top desk

1946 Mollino's work played a pivotal role in the renaissance of Italian design during the mid-1940s. Having trained as an architect at the University of Turin in 1931, Mollino (1905–1973) immediately started to produce work which was radically different from that of his contemporaries, who were concerned with a more rationalist approach to design. Initially, his work was inventive; the roll-top desk, designed for his own apartment in 1946 and made by the small Turin workshop of Aspelli & Varesio, could be transformed into a table by turning over the top and

In his quest to create functional mass-produced furniture, Charles Eames designed this moulded plywood chair.

raising the sides to form the table top. Some of his later work, however, such as the 'Arabesque' tea table of 1950, was even more extreme. It was Mollino's interest in sculpture and organic principles that future designers regarded as the starting point of their own work.

Isamu Noguchi
sofa and ottoman

1946 Born in Los Angeles, Noguchi (1904–1988) was brought up and trained as a cabinet-maker in Japan, returning to America in 1918. After studying with the sculptor Brancusi in Paris during the late 1920s, he again returned to the USA. Noguchi's interest in biomorphic forms can be seen in the table and sofa designs he created for the American manufacturer Herman Miller during the late 1940s. Although his highly individual pieces were often deemed to be too quirky for mass production, Herman Miller showed faith in Noguchi's work by producing the famous 'Parabolic' table in 1949. Noguchi's individualism and free interpretation of the conventional order and structure of objects were perhaps his most notable qualities. His versatility, as a result of the variety of projects he undertook, together with his Oriental influences, enabled him to bring a new approach to many conventional household objects.

Eero Saarinen
'Womb' and 'Tulip' chairs

1946 Saarinen (1910–1961) first trained as a sculptor in Paris in 1930–31 before studying architecture at Yale University in New Haven, Connecticut. Perhaps the most important aspect of his career was his involvement with the Cranbrook Academy of Art in Bloomfield, Michigan, founded in 1932. During the 1930s, Saarinen was director at Cranbrook, from where some of the most significant names in American furniture and design emerged. As a direct result of Saarinen's work with Charles Eames for the 'Organic Design in Home Furnishings' competition at the Museum of Modern Art in New York, which paved the way for the beginnings of organic design, Saarinen designed the 'Womb' chair, which was manufactured by Knoll International. This design reflected not only the use of state-of-the-art technology and new materials but also, perhaps more importantly, the way in which people actually used furniture. Just as the 'Womb' chair was organic and sculptural, allowing the user several possible sitting positions, the 'Tulip' chair, designed by Saarinen in 1957, broke revolutionary design ground. The 'Tulip' chair was designed as the ultimate in fluid sculptural form, to be manufactured in one piece. However, contemporary technology was not up to fulfilling Saarinen's dreams in this regard.

Robert Heritage
'Hamilton' sideboard for Archie Shine

1954 Trained at the Royal College of Art in London, Heritage (1927–) was appointed professor in the School of Furniture Design at his old college in 1974. He designed several sideboards which were manufactured by A. G. Evans, Gordon Russell Ltd, Archie Shine and Race Furniture Ltd. He also designed the 'QE II' chair in 1969 as well as 'Molecula' seating, which went on sale in 1978. During the early 1950s, there was a demand for colour in domestic interiors, and Heritage was one of the prime movers in the transition in British furniture design, giving it a more contemporary look. His furniture is characterized by its long, low-slung and elegant style, mainting its traditional function while adding a modern feel with a clever mix of wood veneers and industrial decorative processes. This is demonstrated by the 'Hamilton' sideboard Heritage designed for Archie Shine, which won a Council of Industrial Design award.

Cesare Lacca
trolley

1955 Lacca was another of the new breed of Italian furniture designers to emerge on to the international scene in the immediate post-war years. His designs have a clarity and elegance typical of the rational approach taken by many of his contemporaries. Lacca's trolley design, for example, has an almost engineered, geometric solution, inspired by futuristic aircraft design. The piece is cleverly constructed, using a mixture of traditional and innovative elements, namely the slender mahogany frame and the new material, plate-glass. Lacca's futurism was always exquisite and is notable for the high standard of craftsmanship and outstanding quality of materials. Overall, his work displays a delicacy which contrasts with the angularity of his constructions.

Franco Albini
PS16 rocking chair

1956 Albini (1905–1978) was also one of the new generation of designers who established a renaissance in Italian furniture and design immediately after the Second World War. Born in Robiate, Como, Albini trained as an architect in Milan and, in 1929, became the first architect-designer to work for Cassina. His appointment came as the company introduced new machinery and decided to move from the home market to a worldwide one. Typical of Albini's work is the PS16 rocking chair. The design was a simple and rational one which, combined with its sculptural aesthetic, resulted in a unique and highly individual piece. The new Italian designers gleaned ideas from contemporary magazines such as *Domus* and *Casabella*, Albini being editor of the latter in 1945–46. All of these designers showed strong individualism and brought Italian furniture design international acclaim.

Jorgen Hovelskov
'Harp' chair

1958 Hovelskov was very much a student of the Danish design tradition, yet with an international flair. His work reflected traditional national themes and concerns, but also showed an awareness of sculptural trends being played out by leading figures in the art world. For example, the influence of the British artist Barbara Hepworth can be seen in his exploration of the space surrounding a form. The 'Harp' chair, perhaps Havelskov's best-known design, has a frame of solid birch, with the seat and back made of flag line strung through the frame in the manner of a ship's rigging. The magnificent construction of the chair harks back to the 1930s revival of Danish crafts and the work of Hans Wegner, who advocated a conscious effort to achieve high-quality manufacture together with an honest use of materials.

Verner Panton
'Cone' chair

1959 Panton (1926–) marked his place in the history of furniture by designing the first one-piece injection-moulded plastic chair. Designed on a cantilevered form, it was produced by Herman Miller of the USA in 1967. Throughout his career, Panton doggedly pursued the unified chair design, at the same time proclaiming his belief that all designers should make a conscious effort to use only the latest materials and technological developments to achieve their goals, throwing off past traditions and looking only to the future. Through the series of 'Cone' chair designs he created in 1959, Panton himself looked to the future. Produced by Fritz

Vernon Panton created the cone-shaped chair he called 'Living Tower' in 1969. It was designed for Fritz Hansen of Denmark.

Hansen of Denmark, the 'Cone' chair created a futuristic form, seemingly born out of fantasy, but actually dependent on the property of the materials used.

Robin Day
Polyprop chair

1963 Born in High Wycombe, Day (1915–) graduated from the Royal College of Art in London in 1939. In 1948, in partnership with Clive Latimer, he gained international recognition by winning the Museum of Modern Art's 'Low Cost Furniture Competition' in New York. On his return to England, Day was approached by the Hille furniture company, which had been looking for a way in to the American market. In 1951, Day was commissioned to design the seating for the Royal Festival Hall, the main building of the Festival of Britain. The 'Butterfly' cocktail cabinet, also made by Hille, is a typical example of innovative and affordable storage furniture which could be bought from some of the

UK's major retail firms. Day's greatest success came in 1962–63, when he designed his low-cost injection-moulded polypropylene chair, which became one of the world's best-selling chair designs.

Roger Dean
'Sea Urchin' chair

1968 This chair is typical of anti-design Pop culture in its exploration of new ways of thinking about the ordinary or household object. Young designers of the 1960s were listening to consumers who were no longer interested in 'well-designed', 'functional' or 'standardized' items, so they began to move towards 'here-and-now' or 'novelty-for-novelty's-sake' designs instead. Dean's work can be seen as a continuation of some of the pioneering ideals established by Charles Eames and Eero Saarinen. The young generation of the 1960s were more affluent than any before them, and it was their disposable income and desire for gimmicky and cheap things which led to outlandish, spontaneous and fleetingly fashionable designs. Both organic and space-age in feeling, the 'Sea Urchin' was conceived for the futuristic home.

Ettore Sottsass
office chair

1970–71 Sottsass (1917–) had two distinguished careers, one as a product designer and the other as a leading figure of the Studio Alchymia group and the co-founder of Memphis. Born in Innsbruck, Sottass worked as a design consultant for Olivetti from 1958, establishing an additional design studio for the company at Ivrea, near Turin, in 1960. During this period, he was concerned primarily with anti-design combined with his love of colour. Examples of his work from this time are his revolutionary 'Valentine' typewriter, designed in 1969, and his office chair of 1970–71. These designs also reflect Sottsas's interest in Pop art by bringing contemporary, culturally significant objects into the office environment and using bold blocks of colour and simple rectilinear shapes.

James Butchart
'Flight' table

1972 Butchart was one of the first of a new generation of graduates who threw off the trappings and excesses of the Pop-inspired furniture and design of the previous decade and returned to a more rational approach. Butchart's work was inspired by the rapidly developing technology and industrial equipment of the 1970s; devoid of unnecessary adornment, it became part of the high-tech movement. This new style was clean and smooth, any colour being an open display of the true colouring of the

Robin Day's revolutionary stacking chair, created from polypropylene and steel, was launched in 1963. Since then, millions have been sold worldwide.

Pesce's 'Dahlia, Uno Duo, Tre' Chair was designed to move with the body, and was characteristic of Pesce's work.

materials used, reflecting the image of industrial machines, aeroplanes and office equipment. The environment, social conditions and economic considerations formed important aspects of the principles behind the work of these new designers.

Frank Gehry
'Three Nesting Chairs'

1972 Born in Toronto, Gehry (1929–) studied architecture at the University of Southern California in Los Angeles before going to Harvard University in Cambridge, Massachusetts. In 1972, he produced 'Easy Edges', perhaps the last truly Pop-inspired series of furniture designs. 'Easy Edges' consisted of 17 pieces of furniture, including the 'Three Nesting Chairs', made of laminated corrugated cardboard and intended for mass production. Gehry's work has always been about challenging the natural or accepted notions of furniture design. His choice of fibreboard or pressed cardboard, a cheap throw-away material, immediately confronted established traditions. Gehry's furniture makes a statement, expressing a new aesthetic through his powerful, surrealistic and sculptural compositions, drawing inspiration from fine art as well as the writings of Marcel Duchamp. The 'Three Nesting Chairs' were manufactured in the USA by Jack Brogan.

Gaetano Pesce
'Dahilia Uno, Duo and Tre' chair

1980 The Italian-born Gaetano Pesce (1939–) transformed international furniture design. Inspired by his interest in Pop art and the soft sculptures of American artist Claes Oldenburg, Pesce developed a radically new look backed up by an innovative use of new materials. In 1969, having studied design and architecture in Venice, he designed the UP series of chairs, made by B&B Italia, which were simple organic shapes made of polyurethane foam. The extraordinary innovation came when the small box containing one of these was opened and out sprang the polyurethane foam, immediately forming the chair. Pesce designed similar 'fun' furniture in 1980 with the 'Dahilia Uno, Duo and Tre' chair and the 'Sunset in New York' sofa, further exploring furniture which moved with the body.

Nathalie du Pasquier
'Royal' bed

1983 Du Pasquier (1957–) is very much a member of a new generation of designers who draw their inspiration from novel sources. She is a self-taught decorative genius who produces striking work in a variety of materials. One of the most important features of her work is its visual

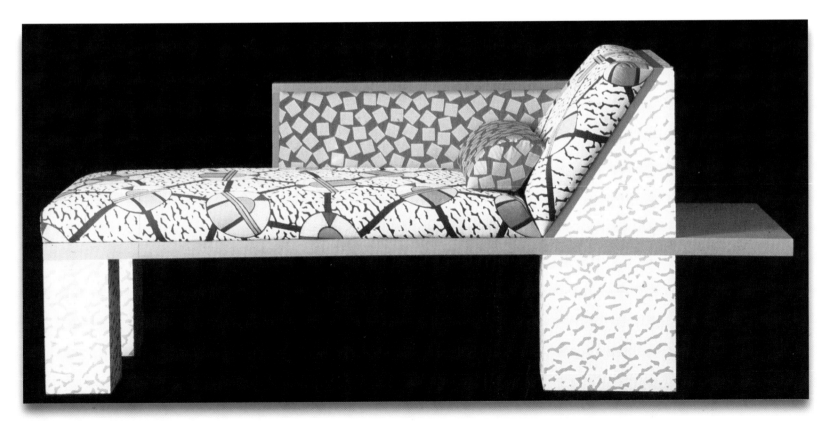

In 1983 Nathalie du Pasquier exhibited her 'Royal' bed (seen here) together with the 'Royal' sofa in the Memphis exhibition.

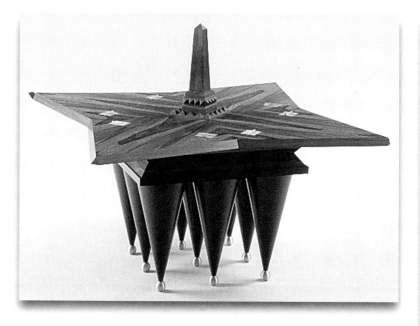

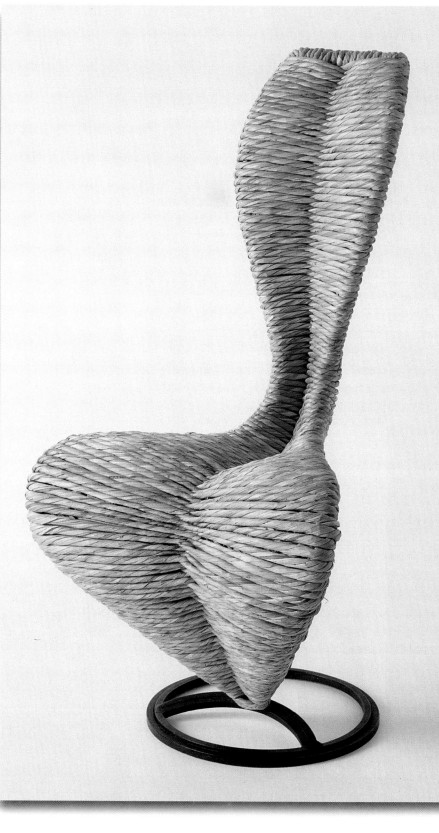

strength, which evolved through her extensive trips to Africa and Australia between 1975 and 1978. In 1981, du Pasquier exhibited pieces in the first Memphis exhibition. Typical of her work for Memphis are the 'Royal' bed and sofa. Her designs are hard-edged with flat, intense colours, and her approach is inspired by the abstract forms of African and Australian objects.

Wendell Castle
Coffee Table

1984 Castle (1932–) has been of enormous importance in the American craft movement, being regarded as the pioneer of the revival of craftsmanship. His work explores the emotional barriers of the viewer or user through both its organic content and its use of lavish and expensive natural materials. Only the finest craftsmen work on Castle's designs, and most pieces are produced only in limited editions. Pieces such as the 'Olympics' desk make no concessions to mass production, while Castle himself, in the true spirit of the Arts-and-Crafts Movement, oversees every aspect of the progress of each piece. The 'Castle' chair, made by Castle and The Gunlocke Company in Wayland, New York, seems to epitomize his belief in the skills of the craftsman together with the search for an emotional content in design.

Tom Dixon
'S-shaped Chair'

1988 Dixon (1959–) is a member of a new generation of British furniture designers and has been making a name for himself

Left: this strikingly unusual coffee table was created by Wendell Castle in 1984. Castle is often regarded as the pioneer of American revivalist craftmanship.

Right: Tom Dixon designed his now-famous S-shaped chair in 1986–87. Since 1991 the chair has been manufactured by Cappellini.

internationally since the 1991 Milan furniture fair. Dixon is particularly interested in bringing out the potential of the materials he works with. His work has been categorized as 'bricolage', which involves the designer making a conscious effort to discover the physical possibilities of his or her chosen materials. In Dixon's case, these are often found materials. His best-known piece is probably the 'S-shaped Chair', manufactured by Cappellini since 1991. Having his work manufactured is an important element in Dixon's philosophy. As a true craftsman, he is keen to be involved with the physical making of his work; if he is not actually involved, then he will work alongside those who are, thereby learning the limitations and restrictions of a material.

André Dubreuil
'Spine' chair

1988 Dubreuil (1951–) is one of a new generation of flamboyant designers who work in a highly personal manner. He prefers to work directly with his material, letting it provide inspiration, rather than spending time at the drawing board. His best-known design is the highly innovative 'Spine' chair, with its sweeping ladder of forged iron pulled into a naturalistic form, showing drama and lyricism yet still owing something to classicism. This chair had a limited production run, each piece being hand made by a highly skilled blacksmith in Dubreuil's native Dordogne. Dubreuil was one of the first artists to gain notoriety for his New Baroque designs, his more self-expressive and exotic work in which his emotions run riot. These one-off pieces are exquisitely crafted with meticulous detail and passion, using etched copper, glass beads and richly enamelled detailing, the shapes becoming more and more fantastic, even erotic.

Mark Robson
GRP chair

1989 Robson (1965–) graduated from the Royal College of Art in London in 1989. In the same year, he pushed furniture design to new heights with the GRP chair manufactured by Fiell, UK. Made of glass-reinforced polyester and covered with a pigmented cellulose finish, this chair brings a new meaning to ideas of personalized seating. Perhaps taking his cue from the world of motor racing, where each driver's seat is moulded specifically for him, Robson developed the idea of fluid, organic form to new limits. Carefully considering the parameters of the material, Robson used his own body as a template for the construction of the GRP chair, allowing the material to follow his body's contours while he assumed different positions. Such progressive design would not have been possible with any other material.

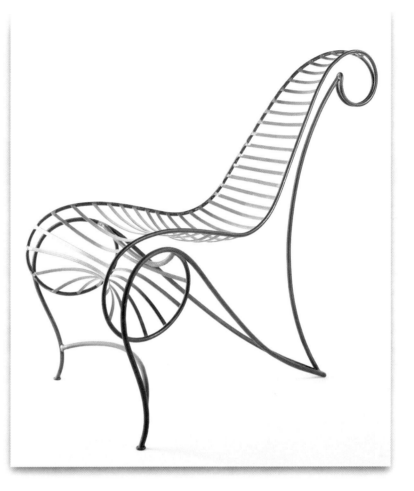

Elizabeth Garouste and Mattia Bonetti
'Africa' table

1990 The work of Garouste (1949–) and Bonetti (1953–) is typical of a new desire to find alternative expression in the field of design. Garouste and Bonetti formed their partnership in the early 1980s with the aim of producing limited production pieces, manufactured through their company BGH, as well as more expensive one-off designs. The 'Africa' table, produced in limited numbers for Neotu, the Parisian gallery, is typical of the work of these New Baroque designers, in this case inspired by tribal and jungle images. The massive elephantine legs, studded with black breast-like knobs, which support the slab top reflect a raw primitivism and create a strong emotional presence. These designers have gone on to create whole interiors, including Christian Lacroix's Paris boutique, incorporating their furniture, objects and custom-designed fixtures to creating modern spectacles while capturing the Baroque sense of inventiveness and pageantry.

In 1986, André Dubreuil developed his 'Spine Chair', so-called because it follows the line of the back. The chair is made from cleverly wrought steel.

Furnishings, Wall Coverings & Metalwork

9

OFTEN WORKING TO COMMISSIONS FROM MANUFACTURERS, A WIDE RANGE OF ARTISTS AND CRAFTSPEOPLE HAVE SOUGHT TO CREATE PLEASING EFFECTS IN COLOUR, TEXTURE AND FORM USING TRADITIONAL MEDIUMS SUCH AS CARPETS AND TAPESTRY. THE INFLUENCE AND APPRECIATION OF THEIR WORKS ARE, UNSURPRISINGLY, MOST CLOSELY FELT IN THE HOME.

Overleaf: Charles Grant's 'Mendip' design in jacquard woven cotton (see page 131).

Left: British designer Walter Crane was famous for his exquisite wallpaper patterns, such as this one, entitled 'Peacock Garden'.

Right: this painted tile is a relatively early Walter Crane design. Its depiction of an elegantly stylized heron with equally stylized fish is typical of Crane's work.

Walter Crane
wall coverings, textiles and carpets

1890–1915 Crane (1845–1915) was one of the most versatile of British designers, working in an extraordinary number of fields at the turn of the century. He trained as a wood engraver and draughtsman, and his early success was as a book illustrator in the early 1860s. He also designed ceramics for Wedgwood and other companies. Crane's most prolific work was, however, reserved for embroidery, wallpaper, printed textiles, carpets, silks, tapestries and book covers, all designed very much in the Arts-and-Crafts style. From about 1890, Crane's work began to have an impact in Europe, and in 1898 he designed the front cover of *Jugend*, the Art Nouveau magazine. By 1902, it was his work that made up most of the British section at the Turin Exhibition. What Crane will perhaps be best remembered for, both in Europe and the USA, are his books on the theory and practice of design.

Josef Hoffmann
wallpaper

1905–15 The textile division of the Wiener Werkstätte, of which Hoffmann (1870–1956) was a founder-member, was set up in 1910, and the first commercial production of wallpaper followed in 1913. The initial principle of the Werkstätte had been to bring together artist-designers and craftspeople to create *Gesamtkunstwerke*, or total designs. Creating total interior concepts was, however, prohibitively expensive, and the Werkstätte increasingly turned to producing and selling separate designs commercially. Wallpaper had been produced before 1913 for specific commissions, but after this date literally thousands of different designs were created by a number of Werkstätte designers. Hoffmann's own early designs tended to be formal and geometric, with simple, repeating, linear motifs, but became freer later in his career. 'Jagdfalke' of 1913 is a design of white, heart-shaped leaves on a black ground interspersed with coloured, bell-shaped flowers.

Ludwig Heinrich Jungnickel
wallpaper

1908 Jungnickel was one of the key designers of the Wiener Werkstätte. The Stoclet Palace, created between 1905 and 1911 in Brussels for the industrialist Adolf Stoclet, was a commission which permitted the Werkstäatte to create a fully cohesive building and interior; in 1908, Jungnickel designed the wallpaper for the nursery. Entitled 'Hochwald', this was a design of stylized, rather fierce, wild animals and birds amongst exotic trees on a black ground. The simplified repeating motifs and dark ground are typical of the period, and the simple forms meshed with complex patterns owe much to French and German medieval tapestry design.

Charles Rennie Mackintosh
textiles

1915–23 Mackintosh (1868–1928) initially designed textiles for Hill House and the Ingram Street tea-rooms around the turn of the century. In 1915, he moved to London, shortly after this receiving his first commercial commission, for a number of textile designs, from Foxton Ltd and Sefton's Ltd. These appear to have been quite successful, though Mackintosh cancelled his agreements just before he left for France in 1923. The work covers several different styles. Some boldly coloured and repetitive designs stress two-dimensionality, thus seeming to fulfil the central tenent of the Arts-and-Crafts Movement, namely truth to materials. In a later phase, Mackintosh's work became looser and more abstract. Later still, he developed more vibrant and fully abstract designs, which in turn gave way to completely geometric designs in strong colours, reflecting the rhythmic, bold patterns of the Art Deco era. 'Waves' is an oustanding example of the latter approach.

Edgar Brandt
iron screens

1920s Brandt (1880–1960), who set up his studio in 1919, was undoubtedly the master craftsman of wrought-ironwork in the 1920s. His work made a dramatic impact at the 1925 Paris International Exhibition, being shown in numerous places, including at the Gate of Honour, the elaborate main entrance. On his own stand was his best-known piece, the spectacular five-panel screen design, 'Oasis'. Made of wrought-iron with brass highlights, this screen, with its multiple central fountains flanked by large, stylized flowers and foliage, is perhaps Brandt's most visually stunning piece. He carried out work for numerous private clients as well as companies, such as Selfridges department store in London, where he designed the lift doors. During the 1920s, he made

Top: *Mackintosh designed this fabric while living in Chelsea, London, in 1916. It is simply titled 'No. 5 in 3 colours'.*

Bottom: *Edgar Brandt's ironwork was always finely wrought and gained him worldwide artistic recognition. He is perhaps most famous for his fire screens.*

numerous designs for firescreens which included exceptionally fine and delicate wrought-ironwork.

Max Peiffer-Watenphul
Bauhaus tapestry

1920s Peiffer-Watenphul (1896–1976) was a typical apprentice of the Bauhaus weaving workshop during the 1920s. The students were encouraged to design bold, formal work with a strong use of colour, reflecting the influence of contemporary developments in painting. Due to a shortage of materials during this period, many of the students were forced to use scraps of material to show tactile qualities to good advantage. Peiffer-Watenphul's tapestries use orange, yellow, blues and greens, together with several reds, against light grey grounds in highly complex, abstract, formal compositions. The work of the textile department, having been allowed far greater freedom than any other department at the Bauhaus, went on to have a considerable influence on the European textile industry, with many students finding good positions within major firms.

Felice and Kitty Rix
wallpapers and textiles

1920s At the Wiener Werkstätte during the 1920s, it was the more imaginative wallpaper designs which proved to be most popular. Many such designs were produced for Salubra Werke and Flammersheim & Steinmann, both companies having approached the Werkstätte for permission to use their designs. Some of the most sought-after work of this period was that of Dagobert Peche and Maria Likarz-Strauss. Kitty (1893–1967) and Felice Rix (1901–), both students in the textile department, carried out numerous designs for both wallpapers and textiles, their work owing much to Peche and Likarz, whom they greatly admired. The Rixes' designs were calm and light, even fashionable, but changed with the death of Peche to linear patterns more closely related to the work of Josef Hoffmann.

Varvara Stefanova
textiles

During the late 1920s, Russian textiles became hugely popular in Britain. This design by Stefanova is typical of Russian Constructivist designs of the period.

1920s Stefanova is generally regarded a pioneer of Russian textile and wallpaper art in the aftermath of the October Revolution. During the 1920s, French textile designers had a significant, but by no means exclusive, influence on the American and British textile industries. During the late 1920s and early '30s, Russian Constructivist textile designs by Stefanova, Liuboc Popova and others were imported into Britain in large numbers. Stefanova's designs, influenced by the

philosophy of Alexander Rodchenko, had a great deal of charm. They generally consisted of simple, geometric patterns composed of bold, angular lines overlaid with circular motifs and Revolutionary symbols. Her colours were striking and, again in line with Constructivist art, few in number. Such designs were, in many ways, far ahead of their time, with features comparable to the Op art of the 1960s.

Maria Likarz-Strauss
wallpaper

1925 Likarz-Strauss (1893–) was one of the leading textile and wallpaper designers of the Wiener Werkstätte, and her bold floral or African-inspired designs are typical of the later Austrian Art Deco style. She worked at the Werkstätte in 1912–14 and continued to create more influential designs after 1920. In 1925, a firm of wallpaper makers in Cologne produced a collection entirely devoted to her work. The pattern 'Siam' was one of the designs. Printed in bold ochres, reds and white on a black ground, this pattern took its inspiration from Oriental architecture, but owes a debt to the Cubist principles of stylization and flattening of form. By the time the Werkstätte folded in 1933, ideas of interior design had begun to change. The influence of the simple, sparse ideals of the Bauhaus were beginning to have an impact, and the idea of covering walls with richly patterned wallpaper was beginning to seem outdated.

Ruth Reeves
textiles

1930 Reeves (1892–1966) was one of only a handful of significant textile designers working in the USA in the 1920s. Following the display of French textiles in a 1926 exhibition at the Metropolitan Museum of Art in New York and other venues, the American public found itself stimulated by the design work coming out of Europe. This growing awareness contributed to a rise in interest in Reeves's and her colleagues' work. 'Homage to Emily Dickinson' by Reeves was one of a series of block-print commissions by the New York department store W. & J. Sloane in 1930. It showed the influence of Raoul Dufy in the use of colour and narrative elements, the latter with a distinctly American flavour. Some of Reeves's other designs, such as 'Manhattan' and 'Electric' in the same series, owe more to the works of Fernand Léger, with whom she worked in Paris, and show a Cubist angularity of form.

Warner & Sons Ltd
textiles

1930–60 Warner & Sons Ltd led the way in British textile manufacture from the 1930s to the 1960s. The company was the first to introduce a greater recognition of the designer's role and was innovative in the use of new machinery and the latest materials. Much of this outlook was due to the managing director, Ernest Goodale, and the foresight of the owner, Sir Frank Warner. In 1932, Goodale was instrumental in the setting up of the Federation of Furnishing Textile Manufacturers (later renamed the Furnishing Fabric Manufacturers Association), with Goodale the first president until he retired in 1968. Goodale brought Alec Hunter to Warner as production manager. In doing so, he added a significant new force to the firm, as Hunter introduced novel contemporary designs by leading British designers to run alongside the firm's traditional lines. This forward-looking pattern was emulated by other British textile firms in the decades which followed.

Alec Hunter
Braintree textiles

1932 In 1932, Hunter (1899–1958) was engaged by Ernest Goodale to join the textile manufacturers Warner & Sons Ltd, at Braintree, Essex, as production manager. Previously, he had been responsible for the first Edinburgh Weavers productions. Hunter brought about

important changes to production methods at Warner & Sons, introducing power looms and new materials. Perhaps even more significantly, he encouraged closer working relationships with outside designers, bringing greater recognition to them. Such cooperation between manufacturers and artists (which was also being advocated by the government) stimulated a range of successful designs from freelance designers and led to the establishment, in 1935, of a special department run by Theo Moorman for exclusive, hand-woven textiles. This department undertook numerous commissions for various exhibitions, including 'Britain Can Make It' and the Festival of Britain. Many of these innovative and contemporary designs were designed by Hunter himself.

This textile was designed for Warner & Sons by Charles Grant, c. 1935. It is a jacquard woven cotton and was entitled 'Mendip' after Britain's Mendip Hills.

Raoul Dufy
tapestry design

1936 Born in Le Havre, Dufy (1877–1953) trained as a painter from 1905 under the influence of Henri Matisse and was associated with the Fauves. He began designing textiles as a result of two projects for Paul Poiret in 1911, producing work of remarkable vigour and colour that drew on techniques borrowed from woodcuts. In 1934, Dufy was commissioned by Marie Cuttoli to design a tapestry to be woven at Aubusson, based on Parisian themes. Then, in 1936, Cuttoli commissioned a second design called *Amphyrite*, whose themes reflected both Dufy's keen interest in the sea and a homage to the city of his birth. Dufy subsequently explored these themes at various times in his career. The two tapestries for Cuttoli demonstrate the spontaneousness of Dufy's work, with the *Amphyrite* tapestry being particularly imaginative in its play with scale from an elevated perspective. Dufy later worked in collaboration with Jean Lurçat, establishing a closer working relationship between the weavers, who until this time had been little more than copyists, and the painters. This experiment broke new ground and was developed in later projects.

Left: this illustration is a detail of Jean Lurçat's apocalyptic tapestry Le Chant du Monde. *The detail is entitled* La Fin de Tout.

Association of Tapestry Cartoon-Painters

1945 The Association of Tapestry Cartoon-Painters might well have been established sooner but for the Second World War. It was in 1945 that Jean Lurçat founded a new movement to encourage the appreciation and use of tapestries, advocating a reassessment of the principles and functions of tapestry weaving in a modern setting. Lurçat was joined by many fellow enthusiasts. The members of this group contributed to numerous exhibitions, conferences and other activities aimed at promoting the art of tapestry. Part of Lurçat's project was to demystify the materials and processes of weaving. This was largely achieved when an interview with him was published in 1947, entitled 'Tapisserie Française'; it was translated into English as 'Designing Tapestry' in 1950. Lurçat was able to communicate his ideas on what could be achieved in modern settings by reductions in colour palettes and the introduction of different materials.

Jean Lurçat
Apocalypse

Right: another poignant detail from Lurçat's Le Chant du Monde *tapestry; this macabre segment is called* l'Homme d'Hiroshima.

1947 Lurçat (1892–1966) revolutionized the art of tapestry, bringing about a new relationship between the weaver and the artist which was essential for the future development of the craft. Perhaps the most significant change occurred when he first saw a Gothic *Apocalypse* tapestry at Angers in 1937. With its limited range of colours, this fourteenth-century tapestry inspired Lurçat's notion that tapestry could

only find an appropriate role in the modern world by restricting the range of colours used and allowing the native qualities of the wool to be shown to good effect. One of the great secrets of the craft was, Lurçat believed, that a successful tapestry owes its strength to strong values in juxtaposition. Lurçat became the resident designer for the Aubusson factory, and in 1945 he realized his ideals when he founded the Association of Tapestry Cartoon-Painters.

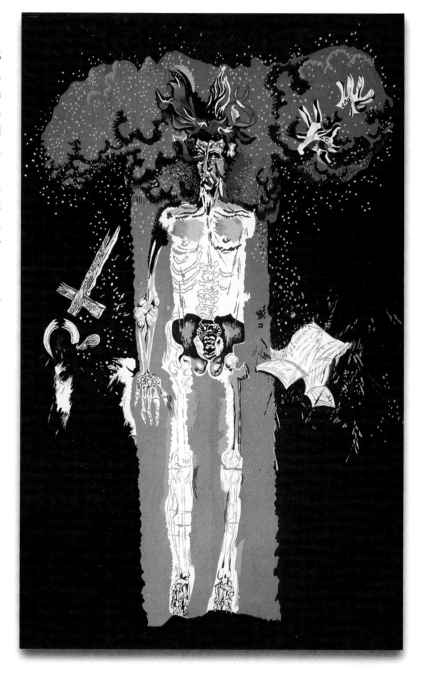

Le Corbusier
tapestry for UNESCO

1950 Le Corbusier (1887–1965) was instrumental in bringing about the next significant stage in the development of tapestry design. He advocated the idea that contemporary tapestry designs should form a pivotal role in the future of the modern interior, assuming the role previously filled by wall paintings. Since Le Corbusier's tapestry designs are, like his furnishings, meant to be appreciated as part of the interior spaces for which they were designed, seeing them out of context does not do them justice. His style, reflected in the commission for the UNESCO tapestry, was heavily abstract, with large blocks of colour playing out a drama, although always with the machine ethic in mind. Le Corbusier approached tapestry designs very much as if they were architectural studies on walls, as can be seen in his *Still-life* tapestry (1954). His designs for wallpaper were ingenious and geometric.

David Hockney
Play within a Play

1963 Hockney (1937–) was a student when he became interested in drawing the attention of the viewer to the surface of the canvas of painted works. In 1963, he developed a series of 'curtain paintings', exploiting the notion of 'surface as boundary'. One work of particular note was his *Play within a Play* (1963), a painting of a tapestry on which he placed a vertical strip of plexiglass to represent a pane of glass protecting the work. This only covered a third of the composition, however, thus inviting the viewer to see it from two different aspects. The floorboard at the bottom indicated that only a shallow space separated the surface of the tapestry from the boundary. In 1969, and again in 1972–73, the Edinburgh Tapestry Company produced tapestries of Hockney's paintings which further explored the boundary theme of the original pictures.

Kaffe Fassett
Yellow Ginger Jar

1980s The work of Kaffe Fassett is recognized as being highly innovative and expressionistic. He is most widely known for his colourful and original knitwear designs, which are inspired by everyday objects. Fassett's use of bold colour and narrative style owes much to the tapestry work of Raoul Dufy, although with his own diverse use of imagery. In the 1980s, Fassett became involved in designing tapestries for Edinburgh Weavers, spending many weeks sitting with the weavers in order to learn the secrets of producing large-scale works. In November 1993, he exhibited his tapestry designs at the Edinburgh

Museum and Art Gallery. Many of these were inspired by objects seen by Fassett on his travels, such as *Yellow Ginger Jar*, based on an Oriental ginger jar and cover. Fassett's work has introduced a new and distinctive pictorial style in tapestry.

Marta Rogoyska
Hot Bird Jungle

1988 Born in England of Polish parents, Rogoyska came to prominence in the 1980s as a weaver of precise contemporary tapestries. Formerly a performance artist, she brings influences of the theatre to her work, which is characterized by her use of bright, bold colours and simple, carefully delineated shapes. These effects are partly achieved through dyeing her own wools, and partly through the use of a tight, hard-twist yarn. Rogoyska's diverse sources include early French tapestry and modern art as well as the theatre, with birds being a recurring theme. The stylized exotic birds of *Hot Bird Jungle* are especially notable. One of Rogoyska's early commissions was from George Howard to make three tapestries for the restaurant at Castle Howard in Yorkshire. The result was her distinctive *For George's Sake I, II and III*.

Kaffe Fassett is best known for colourful knitwear designs, inspired by everyday and household objects.

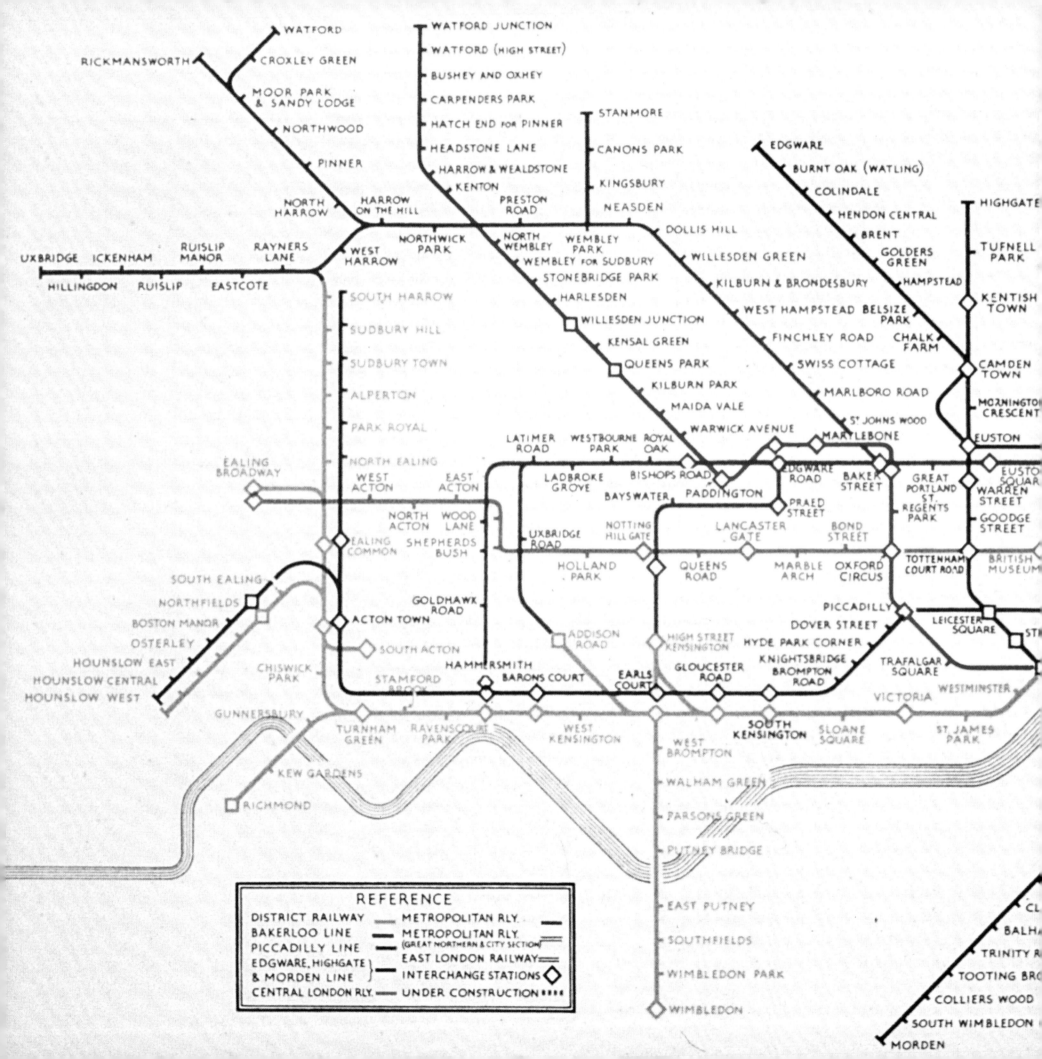

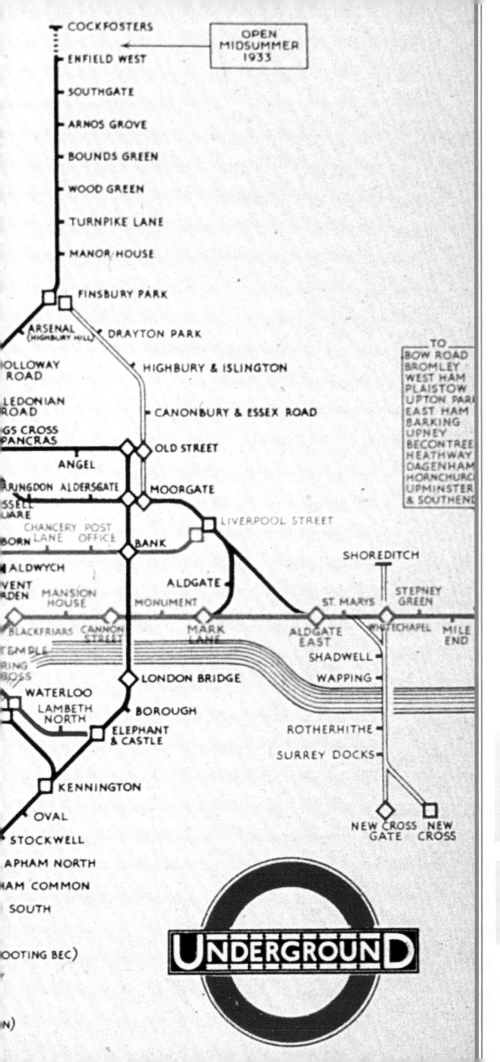

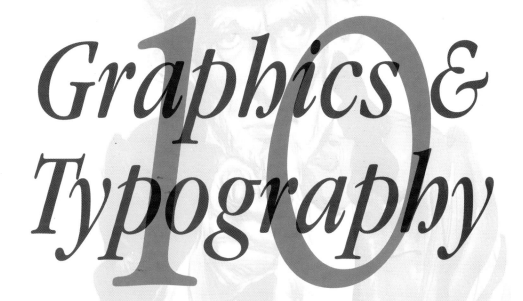

Graphics & Typography

10

GRAPHICS AND TYPOGRAPHY ARE PRESENT IN ALMOST EVERY ASPECT OF OUR VISUAL LANDSCAPE, YET THEY CAN BE CONSIDERED THE MOST NEGLECTED OF ALL ART FORMS. MARVELLOUS WORKS SUCH AS HENRY BECK'S CLASSIC LONDON UNDERGROUND MAP AND ERIC GILL'S GILL SANS TYPEFACE SERVE TO REMIND US OF THE ARTISTRY AND SKILL THAT GOES INTO GRAPHIC AND TYPOGRAPHICAL DESIGN.

Gustav Klimt
Beethoven Frieze

1902 In 1902, the artists of the Vienna Secession devoted their annual exhibition to Ludwig van Beethoven, who had composed his most important works in that city. All the exhibits at the show – even the catalogue – were conceived to support and enhance the central work, a monumental statue of Beethoven by Max Klinger. The contribution by Klimt (1862–1918) was a seven-part frieze, on three walls, symbolizing Beethoven's Ninth Symphony. Brilliantly coloured and textured, and contrived using gold and silver leaf, glass and mirrors, the frieze contained no direct references to Beethoven's music. Instead, it was a highly personal, allegorical expression of the emotional impact of great music on a particular listener. As with much of Klimt's art, the frieze's audience found it too challenging, and it is only in recent years that it has found its place in the history of art.

Overleaf: Henry Beck's famous London Underground map (see page 140).

Right: part of Klimt's seven-section Beethoven Frieze, symbolizing Beethoven's Ninth Symphony. One of Gustav Klimt's most breathtaking works of art.

Winsor McCay
Dreams of a Rarebit Fiend

1903 McCay (*c.* 1869–1934) is regarded as the first great practitioner of both the comic strip and animated film. He created the first animated film to contain backgrounds, *Gertie the Dinosaur*, and went on to make a further 10 animated films which influenced Walt Disney himself. McCay's strip *Dreams of a Rarebit Fiend* explored a surreal world in which a character's taste for rich cheese rarebits produced nightmares and other fantastical sleep visions. Intended for adults, the strip contained disquieting elements of deformity, cannibalism and death. McCay's elegant work was highly original and displayed an enormous fascination with the irrational. His trademark use of dream imagery was a direct progression from the nonsense literature of such British authors as Edward Lear and Lewis Carroll.

Lyonel Feininger
Wee Willie Winkie's World

1906 The American artist Lyonel Feininger (1871–1956) studied art in Germany, where he was a popular radical political cartoonist. In 1906, the *Chicago Tribune*, aware of the sophisticated pictorial satire being produced in Germany at the time, recruited Feininger to produce a cartoon along similar lines for their Sunday newspaper. In doing so, they hoped to appeal to the large, cultured German-American population of Illinois, still nostalgic for the art and literature of their native country. Feininger used four colours and an innovative mix of sizes and shapes for his strip *Wee Willie Winkie's World*, which presented the daydreams of a small child who believed ordinary objects were fabulous creatures. Inexplicably, the strip failed within a year. Feininger went on to become a founding member of the Bauhaus and to develop his own Expressionist style, with architectural forms and interpenetrating prismatic planes of colour and light.

F. W. Goudy
Goudy Old Style typeface

1914 Goudy (1865–1947), a printer and designer of typefaces, established his business in New York, where he also lectured on typography. Goudy designed more than a hundred new typefaces, among them Garamond, Goudy Old Style, Forum and Trajan, produced for American Type Founders and the Lanston Monotype Machine Co. Goudy Old Style, in particular, is outstanding for the strength and beauty of its form and allows any author's work to reach the public with unusual grace and felicity. Goudy was also a fine calligrapher, but tragically many of his drawings were destroyed when his workshop burned down in

1939. One of the century's creative giants of type design, he received many graphic-arts honours, including the Gold Medal of the American Institute of Graphic Arts.

Norman Rockwell
Saturday Evening Post covers

1914–61 Rockwell (1894–1978), the American painter and illustrator, enjoyed an immense and lifelong popular success with his covers for the *Saturday Evening Post*, painting 317 covers over a period of 47 years. Rockwell's great gift was as a pictorial storyteller, and in his highly skilful, almost photographic style, he portrayed anecdotal scenes of American life so packed with detail – often humorous – that events both before and after the scene are evident to the viewer. His subjects were small-town life and everyday family situations, all familiar to his audience and perhaps portraying Americans as they wished to see themselves: modest, unpretentious and free from malice. At a time of giddy change in the wider world, Rockwell's illustrations were reassuring as well as entertaining.

J. M. Flagg
'I Want You for US Army' poster

1917 James Montgomery Flagg (1877–1960) was an American illustrator, poster artist and portrait painter. Based on Alfred Leete's famous British recruiting

One of Norman Rockwell's famed covers for the Saturday Evening Post, entitled 'Freedom from Want'.

poster depicting Lord Kitchener, *Your Country Needs You* (1914), one of America's most famous recruiting posters, *I Want You for US Army*, was produced by Flagg in 1917. Its dashing line, confident draughtsmanship and patriotic red, white and blue colouring emphasize the message. Uncle Sam, with white whiskers and top hat, is a powerful symbolic figure, and the perspective of the pointing finger involves the viewer on a personal basis. The figure of Uncle Sam derived from earlier American folkloric figures (such as Yankee Doodle, a lean gentleman in top hat and striped trousers) representing the USA. In this instance, he is a self-portrait of Flagg. The poster was so successful that it was reissued during the Second World War.

Left: J. M. Flagg's US Army recruitment poster from the First World War was based on the famous British poster of 1914, which depicted Lord Kitchener.

Right: Paul Colin's celebratory poster of Josephine Baker's La Revue Négre *hit the streets of Paris in 1925.*

Paul Colin
Josephine Baker poster

1925 In October 1925, the Jazz Age arrived in Paris in the shape of 20 American musicians and performers from Harlem called La Revue nègre. This electrifying troupe starred the unforgettable Josephine Baker, whose entry on to the stage of the Champs-Elysées Theatre caused a sensation. Colin (1892–1985), then a young artist, created a poster for the revue which captured all the reckless energy of his subject. His celebration of the so-called 'black craze' was influenced by African sculpture as well as Cubism and Art Deco. *L'art nègre* became a dominant force among avant-garde artists, who perceived a pure and intuitive creative impulse missing in over-refined Western art. Colin and Baker became lovers, and Colin later produced many other posters and programmes documenting her remarkable career.

Charles Gesmar
Paris Casino poster

1925 Gesmar (1900–1928) worked in the mainstream of French commercial art of his time. During the 1920s, posters promoted mainly theatrical events, continuing to draw heavily on the rich traditions of artists such as Alphonse Mucha. However, poster art was moving inexorably in the direction of advertising, whether of travel opportunities, exhibitions or luxury goods of all kinds. Gesmar's light and engaging style was ideal for the posters he produced for the 1920s music-hall sensation Mistinguett, for whom he designed not only posters but also costumes, stage sets and programmes. His poster for the Paris Casino is characteristic, vying as it did as an advertising medium with the developing power of radio.

Charles Loupot
Paris Exhibition poster

1925 The Swiss-born Loupot (1898–1962) was one of the most highly regarded poster artists in France during the first half of the twentieth century. The opulent Paris Exhibition of 1925 had been planned for 1915, but was postponed when history intervened. Its aim was to showcase French design and provide a forum for improvement to its standards. Loupot's light and charming poster was ideal, representing the summit of Art Deco style. After the Second World War, he began a long association with the manufacturers of the apéritif St Raphael, producing advertisements which were landmarks in graphic design. Loupot created their logo, using an extravagant and flexible design, and introduced the two waiters in silhouette, one white and one red, which have been the firm's trademark ever since.

Herbert Bayer
Universal sans serif typeface

1926 Bayer (1900–1985), the director of the Graphic Design School in Germany's Bauhaus, designed his Universal sans serif typeface to stress the objective use of type for the clear and factual presentation of graphic information. Bayer believed in the need to integrate all aspects of artistic creativity into the modern scientific world and argued that old-style faces, with their capital letters and serifs, derived from handwriting and were incompatible with the modern age. In particular, he felt that the German Fraktur script evoked the 'old way' of doing things. Universal, with its simple, geometric design stripped of all ornament and without serif letters, stressed its harmony with modern methods of typography and printing.

Eric Gill
Gill Sans typeface

1927 Gill (1882–1940), the great English craftsman, fully explored the relationship between art and craft, being himself a sculptor, sign maker, woodcut artist and carver of stone letters, as well as a religious thinker, essayist and lifelong campaigner against 'aesthetic snobbery'. With the encouragement of the typographer Stanley Morison, Gill began to design type for the printing trade. His first face, the classical roman Perpetua, was finally released in 1929, some years after its inception, but his most famous face is the sans serif Gill Sans. Drawn as they were by an artist, the letters contain subtleties and refinements which make this a most satisfying face, and it has remained in common use, especially for official forms and publicity material.

Top: Bayer designed Universal Sans Serif as a reaction against typefaces which mimicked handwriting. He considered them too old-fashioned for modern usage.

Bottom: *Eric Gill designed the Gill Sans typeface in 1927. It is still widely used today.*

abcdefghijklMNOPQ
rstuvWXYZ
abcdefghijkLMN
opqrstu
VWXYZ

Paul Renner
Futura typeface

1927 The German typographer Paul Renner (1878–1956) began his career as a painter. He launched his famous Futura face in 1927, and it quickly proved to be a most practical face for official use. Renner used it on his avant-garde posters, together with his trademark diagonal orientation and abstract shapes. Futura, influenced by Herbert Bayer's Universal face, was one of the first faces to employ a completely even stroke throughout the alphabet. As with Universal, the letters are based on squares and circles, but Futura is rigid in its geometry and has as many interchangeable components as possible. With its elegance and commanding visual power, it is still in wide use today in a number of variations.

Jean Dupas
gouache-and-ink drawing

1928 The Art Deco style of Jean Dupas (1882–1964) is characteristic of the period between the two World Wars. He drew on Modernist themes, and many of his works were displayed at the Decorative Arts Salon in Paris rather than at the annual Salon for painting. Dupas produced designs for the Sèvres manufactory for the 1925 Paris Exhibition and later worked on a series of advertisements for Saks and for the London Passenger Transport Board. His style was abstract; he specialized in lissome damsels, often somewhat elongated and presented in titillating poses. Dupas's sensitive 1928 gouache-and-ink drawing is typical of his work of the period.

The Futura typeface was influenced by Herbert Bayer's Universal Sans Serif face. Futura was designed in 1927 and is still in common use.

Chester Gould
Dick Tracy

1930s *Dick Tracy*, the detective comic strip, was the first popular 'cops-and-robbers' series, and the forerunner of all other series involving the police; 'Dick Tracy' has since become a nickname for all plain-clothes detectives. The strip, first distributed in 1931 by the *Chicago Tribune* and the New York News Syndicate Inc., ran until Chester Gould (1900–1985), its author, retired in 1977. Its loud and clear support for tough law enforcement and its message that crime does not pay were very popular. Gould was a self-taught artist who found his niche with *Dick Tracy*. He used hard outlines and bright colours to project a clean-cut hero whose respectable methods triumphed over criminals who were grotesquely caricatured to contrast with his own squeaky-clean image.

Henri Matisse
Poésies de Stéphane Mallarmé

1932 Matisse (1869–1954) began his adult life as a lawyer, but after an illness he gave up the law and went to Paris to study art. Although taught in a conventional manner, he was influenced by Paul Gauguin, Paul Cézanne, Vincent van Gogh and, later, by the Pointillist painting of Henri Cross and Paul Signac. Matisse's vivid use of colour and distortion of shapes displayed an extreme emotionalism which led him and his companions to be dubbed the Fauves. His sophisticated etchings to illustrate a volume of Stéphane Mallarmé's poems are not literal illustrations of them, but rather intuitive works of art that balance the black type and white page to create a harmonious whole.

Henry Beck
London Underground map

1933 By the late 1920s, the London Underground system had grown enormously, and the old-style map, originally created in 1908, had become a confusing mass of snaking lines. Henry Beck (1903–1974), an engineering draughtsman with London Underground, designed a new version and revolutionized the way the world saw railway maps. Rather than basing his map on geographical fact, he used the principles of electrical circuit diagrams to display the system, so that lines met only at right or 45-degree angles, with stations placed to give the central area more prominence in relation to outlying areas and not to show their actual distance from one another. Beck gave interchanges a distinct convention and used colour to identify the different lines. This type of clear diagrammatical map is now in use for transport systems all over the world.

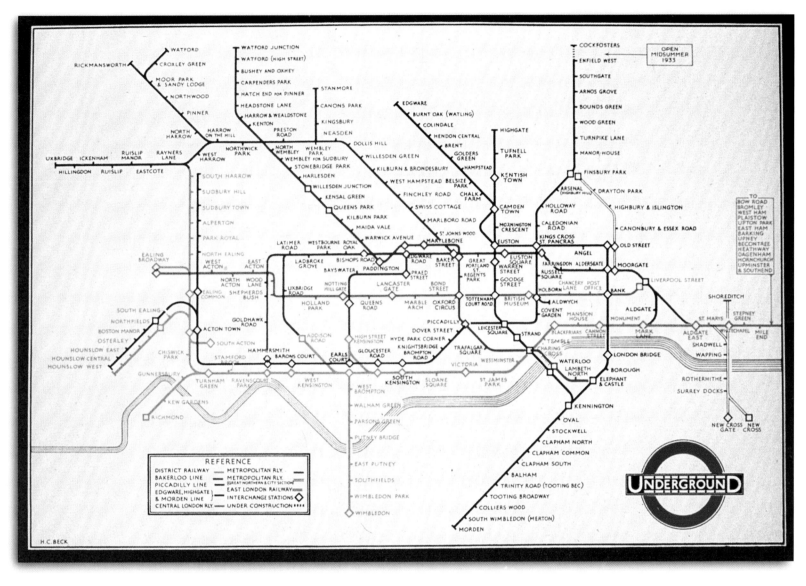

A. M. Cassandre
Dubonnet poster

1934 A. M. Cassandre was the pseudonym of the French graphic artist Adolphe Jean-Marie Mouron (1901–1968). In the years following the end of the First World War, poster art, growing into a powerful advertising phenomenon, was used to market the new luxury and escapism. Between 1923 and 1936, Cassandre designed a series of brilliant and highly influential posters which dominated French advertising. From 1927, he showed a growing interest in the typographic element of advertising posters, believing it to be an integral part of the design. Indeed, words were usually the starting point for his designs. Cassandre's set of three posters advertising Dubonnet cleverly spell out the word

'Dubonnet' gradually – Dubo – Dubon – Dubonnet – implying (in French) something good, which is also the name of the product.

W. A. Dwiggins
Electra and Caledonia typefaces

1935; 1939 William Addison Dwiggins (1880–1956) was an American designer whose skills encompassed calligraphy, typography, book design and illustration; he was also a puppeteer and writer and is believed to have been the first person to use the term 'graphic designer', in 1922. Dwiggins started his commercial life as a calligrapher and graphic artist, from the mid-1920s working for the publisher Alfred A. Knopf in New York. He later designed or illustrated books for such authors as Edgar

Henry Beck's map of the London Underground system revolutionized railway maps. It has become a worldwide prototype.

Allen Poe and H. G. Wells. His work often integrated decoration, illustration and calligraphy in one, and the exuberance and modernity of his style revolutionized the look of books and magazines. Dwiggins designed four of the Linotype faces most widely used in the USA and Britain, including Electra and Caledonia, which combine liveliness of action with superb discipline.

Paul Rand
Subway poster

1947 Rand (1914–) was one of the most influential and innovative young American designers after the Second World War. He reworked elements of modernist design to produce his own flexible visual language, in which the elements of the design were typically mixed together in an expressive combination of photomontage, collage and type. His 1947 poster, itself promoting the use of subway advertising posters, was bold and simple, with shapes signifying a target. The message, 'Subway Posters Score', was direct and compelling. With his magazine covers and advertising billboards, Rand played a major role in changing the way in which words and images could combine to convey a single image. Rand designed the IBM corporate logo in 1956.

Irving Penn
Vogue magazine cover

1950 The American photographer Irving Penn (1917–) has always considered himself a journalist. His incisive portraits and sophisticated pictures for fashion magazines, in particular for *Vogue*, are austere images communicating the idea of luxury and elegance through compositional refinement and clarity of line. Penn eschewed the use of props or backgrounds, instead focusing on the creation of an atmosphere of serenity through tonal subtleties and simplicity. He joined *Vogue* in 1943, designing photographic covers. His work epitomizes the post-war 'New Look', in which restraint and elegance combined to produce formal refinement.

Charles Schulz
Peanuts

1950– Schulz (1922–) wanted from childhood to be a cartoonist, and in 1950 he sold his *L'il Folks* to United Features Syndicate, who distributed it under the title *Peanuts*. This comic strip became Schulz's life work. His main character is Charlie Brown, representing Everyman. Others include Snoopy the Beagle, with his rich fantasy life and dreams of glory; Linus, with his ever-present security blanket; and the domineering Lucy. All are sharply defined and offer universal truths not just about childhood but about life itself. Schulz's humour is dignified, subtle and almost never topical, and his drawing is spare and precise. *Peanuts* is one of the most popular strips in history, appearing in more than 2,000 newspapers and translated into more than 25 languages. Spin-offs include animated television films, scores of licensed products and hundreds of books.

Irving Penn's cover designs for Vogue *epitomized the post-war 'New Look'. This is a cover from British* Vogue *and dates from June 1950.*

VOGUE

The Black a
White Id

London Seas

JUNE 1950
PRICE 3/-
THE CONDE NAST PUBLICATIONS LTD

M. C. Escher
Gravity

1952 The unique designs of Dutch artist Maurits Cornelis Escher (1898–1972) are based on complex mathematical concepts. Although without training as a scientist, Escher often felt that he had more in common with mathematicians than with his fellow artists. His search was for a visual form which would interpret as clearly as possible his mental image. Drawn with great technical skill and ability, many of his designs are perspective puzzles containing paradoxes and illusions, creating bizarre optical and conceptual effects. *Gravity*, a lithograph with watercolour, is a characteristic piece. Its starry shape writhes with arms which appear not to be fixed in place, and whose hands seem to move independently. Escher's work is of great interest to mathematicians and cognitive psychologists as well as to the general public.

Salvador Dalí
Don Quixote

1957 The Spanish artist Salvador Dalí (1904–1989) combined great technical ability with a variety of artistic styles. He is probably best known for his Surrealist work, in which the commonplace is juxtaposed with the bizarre to create enigmatic, dream-like images. He frequently used double images, capable of interpretation on two levels at once, as well as other visual tricks. Dalí's genius blended with a rampant commercialism, and his prodigious energy sustained a vast Dalí industry in which his madness was artificially sustained as part of the myth. In 1957, he completed the illustration of Miguel de Cervantes' famous work *Don Quixote*, in which he used abstract calligraphy created in a number of more or less improbable ways, together with a brilliant colour palette.

Martin Sharp
Jimi Hendrix poster

1960 The Australian designer Martin Sharp began his career working for the revolutionary Australian magazine *Oz*, moving to Britain when the magazine began to be published there. His influences were those of the comic strip and the burgeoning drug culture of the 1960s. In his work, bizarre and erotic elements jostle with surreal and psychedelic themes. Sharp designed the famous cover for Cream's LP *Disraeli Gears*, with its hallucinatory mix of peacocks, flowers and clocks. Perhaps his most famous work is a portrait of Jimi Hendrix, which, released as a poster, was to be found on every student's bedroom wall. The singer is shown as an integral part, and at the centre, of a dazzling explosion of colour, truly a visual shout.

Peter Blake
Sgt Pepper's Lonely Hearts Club Band cover

1967 The English painter Peter Blake (1932–) became one of the leading exponents of Pop art during the highly creative 1960s. He borrowed imagery from comics and advertisements to create a style in which sophistication jostles with naïveté. Blake's design for the cover of the Beatles' album *Sgt Pepper's Lonely Hearts Club Band*, with its line-up of iconic figures, marijuana plants and early glam-rock look, is a heady evocation of the Swinging '60s. The album cover was the first to feature printed lyrics and was an early example of the gatefold sleeve.

One of the most famous album covers of all time, the Beatles' Sgt Peppers Lonely Hearts Club Band has become an icon of pop art design.

Michael English
Coke

1970 Michael English, the British graphic artist, used mass-media and science-fiction references in much of his work, and his techniques made great use of bizarre and erotic effects. The Surrealist influence is often deliberately confused with other stylistic references. English's vivid airbrushed colours, used on many posters, created a deliberately chaotic effect to contrast with the drab, wordy posters of Britain in the '50s. His 1970 poster *Coke* hums with references to graffiti. Coca-Cola was one of the very first brands to equip itself with a recognizable and distinctive logo, and it was also closely linked with the American lifestyle. English's poster linked Pop art with this world-wide symbol to change the way in which Coca-Cola was seen by millions.

Garry Trudeau
Doonesbury

1970– New Yorker Trudeau (1948–) won the Pulitzer Prize in 1975 for his controversial satirical strip *Doonesbury*, the first time the prize had been won by a cartoonist. Trudeau attended Yale University in New Haven, Connecticut, where he drew a strip parodying leading college personalities. Noticed by a wider public, he was quickly offered a contract to draw a cartoon strip for the Universal Press Syndicate. *Doonesbury* made its debut in 1970 in 30 newspapers, including the *Washington Post*. Several papers, nervous of the strip's political edge, dropped it only to be forced by an outcry from their readers to reinstate it. Today, *Doonesbury* is syndicated in more than 1,400 newspapers worldwide.

Top: Michael English used many design elements in his Coke poster. His style has been called Pop Art and Surrealism and is a blend uniquely his own.

Bottom: Garry Trudeau, the creator of Doonesbury, *was the first cartoonist to win the Pulitzer Prize, which he received in 1975.*

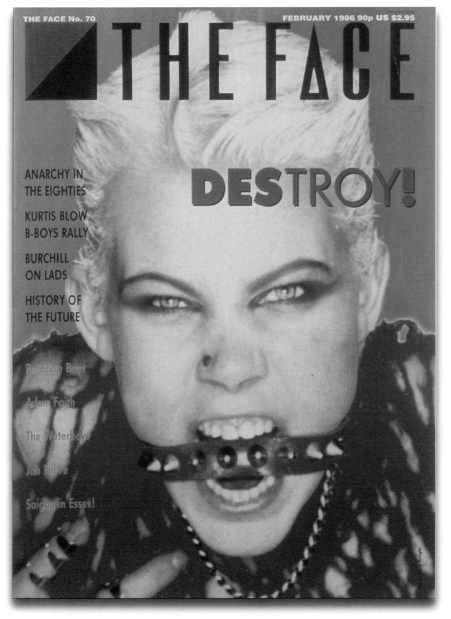

Twen magazine cover

Hans Feurer
Twen magazine cover

1971 The Munich-based magazine *Twen* was launched in 1959, with Hans Feurer as its art director. The magazine's design was, from the start, a spectacular mix of words and images, with photographs and editorial content cropped or manipulated for graphic effect. These powerful images linked the aims of the designer with the needs of the consumer. The design of *Twen*, using heavy black sans serif type, had a strong influence on other magazines starting in the 1960s, such as the British women's magazine *Nova*, launched in 1965. The dynamic covers for the magazine provided a gateway into the editorial content, aimed at the young, free-spending children of a revived Germany.

Neville Brody
The Face *magazine*

1980s Brody (1957–) is the best-known British graphic designer of his generation. He began his career designing record covers, and from 1981 to 1986 was art director of the ground-breaking British style and music magazine *The Face*. Brody, heavily influenced by the chaotic ethos of punk, used computers to manipulate new and existing letter forms to create a look independent of the limitations imposed by old-fashioned printing techniques. He used typography as a visual language, shaping and emphasizing the editorial message of the text. As a highly influential carrier of consumer information to free-spending young people, *The Face* transformed the way in which readers and designers approached the medium. The magazine has influenced high-street shop design, as well as every other area of visual communication.

Barbara Kruger
Your glutton for punishment is on a diet

1982 Kruger's (1945–) background is in the production of advertising photo layouts. In her later work, she would take a photograph which an informed viewer would see as ironic and caption it with a slogan. Kruger always used the typeface Futura Italic, and her feminist, anti-consumerist images and slogans quickly became recognized. In addition to her notable work *Your Glutton For Punishment Is On A Diet*, Kruger juxtaposed a picture of a mushroom cloud with the caption 'Your Manias Become Science', and printed 'I shop therefore I am' on shopping bags in 1989. It is a measure of her success that words, or words and images, have come to be accepted as art in their own right. But now that typography is available to many people via home computers, Kruger's work has been largely robbed of its impact.

Left: Neville Brody's cover designs for The Face *magazine broke new design ground. This cover is from February 1986.*

Right: 'Your glutton for punishment is on a diet' is characteristic Kruger. In her hands the juxtaposition of words and images become a new art form.

LOW TO MIDDLE TAR As defined by H. M. Governm

rning: **SMOKING CAN CAUSE HEART DISEASE** Health Depart

Advertising, Logos & Packaging

11

THE GROWTH OF THE CONSUMER SOCIETY HAS OPENED UP A WEALTH OF POSSIBILITIES IN THE WORLD OF ADVERTISING. LARGE CORPORATIONS UNDERSTAND THE VALUE AND SIGNIFICANCE OF THE VISUAL IMAGE OF THEIR BUSINESS AND THEIR PRODUCTS. PRODUCT PACKAGING DESIGN IS NOW A HIGHLY SPECIALIZED ACTIVITY AND SOME LOGOS HAVE BECOME ICONS OF THE TWENTIETH CENTURY.

Peter Behrens
packaging for AEG, Berlin

1907 The German architect and industrial designer Peter Behrens (1868–1940) set new trends in industrial design. In 1903, he was appointed director of the School of Applied Arts in Düsseldorf, and four years later he became artistic adviser to the German General Electric Company (AEG) in Berlin. Behrens's association with AEG marked a turning-point in industrial design. In addition to designing factories and showrooms, he also designed the company's stationery, catalogues, packaging, products and lighting equipment. In fact, his appointment marked the emergence of a new phenomenon – corporate identity – whereby a designer is responsible for all of a company's visual concerns. When Behrens designed the AEG logo, he simplified it dramatically to just three letters in a rectangle, and the strong, clear lettering remains the basis of the logo used today.

Root Glass Company
Coca-Cola contour bottle

1916 Originally a mixture of nut oil and sugar, the Coca-Cola drink was invented in 1886 by Dr John S. Pemberton, a chemist from Atlanta, Georgia. The same year, Frank Robinson took over promotion and advertizing of the new product and devised the Spencerian script of the original Coca-Cola logo and coined the slogan 'Delicious and Refreshing' that accompanied the name. The use of logo and product design went on to become a highly significant aspect of the success of the Coca-Cola brand. The first appearance of the 'classic' Coca-Cola bottle was in 1916 when the bottlers approved a unique 'contour' shape designed by the Root Glass Company of Terre Haute, Indiana. This distinctive visual shape became hugely popular and was used in advertizing to symbolize the youthful exuberance of America. Later in the century, Coca-Cola would reinforce its corporate messages using advertizing agencies to inform the world that Coke 'Is It', 'Adds Life' and is the 'Real Thing'.

René Lalique
Worth perfume bottle

1920 Lalique (1860–1945), a French jewellery designer and glass maker, is best known for his use of unusual materials and innovative styles in jewellery and glassware. His interest in glass resulted in his designs for mass-produced moulded perfume bottles. In 1920, the success of these early designs allowed Lalique to establish his own glass factory, where he developed the style now known as Art Deco. The sleek, stylized formulations of these designs exerted a profound influence on Lalique's contemporaries, who saw in Art Deco a bold statement of the drive and

power of the Industrial Age expressed with elegance. The mass-produced perfume bottle had a profound effect on the perfume industry, with manufacturers producing individual shapes which became both their trademarks and their product identities. In 1920, Lalique designed the classic statuesque perfume bottle for Worth, which was sculpted from vivid green glass.

Gabrielle 'Coco' Chanel
Chanel No. 5 perfume

1921 Chanel (1883–1971) was one of the most celebrated Parisian couturiers of the century. Her accessories and perfumes, notably Chanel No. 5, became world-wide synonyms for luxury and chic. Nowhere is packaging more important than in the perfume industry, and the design of the bottle is always crucial to a scent's eventual success. The Chanel

Overleaf: Nigel Rose's highly original cryptic cigarette advert (see page 151).

Right: an early Coca-Cola advertising coupon dating from the 1900s. Coca-Cola represents the advertising success story of the twentieth century.

No. 5 bottle has changed 15 times since its introduction in 1921, but remains the essence of simplicity, with a square form, plain wedge stopper and minimal white label. The bottle became a fashion necessity when, asked what she wore to bed, Marilyn Monroe replied, 'Chanel No. 5'.

Walter Dorwin Teague
Ivory Soap packaging for Procter and Gamble

1940 The name 'Ivory' was first used by its American manufacturer, Procter and Gamble, in 1879, and the traditional appearance of the packaging remained virtually the same until a redesign was commissioned in 1940. The designer responsible for Ivory's new look was Walter Dorwin Teague (1883–1960), one of the personalities who helped to establish industrial design as a separate discipline and recognized profession. Teague's new Ivory packaging reflected post-war austerity, with a purposely understated appearance which fit the American market perfectly. Soap was a necessity, and its packaging needed to reflect that. Teague went on to design the packaging for Downy Fabric Softener, with its characteristic curved blue plastic bottle and moulded handle; this packaging became so immediately identifiable that it has not changed to this day.

Salvador Dalí
window displays for Bonwit Teller, New York, New York, USA

1941–42 Dalí (1904–1989) was one of the most influential and unique painters of the twentieth century. Influenced by the Futurists and Giorgio de Chirico, he became a leader of the Surrealists and was notorious for his flamboyant eccentricity. Like many of the Surrealists, he designed

shop windows, and he was responsible for turning the window of Bonwit Teller in New York City into what *Vogue* magazine described as a 'cause célèbre against artistic censorship'. The magazine reported: 'The window of this prestigious shop consisted of walls covered in pink satin, with hand mirrors everywhere and a bathtub in the middle, out of which protruded disembodied hands holding mirrors; the mannequin was wrapped in feathers, with insects crawling in her hair. And this was the toned-down version of Dalí's blueprint; in retaliation he smashed the glass with a sledgehammer'.

Raymond Loewy
Coca-Cola fountain dispenser and cooler

1950s The outstanding packaging and design traditionally associated with the Coca-Cola soft drink product has played a vital role in the success of probably the most instantly recognizable brand of the twentieth century. During the Second World War, the Coca-Cola company had consolidated world-wide sales by making the product available to all American service personnel overseas. In 1950s America, teenagers were being discovered as an important domestic market for popular music, fashion, food and drinks. The highly influential French-born designer Raymond Loewy (1893–1986) played an important role in the use of design to influence this generation of consumers with his distinctive designs for fountain dispensers and drinks coolers that have become much-emulated design classics in their own right.

Paul Rand
IBM and UPS logos

1956; 1961 The American designer Paul Rand (1914–) became art director of *Esquire* and *Apparel Arts* at the age of only 23, incorporating into these magazines design elements pioneered by the European Modern Movement in the early 1930s. When he joined the William H. Weintraub advertising agency in 1941, Rand specialized in corporate

Top: Walter Teague's design for Proctor & Gamble's 'Ivory Soap' packaging was unveiled in 1940. The packaging reflected the austerity of wartime.

Bottom: Paul Rand designed IBM's company logo in a style reminiscent of nineteenth-century wood-block lettering.

design. Later, he worked on a new corporate-identity programme for IBM, which reflected a move away from the pre-war New Typography Movement. His trademarks became the focus of marketing programmes the world over, as well as icons of the century, especially his work for IBM and his designs for the American Broadcasting Company (ABC) and the United Parcel Service (UPS). For UPS, he simplified the existing logo, designed in 1937, to a more refined version, abbreviating the original shield and adding a rectangular package.

Landor Associates
corporate identity for British Airways

1983 In the 1980s, a trend towards total redesign of corporate image developed alongside a reorganization of working practice. One of the most successful examples of a corporate overhaul was Landor Associates' work for British Airways. The San Francisco company, founded by the German Walter Landor, was an analytical, research-based organization, and they saw immediately that the British Airways (then called British Air) corporate image was crude and brash. They changed the colour scheme to dark blue with a rich red and light grey background, and exchanged the Union Jack for a subtle grey coat of arms. The new impression was one of quality, service and dignity, and the design was implemented across the airline, from baggage labels to the aircraft themselves. While the new design was mocked as being old-fashioned, the critics were wrong. As a result of its new image, British Airways was one of the few big airlines to be in profit in the next decade.

Top: in 1961, Paul Rand updated the UPS logo – originally designed in 1937. Rand kept the essential elements, but refined and simplified them.

Bottom: in the 1980s, the distinctive red, blue and grey logo of British Airways reinforced one of the world's most recognizable corporate identities.

Nigel Rose
Benson and Hedges shaved pack

1985 The influential advertising campaign launched by Benson and Hedges cigarettes in 1985 featured a series of increasingly cryptic posters, of which Nigel Rose's design, for the Collett Dickenson Pearce agency, was one of the most successful. The poster shows the characteristic gold packaging of the cigarettes, with a razor and a piece of foam set on a gleaming background. The name of the product has been shaved off the packaging, but the gold suggests it. This campaign set off a series of copy-cat advertisements in the cigarette industry, including the enigmatic Silk Cut ads, and by the 1990s, it was only possible to associate the advertisements with cigarettes by means of the health warning set below the image.

Oliviero Toscani
Benetton advertising campaign

1991–92 The Italian designer and photographer Oliviero Toscani has produced some of the most controversial advertising posters of the twentieth century for the Italian clothing company Benetton. Using arresting, often violent images, Oliviero followed an existing trend towards cryptic advertisements by juxtaposing arresting and imaginative scenes, unrelated to the Benetton product, with the simple but colourful slogan 'United Colours of Benetton'. Some of the more controversial images included a man dying of AIDS, a woman giving birth, a burning car and a colourful parrot on the back of a zebra. While critics have complained that the images are irrelevant to the product, the advertisements are immediately recognizable and have heightened Benetton's profile by making the company appear to be a trend-setting organization – at all costs.

Top: Nigel Rose's cryptic Benson & Hedges advert set the standard for cigarette advertising and became the catalyst for a series of copycat campaigns.

Bottom: Oliviero Toscani's advertising campaign for Benetton has produced some of the world's most controversial and highly criticized posters.

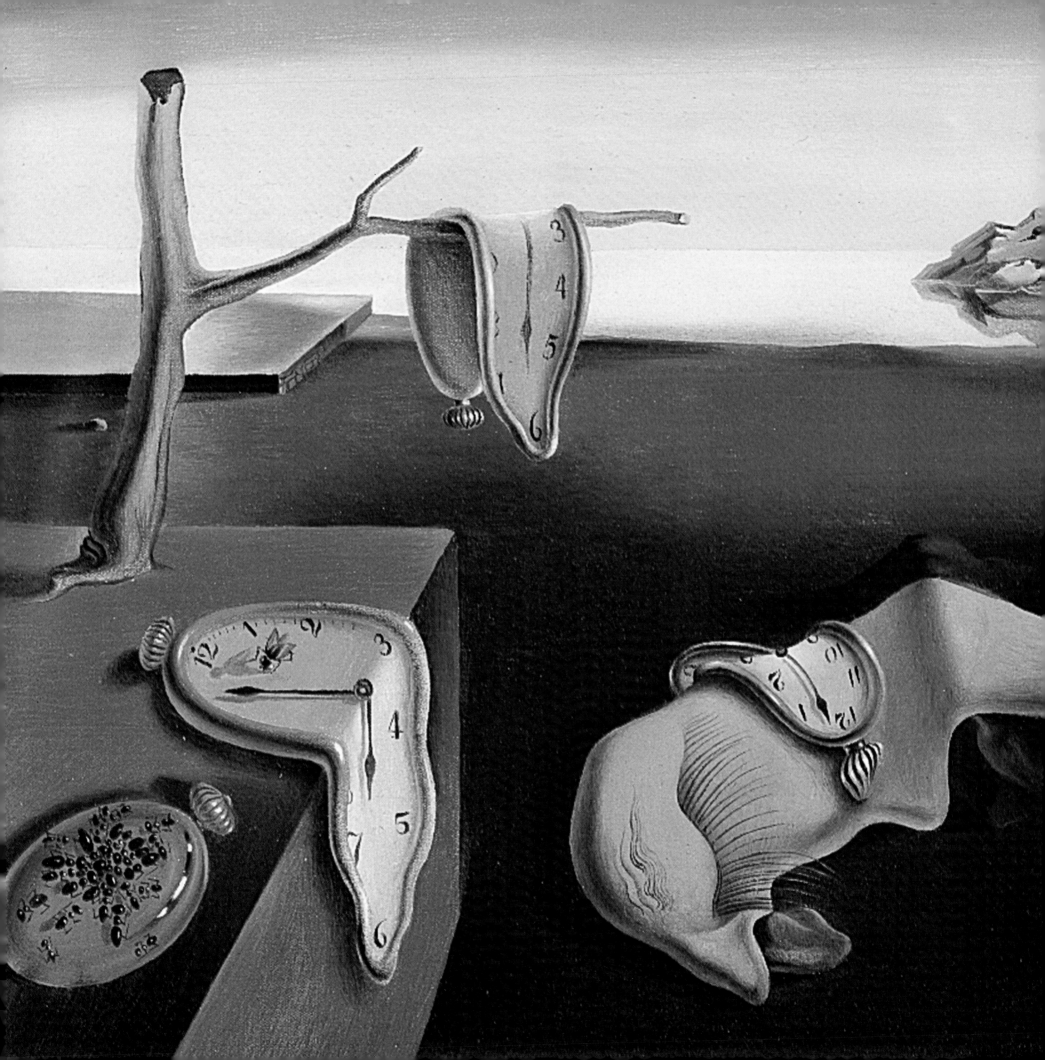

Painting, Sculpture, Prints & Environments

12

THROUGHOUT THE TWENTIETH CENTURY, THE WORLD OF FINE ART HAS SEEN AN ASTONISHING DIVERSITY OF STYLES AND MOVEMENTS, INCLUDING MODERNISM, ABSTRACT EXPRESSIONISM AND POP ART. WORKS IN A VARIETY OF MEDIUMS REVEAL THE INNER PASSIONS, IDEAS AND PHILOSOPHIES OF A WIDE RANGE OF ARTISTS FROM AUGUSTE RODIN TO BARBARA KRUGER.

Auguste Rodin
Monument to Victor Hugo

1889–1909 One of the most prolific sculptors of the late nineteenth and early twentieth centuries, Rodin (1840–1917) was heralded as bringing new life to a dying art. He completed his first masterwork, *The Vanquished* (later called *The Age of Bronze*), in 1876 after a trip to Italy. This sculpture led to the first of many public controversies which were to beset Rodin throughout his career. Accustomed to the highly artificial appearance of most nineteenth-century Academic sculpture, the critics refused to believe that Rodin was able to model a figure so realistically without making plaster casts of a live sitter first. Nonetheless, during the 1880s, he became one of the most successful French artists. He received many commissions for public monuments, including the Burghers of Calais (1884–95) and the *Monument to Victor Hugo*. Rodin also produced numerous small, intimate sculptures, including *Eternal Spring* (1884).

Paul Cézanne
Mont Sainte-Victoire

1902–6 Cézanne (1839–1906) is considered by many to be the father of twentieth-century painting. His early work in Paris in the 1860s was crude, but in 1872, while working with fellow painter Camille Pissarro, he turned to an Impressionist style, with a lighter palette and small brush strokes. This style developed during the 1880s into a constructive one based on hatched brush strokes

and blocks of colour. During this period, Cézanne lived at his family home in Provence and worked on landscapes, still-lifes and portraits, such as *The Card Players* (1885–90), in which he achieved a sense of monumentality for the first time. Towards the end of his life, his style became more abstract, and he concentrated on fewer subjects, one of which was the landscape around Mont Sainte-Victoire.

Aristide Maillol
Jeune Fille se Voilant

c. 1905 The French sculptor and graphic artist Aristide Maillol (1861–1944) is mainly known for his female nudes, representing his interest in timeless serenity as opposed to fleeting expressions and emotions. Maillol sought the eternal rather than the momentary, and challenged his contemporary Rodin,

Overleaf: Salvador Dalí's The Persistence of Memory, *from 1931 (see page 164).*

Top left: this imposing bronze is Auguste Rodin's Monument to Victor Hugo. *It took the sculptor ten years to complete.*

Top right: Aristide Maillol is best known for his sculptures of female nudes, such as this piece called Jeune Fille se Voilant.

Bottom: Paul Cézanne was an important member of the Impressionist movement. His La Montagne Ste Victoire *now hangs in London's Courtauld Gallery.*

who used rough surfaces, fluid shapes and intense energy to express his view of the human condition. Maillol began sculpting when he was almost 40, and his early large sculptures include *The Mediterranean* (c. 1901) and *Action Enchained* (c. 1905), a monument to the revolutionary Louis Auguste Blanqui.

considered a shockingly brutal destruction of the human figure unparalleled in Western art, and a turning point for both Picasso and twentieth-century art in general. The geometric nature of Cubism is evident in the women's figures. *Mother and Child*, another important painting, represents the artist's move away from Cubism to monumental, classically modelled figures.

 **Pablo Picasso**
Les Demoiselles d'Avignon and Mother and Child

1907; 1921–22 Born Pablo Ruiz y Picasso (1881–1973), Picasso was the most influential and successful artist of the twentieth century. Painting, sculpture, graphic art and ceramics were all profoundly and irrevocably affected by his genius. His Blue Period (1901–4) was stimulated by his exposure to life in Paris, while in his Rose Period (1905–6), Picasso painted harlequins and circus performers in a lighter, warmer colour scheme. After 1908, he joined with Georges Braque and other like-minded artists to explore the representation of three-dimensional objects on a two-dimensional surface by means of overlapping planes. This early phase of the Cubist movement is called Analytical Cubism. By 1912, Picasso, Braque and Juan Gris were introducing textured materials such as chair caning and wallpaper, in the form of actual materials or painted imitations, into their works. This reconstitution of reality, called Synthetic Cubism, proved to be of fundamental importance to the development of modern art. Perhaps the most important of Picasso's paintings is *Les Demoiselles d'Avignon*,

Pablo Picasso painted Les Demoiselles d'Avignon *in 1907, during his early experimentation with Cubism.*

Konstantin Brancusi
The New-Born, The Kiss and The Beginning of the World

1908; 1915; 1924 The Romanian-born sculptor Brancusi (1876–1957) went to Paris in 1904. He was determined to move towards abstraction in his work, aiming to capture the essence and spirituality of a subject. Brancusi was influenced by African tribal masks and objects and by Romanian folk art. The first important example of his personal style is the stone sculpture *The Kiss*, which was erected over a friend's grave in the Montparnasse Cemetary in Paris. This work is typical in its compactness and simplicity of form. Around 1910, Brancusi began to produce non-representational sculptures in marble or metal, concentrating on two basic themes: variations of the egg shape and soaring birds. Among these works is *The New-Born*, which exemplifies his sensuous, simply modelled, contemplative and mystical style. His stone and metal sculptures include *The Beginning of the World*; these were the media he used most frequently.

Konstantin Brancusi sculpted Le Baiser *('The Kiss') in 1908. It was placed over the grave of one of his friends.*

Henri Matisse
The Dance

1910 The French artist Henri Matisse (1869–1954) used colour as a means of expression rather than description and deliberately flouted the conventional rules of drawing and perspective. As a member of the Fauves, he developed his use of colour. By 1910, he had come to believe that enjoyment could be gained by studying a painting's essential lines with care. *The Dance*, a series of large canvases commissioned by Matisse's patron Shchukin in 1909, is an excellent illustration of this dictum, using just three colours to enhance the supple circle of dancers. Under the influence of Cubism, Matisse's palette became more sombre, and his shapes took on a geometrical severity for a time, as in The *Moroccans* (1916) and *The Piano Lesson* (c. 1917). During the 1920s, his colours brightened again, and his patterns became more complex, especially in his Odalisques, female nudes posed against the arabesques of North African fabrics. His sculpture is characterized by the flowing, semi-abstract forms of *The Serpentine* (1909) and *The Back* (1909–30), a series of monumental figure studies. Matisse's greatest accomplishment, apparent in all his work, was to liberate colour and utilize it as the foundation of a decorative art.

Edvard Munch
Children in the Street

1910 The Norwegian painter and graphic artist Edvard Munch (1863–1944) was one of the great masters of modern European art and a key figure in the development of Expressionism. His tragic early life left its mark, as can be seen in images which reveal a highly emotional and tormented sensibility. After briefly adopting the precepts of Impressionism, Munch set out to record the anguished psyche of modern humanity. In several stunning Expressionist paintings such as *The Scream* (1893), he created stark and terrifying images of alienation and despair. Munch's works of the 1890s heavily influenced the founders of German Expressionism. In 1908, he suffered a severe nervous breakdown, and although he recovered, his later work shows less visible emotion and torment. One notable exception is *Children in the Street*, which displays great boldness and a type of expressive abstraction in which recognizable forms dissolve into symbols or icons.

Georges Braque
The Portuguese and Guitar and Jug

1911; 1927 Along with Picasso, the French painter Georges Braque (1882–1963) is usually credited as the inventor of Cubism. Originally

influenced by Impressionism and Fauvism, he painted his earliest Cubist landscapes in 1909, inspired by Paul Cézanne. While these tend to be flat, angular pictures in grey tones, Braque's still-lifes developed into multifaceted structures. He invented the method of sticking pieces of wood engraving and marbled surfaces on to canvas; an early picture using this technique is The Portuguese. Braque also pioneered the technique of mixing paint with sand to produce interesting textures. *Guitar and Jug* reflects Braque's Synthetic Cubism and is notable for its stylistic coherence, its rounded, almost Baroque forms and its unusual lighter colours. In the 1920s and '30s, his work became more harmonious and lyrical, reflecting contemporary interest in French classical traditions.

Fernand Léger
The Wedding

1911–12 The French painter Fernand Léger (1881–1955) was a major figure in the development of Cubism and an important documentor of modern urban and technological culture. Trained in an architect's office, he was fascinated by industrial technology and by the dynamic shapes of machinery and construction work. By 1911, he had become a key member of the evolving Cubist movement. Léger's personal style is characterized by tubular, fractured forms and bright colours highlighted by their juxtaposition with cool whites. Major works of his Cubist period include *The Wedding*, *Woman in Blue* (1912) and *Contrasts of Forms* (1913). He is best known for his dynamic use of pure colour, which he

Henri Matisse's controversial La Danse *('The Dance'), was created in 1910. Today it can be seen in St Petersburg's Hermitage Museum.*

released from its figurative function to become purely decorative. Follwing the First World War, Léger concentrated more on urban and machine imagery, favouring sharply delineated, flat shapes and colour areas, as well as combinations of human and mechanical forms.

Umberto Boccioni
Unique Forms of Continuity in Space

1913 The Italian painter and sculptor Umberto Boccioni (1882–1916) was a firm proponent of Futurism, advocating a complete break with previous artistic styles. His first exhibited work was a series of city paintings in which he tried to express the speed and violence of modern life. Inspired by Tomasso Marinetti's 'Futurist Manifesto', Boccioni wrote 'Manifesto of Futurist Painting' in 1910 and 'Manifesto of Futurist Sculpture' in 1912. The only sculptor in the Futurist movement, his aim was to suggest movement by superimposing sequences of images and multiple viewpoints. His painting moved towards abstraction, while in sculpture he used mixed media, such as iron, wood and glass. *Unique Forms of Continuity in Space* avoids straight lines in favour of what Boccioni called 'lines of force'. The sculpture represents the male figure streamlined by speed with 'pure plastic rhythm' to show the action of the body rather than the body itself.

Marcel Duchamp
Nude Descending a Staircase

1913 An American artist of French birth, Duchamp (1887–1968) studied in Paris, but spent most of his working life in the USA. His early portraits and landscapes were influenced by Neo-impressionism and Cubism, but he first caused a sensation at the 1913 Armory Show in New York City with his controversial painting *Nude Descending a Staircase*. This work, which shows the movement of a semi-abstract figure in a number of curved and straight planes, upset the older Cubists. Around this time, Duchamp was developing the fundamental principles of Dada with Guillaume Apollinaire and Francis Picabia, and he decided to abandon conventional materials for the first of his sculptures known as ready-mades – ordinary objects which he signed and titled. These included a bicycle wheel mounted on a kitchen stool, a bottle rack and a urinal, the last of which Duchamp entitled *Fountain*. One of his achievements was to break down the conventions around what constitutes art and good taste. From 1915 to 1923, Duchamp was engaged in a major work entitled *The Bride Stripped Bare by Her Bachelors*, Even, a glass and metal structure which remained unfinished. During the 1920s, he was instrumental in bringing Dada to the USA. He also made a number of elaborate machines which served no purpose.

Right: Marcel Duchamp was influenced by Cubism and helped to develop Dadaism. His Nude Descending a Staircase *can be found in the Philadelphia Museum.*

Opposite: Ernst Ludwig Kirchner was one of Germany's foremost Expressionist painters. In 1913 he painted Five Women on the Street.

Wassily Kandinsky
The Black Arch

1913 The Russian-born painter Wassily Kandinsky (1866–1944) is considered by many to be the founder of abstract art. In 1907, he exhibited with the German Expressionist group Die Brücke, and in 1909 he founded the New Association of Munich Artists. In 1910, Kandinsky executed his first abstract painting and wrote his famous theoretical study Concerning the Spiritual in Art (1912). In 1911, along with August Macke, Franz Marc and, later, Paul Klee, he founded the group known as Der Blaue Reiter; in 1925, he became a teacher at the Bauhaus. Over the next decade, Kandinsky's painting evolved from the Expressionistic, highly coloured improvisations of his early period towards more precisely drawn and geometrically arranged compositions. *The Black Arch* illustrates his abandoning of the tradition of spatial illusion, affirming the two-dimensional character of the canvas and the arbitrary nature of pictorial space.

Ernst Ludwig Kirchner
The Street

1913 Kirchner (1880–1938) was a leading German Expressionist painter with a precocious skill at graphics. He first studied architecture, but turned to painting in Munich (1903–4). In Dresden (1905), he became a founding member of Die Brücke. Kirchner's skill at engraving led him to produce unusually tense images in which areas of vivid colour were contained within austere and compact draughtsmanship. His *Self-Portrait with Model* (1907) shows the artist wearing a brightly striped robe and a violent, mask-like expression. In *The Street*, the expression of pain is even more aggressive. Kirchner transformed the long dresses and feather boas of his time into barbaric costumes. During this period, he replaced his bright palette with a darkly shadowed one. Kirchner's bitter view of his world is expressed clearly in his savage, yet highly acclaimed woodcuts, lithographs and etchings, of which he produced about 2,000.

George Grosz
Suicide and God with Us

1916; 1920 The German-American painter, caricaturist and graphic artist George Grosz (1893–1959) is best known for his 1920s satires of the Weimar Republic. After studying in Berlin, Grosz worked as an illustrator. He served in the German army during the First World War and spent time in a military mental institution; his experiences motivated his anti-establishment caricatures. In 1919, Grosz joined the Club Dada in Berlin, and in 1920 he organized the First International Dada Fair. His kaleidoscopic images of post-war Berlin give a strident portrait of a

dislocated society, as in *Dedicated to Oskar Panizza* (1917–18). The first of Grosz's many portfolios to be confiscated by the police was *God with Us*, a satire on German society. *Suicide* is considered to be a reflection of Grosz's mood and temperament; the painting uses a shattered and claustrophobic perspective and acidic colours to reinforce the dark subject-matter: prostitution, drink and death.

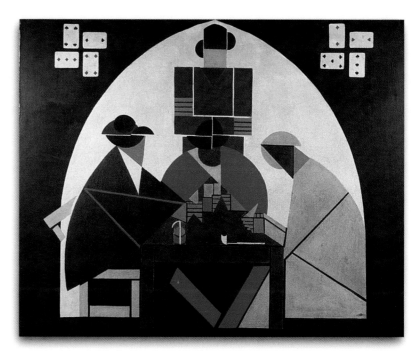

Jean Arp
Forest Form

1917 Arp (1887–1966), a French sculptor, painter and poet, was influential in the development of many of the important movements of his time. In 1912, he exhibited at Der Blaue Reiter's exhibition in Berlin; he showed work at the Expressionist Autumn Salon the following year. Influenced by his contacts with the French avant-garde, Arp began to experiment with abstract paper compositions and collages, designed according to chance, and in 1916 he was one of the founder-members of the Dada movement. Over the next two decades, Arp developed his trademark abstract organic style, a type of sculpture that conveys a sense of plants and animals without reproducing their shapes. His reliefs and sculptures have had a strong effect on the sculpture of this century. *Forest Form* is one of a series of abstract polychrome relief carvings in wood that Arp made during his early invovlement with Dada.

Theo van Doesburg
Card Players

1917 Van Doesburg (Christian Curil Marie Kupper; 1883–1931) was an influential Dutch painter, teacher and theorist. In 1915, he met Piet Mondrian, with whom he formed the group known as De Stijl; he later taught at the Bauhaus in Weimar. Van Doesburg called his own theory of painting Elementarism, a system asserting that the basic elements of painting are lines and shapes. His pictures reflect this theory in their firm, rectilinear shapes and total avoidance of any representational references, as in *Card Players*. Van Doesburg devoted much of his life to promoting De Stijl's ideas through his writings, lectures, art and architecture.

Top: Theo van Doesberg created his own style of painting he called Elementarism. He painted The Card Players *in 1917.*

Bottom: Kasimir Malevich was an important exponent of abstract art. This work is entitled Two Suprematist Figures.

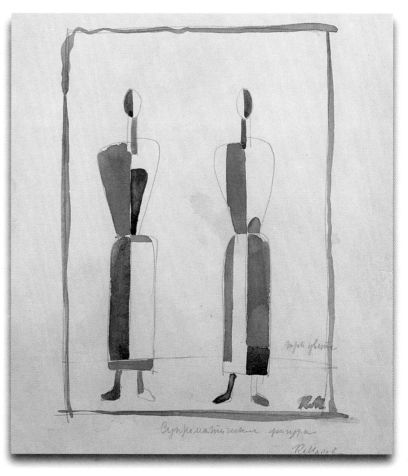

 ### Paul Klee
Once Emerged from the Grey of Night

1917–18 Klee (1879–1940) was a Swiss-born painter and graphic artist whose highly personal, delicate paintings combine music, poetry, primitive lyricism and technical exactitude. His work went beyond Cubism, Surrealism and the abstract in a unique way, transcending the formalism of the majority of modern movements to arrive at what the artist himself called the 'core of energy'. Klee saw art as something which excluded all naturalism, although being a life-giving force, the work of the artist might appear similar to that of nature. Music is constantly present in his work, and a large number of his paintings and drawings are exact graphic transmutations of lines of music, together with their rhythmic harmonies, measures, textures and colours. Klee's early works are mostly etchings and pen-and-ink drawings. These combine satirical, grotesque and surreal elements. His friendship with the painters Wassily Kandinsky and August Macke prompted him to join Der Blaue Reiter, an Expressionist group. His fascination with colour led to compositions of coloured squares with the radiance of mosaics. Klee often incorporated letters and numerals into his paintings, as in *Once Emerged from the Grey of Night*.

Kasimir Malevich
Two Suprematist Figures

1918 The Russian painter Kasimir Malevich (1878–1935) was an important exponent of abstract art. His early work was influenced by the Fauves. In later compositions, such as *Woman with Baskets: Dynamic Arrangement* (1912), he worked in a Cubist style. By 1915, he had developed a style which he called Suprematism, maintaining that pure feeling without any reference to the visual world was the supreme aim of all art. Forms were reduced to their basic geometric shapes, painted in flat, pure colours. Malevich's theory of Suprematism inspired his series of paintings in which white geometric shapes are set against white backgrounds, as in his *Suprematist Composition: White on White*. This work was intended to represent the abstract to end all abstracts. Once he had finished it, Malevich reverted to figurative painting, such as *Two Suprematist Figures*.

Egon Schiele
The Family

1918 The Austrian Expressionist Egon Leo Adolf Schiele (1890–1918) was a highly controversial erotic artist, and his treatment of the nude figure suggests a lonely, tormented spirit haunted rather than fulfilled by his sexuality. At first strongly influenced by Gustav Klimt, whom he met in 1907, Schiele soon achieved an independent anti-classical style in which jagged lines arose more out of psychological and spiritual feeling than out of aesthetic considerations. Schiele painted a number of outstanding portraits, such as that of his father-in-law, Johann Harms (1916), and a series of unflinching and disquieting self-portraits. Late

Egon Schiele's The Family *was painted in 1918, the year of his death. Today it hangs in Vienna's Österreichische Galerie.*

works such as *The Family*, which reveal a new-found sense of security, made Schiele one of the most important Expressionist painters.

Vladimir Tatlin
Monument to the Third International

1919 The Russian painter and sculptor Vladimir Yevgrafovich Tatlin (1885–1953) was the founder of Constructivism, an approach which grew out of his interest in exploring the sculptural possibilities of various modern materials, such as glass, concrete, wire and sheet metal, through abstract reliefs and constructions. An encounter in 1913 with Picasso revolutionized Tatlin's outlook and prompted him to launch his artistic experiments. In 1919, he began plans for a concert-lecture-exhibition hall to be called *Monument to the Third International* (the project never progressed beyond a scale model). A union of architecture, sculpture, light, painting and motion, this complex was to have consisted of two cylinders and a glass pyramid rotating at different speeds and encircled by a spiral tower 400 m (1312 ft) high.

El Lissitzky
Construction Proun 2

1920 Eliezer Markovich Lissitzky (1890–1941) was a Russian painter and designer who enthusiastically employed the vision and ideology of abstract art. It was largely through his efforts that Suprematism and Constructivism, both early forms of abstraction, were first understood in Western Europe. Lissitzky studied engineering in Germany and at the invitation of Marc Chagall returned to Russia in 1919 to teach at the Vitebsk art school. Around this time, he began to paint what he called *Prouns*, geometrical abstractions influenced by the work of Kasimir Malevich. Lissitzky's *Prouns* convey an architectural feeling for clarity and order by means of simple arrangements of lines, squares and rectangles. He is credited with the idea that modern abstract works should be viewed in a museum setting in accord with their particular style.

Max Ernst
The Celebrated Elephant

1921 The German-born painter Max Ernst (1891–1976) became the leader of the Dada group in Cologne in 1919 and was a founder-member of Surrealism in Paris in 1921. Ernst was particularly well known for collages using printed matter; he invented the technique of frottage, using pencil rubbings of leaves and the grain of wooden floors, for example, to suggest the workings of the unconscious mind. His compositions are full of disturbing and absurd images; these reflect his

Eliezer Markovich Lissitsky created Construction Proun 2 *in 1920. His* Prouns *provide the viewer with a feeling of architectural clarity.*

fascination with the art of the insane. *The Celebrated Elephant*, part elephant, part bull, part machine, is one of his early expressions of this private mythology. After being interned in southern France (1939–40), Ernst spent the Second World War in the USA. In New York, he worked with André Breton and Marcel Duchamp on the magazine *V V V*, which published the work of exiles from Nazi Germany.

Juan Gris
Le Canigou

1921 Born in Spain as José Victoriano Gonzalez, Juan Gris (1887–1927) went to Paris in 1906 and lived with Picasso for a time. He did some collages and work for illustrated papers, but all his painting was Cubist in style. Gris's brand of Cubism, more mathematical than that of Picasso or Georges Braque, took simple, fragmented shapes as the bases for still-lifes, landscapes or portraits in bright colours. Rather than working from the object and reducing it to its abstract formal properties, he started with the abstract in an attempt to work towards a new reality. In the 1920s, Gris designed costumes and scenery for the Ballets Russes. He also completed some of the strongest of his Cubist paintings, compressing exterior landscapes and interior still-lifes into bold compositions such as *Le Canigou*.

Piet Mondrian
Composition in Red, Yellow and Blue

1921 Mondrian (1872–1944) was among the most prominent of the century's geometric painters, evolving an austere art of black lines and coloured rectangles placed against white backgrounds. He developed a style which banished the conventions of three-dimensional space and the curve. Mondrian moved these simple elements around the canvas until he found a perfectly balanced composition. He aimed to create an objective, disciplined art whose laws would reflect the order of the universe. Having begun his career painting conventional Dutch landscapes, after 1908 Mondrian began to turn away from the imitation of nature. In 1911, he discovered the Cubist works of Picasso and Georges Braque and was soon producing his own version of Cubism. In 1916, Mondrian and several other Dutch artists formed De Stijl, which published its own periodical in which Mondrian explained his ideas. He believed straight lines joined at right angles expressed perfect equilibrium; he used red, yellow, blue, black, white and grey because they are not found in their purest form in nature and were therefore the most abstract colours. *Composition in Red, Yellow and Blue* is therefore an expression of a spiritual and harmonious conception of the universe and of humanity's place in it.

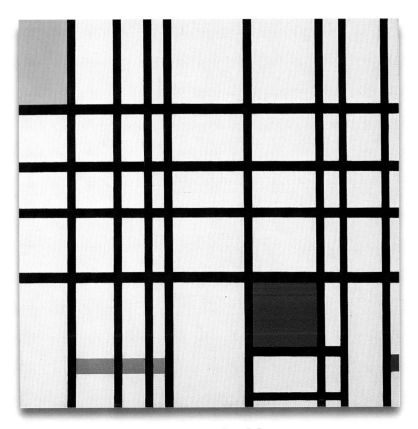

Jacques Lipchitz
Figure

1926–30 The French sculptor Chaim Jacob Lipchitz, known as Jacques Lipchitz (1891–1973), was a vital figure in the development of modern sculpture. He achieved acclaim early in his long career for his Cubist works, developing an individual abstract style and making what he called 'transparent sculptures'. His later figures and animals in bronze were more dynamic and not abstract. Lipchitz's work is unified by several recurring themes, including musicians, mother-and-child groups, portraits and improvisations. His early masterpieces, inspired by Juan Gris and Picasso, include *Man with a Guitar* (1916). In *Figure*, Lipchitz used a strict mathematical composition, showing an amalgamation of architectural forms as a lyrical, harmonious whole. After emigrating to the USA in 1941, he developed a massive, vigorous style which culminated in his monumental Peace on Earth (1967–69).

Henry Moore
Maquette for a Draped Reclining Woman

c. 1930s Moore (1898–1986) was influenced early on by Surrealism, as well as by African, Cycladic, Egyptian and pre-Columbian art. He liked to work with organic materials, particularly stone. His first major public

Piet Mondrian was the foremost member of the Dutch group De Stijl. This piece is titled Composition in Red, Yellow and Blue.

subconscious, but soon developed his own techniques focusing on hallucinations and dreams. Dalí famously claimed that artists should develop their own paranoias and delusions in order to feed their work. His startling nightmare images were inspired by Freudian theory mixed with shocking photorealism. In *The Persistence of Memory*, the melting clocks are characteristic motifs and were intended to create a sense of unease in the viewer. Dalí made two Surrealist films in collaboration with Luis Buñuel, *An Andalusian Dog* and *The Golden Age* – but was rejected by other Surrealists in 1937 for his stance over the Spanish Civil War and because his work was becoming more conventional. He moved to the USA, where his talent for self-publicity was more fully appreciated and gained him widespread notoriety. In the 1940s, he converted to Roman Catholicism and turned to painting religious subjects. In these later works, his unique form of Surrealism remains evident although it is less prominent than before.

Joan Mirò
Painting

1933 The Spanish painter Joan Mirò (1893–1983) was a leading exponent of abstract and Surrealist art. Mirò was influenced much more by the Fauves and the primitivism of Henri Rousseau than by the rigours of Cubism. His first paintings in Paris combined extreme realism and

Top: Maquette for a Draped, Reclining Woman *is one of Henry Moore's most distinctive sculptures. The pose is characteristic of his later works.*

Bottom: Salvador Dalí *painted* The Persistence of Memory *in 1931. At the time, he expressed surprise that no other artist had thought to paint soft clocks before.*

commission was a relief entitled *North Wind*. Carved for the London Transport Office, it exemplified his simple yet monumental style. Moore revived the tradition of direct carving into stone or wood, emphasizing the natural textures of his materials. His works consistently reflect the contours and qualities of landscape, and as a result the simple, solid shapes have a powerful, brooding quality. During the Second World War, Moore made many drawings of people sheltering in Underground tunnels at night and during air raids. He made these works in ink, chalk and watercolour. In his later work, two consistent themes are mothers with children and reclining figures, and even his most abstract works have a naturalistic aspect.

Salvador Dalí
Persistence of Memory and The Sacrament of the Last Supper

1931; 1955 Dalí (1904–1989), a Spanish artist, was associated with Cubism, Futurism and metaphysical painting before becoming one of the best-known Surrealists. He studied in Madrid, but moved in 1928 to Paris, where he was influenced by the works of Joan Mirò and Picasso. He joined the Surrealists in 1929, fascinated by their interest in the

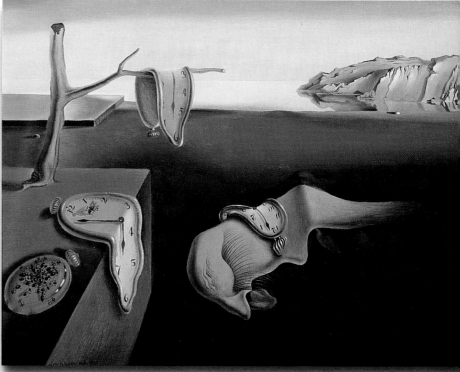

geometrical abstraction, often inspired by the austere landscape of his Catalan homeland. In the 1920s, Miró began to experiment with Surrealism, and from 1924 onwards he was a key figure in the circle of André Breton and other Surrealists. Throughout the late 1920s and 30s, he experimented with ever-freer compositions based on the interplay of elements rather than on a design imposed by the artist. In works such as Painting. Miró's debt to collage is noticeable in the loose organization of the composition. He was best known for the humour and idiosyncratic vision he brought to Surrealist art.

René Magritte
La Condition Humaine II

1934 Born in Belgium, Magritte (1898–1967) was a leading painter and theorist of Surrealism, often using fantastic and dream-like images to question concepts of definition and representation. He worked as a commercial artist for some years, but by 1925 was concentrating almost entirely on Surrealist works. Almost all of Magritte's paintings feature some sort of visual paradox: a sky in which the clouds have turned into bread; a pipe with the caption 'This is not a pipe'; a steam engine emerging from a fireplace. This interplay between precisely drawn objects and abnormal settings and features is based on the idea that realism is only one way of depicting the world. In *La Condition Humaine II*, Magritte forcefully demonstrated the paradoxes of perception by placing a painting showing a landscape view within the window overlooking an identical view. His paintings show both humour and insight.

The Human Condition II, *by René Magritte, shows a canvas in front of a window from which can be seen a continuation of the same image.*

portraying their subjects as aggressive and, at the same time, erotic. In 1963, the artist moved away from New York City, where he had been living, and began to paint lyrical landscapes whose lushness is at times reminiscent of Rubens.

Frida Kahlo
Self-Portrait with Cropped Hair

1940 The Mexican artist Frida Kahlo (1907–1954) spent most of her creative life in the shadow of muralist Diego Rivera, with whom she had a turbulent marriage. Kahlo has become something of a cult figure partly because from the mid-1940s she suffered from spinal problems and, though bedridden, continued to paint, often in terrible pain, until her death. Wide recognition of her work came only posthumously. Over Kahlo's relatively short working life, she produced almost 200 paintings, mostly self-portraits, which address contemporary and feminist issues. *In My Birth* (1932), Kahlo gives birth to her herself, with her adult head forcing its way out of her womb into the world. The concept of Woman as Earth or Nature was extremely important to all Surrealists, as well as to other artists. In *Self-Portrait with Cropped Hair*, we see Kahlo as both feminist artist and Surrealistic object.

Edward Hopper
Chop Suey

1942 Hopper (1882–1967) was influenced by his teacher Robert Henri, a member of the Ashcan School. Hopper's work received little recognition until the 1930s, when his scenes taken from small-town life in New York or New England came to the fore as exemplars of the new American Realism. He transcended the social realism of the Ashcan School to achieve more truthful renderings of the anonymity and loneliness of people in crowds, for example. Hopper's best-known painting is probably *Nighthawks*, which shows four men sitting in a diner, viewed through the window. It is night, and the interior of the diner is harshly lit, in contrast with the shadows outside. Similar in content is *Chop Suey*, illustrated here. Hopper's painting centres on a psychological investigation into the characteristics of American experience, in terms of both human life and landscape. He presented his subject-matter in the manner of a detached reporter with a slightly poetic bent. All of Hopper's work is characterized by an emphasis on the structure and coherence of pictorial design, with a strong geometry of verticals, horizontals and diagonals. In later years, it evolved towards a greater purity, showing the artist's increasing ability to integrate patterns of light and shadow and his interest in the monumentality of architecture and frontal figures.

Willem de Kooning
The Visit

Willem de Kooning painted The Visit *in 1966. It was one of his first major works, executed originally in line with colour added at a later date.*

1940 De Kooning (1904–1997), born in the Netherlands, moved to the USA, becoming naturalized in 1926. He worked in a wide range of styles and in both colour and monochrome, but is probably best known as one of the leading proponents of Abstract Expressionism. His first major works, of which *The Visit* is one, use line, with colour added later, to create fluid, abstract forms. In 1946, de Kooning began a series of black-and-white paintings in which abstract forms overlap and interpenetrate. His controversial series of portraits of women, exhibited in 1953, signalled a return to the figurative, with violent slashes of colour

Edward Hopper's early influence was the Ashcan School, but his later pieces are described as American Realism. This work is titled Chop Suey.

Barbara Hepworth
Pelagos

1946 Hepworth (1903–1975), an English sculptor, is renowned for her non-representational sculpture whose forms combine geometric and organic elements. Having studied sculpture at the Royal College of Art in London, she travelled to Italy in 1924, sketching Romanesque and early Renaissance sculpture and architecture and acquiring technical facility in the traditional Italian mode of direct marble cutting. From her return to England in 1926 until 1934, Hepworth created figurative pieces in stone and bronze which varied in their degree of abstraction. Her mature, direct-cut style evolved out of *Pierced Form* (1931), in which she explored the possibilities of the penetration of closed form by light and air. By 1937, Hepworth had begun to employ colour. *Pelagos* illustrates the compact, simplified forms she preferred.

Jackson Pollock
Frieze

Jackson Pollock created his works by dripping, pouring and hurling paint onto the canvas. This piece is titled Frieze.

1947 The controversial painter Jackson Pollock (1912–1956) was a central figure of American Abstract Expressionism, producing art which was both intensely personal and violently emotional and anarchic. By the mid-1930s, he had developed a dark style which he used while working on the Federal Art Project between 1938 and 1942. Pollock's first solo show included paintings representative of his increasingly vivid style, such as *The She Wolf* (1943). By 1947, he was relying on a type of painting that was expressive in form, but with imagery derived from the unconscious or from myth. Gradually, the surface of these paintings became more homogeneous as the figures became less easily separated from the grounds. Pollock perfected new techniques of application, dripping paint from tins and pouring and hurling it on to unstretched canvases placed on the floor, as in *Frieze*. From 1950 onwards, often working only in poured black paint, he began to reintroduce more explicit figures into his skeins of lines. In his final years, Pollock drew on the various innovations he had pioneered, occasionally using human and anatomical imagery and creating both dynamic swirled and dripped colour paintings and smaller black-and-white studies. Pollock's reputation has continued to grow since his death in a car crash on Long Island.

Alberto Giacometti
L'Homme qui Marche I

1950 Born in Switzerland, Giacometti (1901–1966) was taken up by the Surrealists in the late 1920s, becoming their favourite sculptor in 1932, when he exhibited The Palace at 4am, a highly individual open-cage construction of sticks, glass and wire. Giacometti became disillusioned with the politics of the Surrealist movement, however, and left in 1935 to pursue his own goal, which was to represent objects in the most truthful, realistic way possible. He was obsessed with spatial relationships, and many of his works comprise groups of thin, elongated

human figures with rough-textured surfaces, supposedly seen from a distance. These solitary figures, as in *L'Homme qui Marche 1*, have been interpreted as a metaphor for human beings standing alone in the void of existence. Giacometti's sculptural technique was unique for his time.

Mark Rothko
Number 10

1950 The Russian-born American artist Mark Rothko (1903–1970) was the most transcendental painter associated with Abstract Expressionism. His early paintings of the 1940s are luminously pale scenes made up of indistinct shapes suggesting primitive life-forms floating over a background of banded colours. In 1947, Rothko attempted to universalize his art by working with various arrangements of hovering, rectangular areas of colour. Over the next three years, this format was reduced and solidified into his mature style: two to five rectangles of glowing colour suspended one above another against a luminous field. *Number 10* is one of these. The emptiness of Rothko's paintings symbolizes humanity's spiritual yearnings; like religious icons, these pictures are intended to evoke humility and exaltation in the viewer. From 1958 onwards, his works became increasingly austere.

Lucian Freud
Girl with a White Dog

1951–52 The early work of British painter Lucian Freud (1922–), grandson of Sigmund Freud, portrays people and plants in a bleached, realistic style with hard lines and an almost Surrealistic

aspect. From the 1950s, though, his paintings became more truthful and meticulous, focusing on nudes in squalid settings. His models tend to be people who are known to him; sometimes overweight, they are splayed across beds or chairs in uncomfortable-seeming poses. Typical of Freud's work are *Naked Man, Back View* (1991–92) and numerous self-portraits. *Girl with a White Dog* portrays the artist's first wife, Kathleen, with an English bull terrier, and is emblematic of Freud's mastery and near-obsessive portrayal of human flesh, with all its flaws exposed. While his brutal portraits can discomfit the viewer, his meticulous rendering, lucid detailing and tactile richness have prompted critics to call him the greatest living realist painter.

Allan Kaprow
Happenings

1959 Kaprow (1927–) is an American painter, assemblage artist and art theorist who created the art form known as the happening. His early paintings were Abstract Expressionist compositions. Kaprow also experimented with collages and assemblages composed of non-traditional materials. Inspired by the composer John Cage and his belief in the effectiveness of unfocusing the spectator's mind in order to make him more aware both of himself and of the world around him, Kaprow began to create environmental works which integrated space, materials and colour in events staged by artists. These performances were designed to add another dimension of reality and even direction to art. Other painters such as

Alberto Giacometti's solitary figures (such as L'Homme qui Marche I*) are seen as a metaphor for man standing alone in the void of existence.*

Left: *Robert Rauschenberg is a leading figure in the Pop Art world. He is also an important exponent of environmental art and experimental theatre.*

Right: *Yves Klein invented a colour of his own, International Klein Blue (IKB). The dramatic effect of the colour can be seen in* Venus Bleue.

Jim Dine and Claes Oldenburg staged elaborate live tableaux along similar lines. Since 1960, Kaprow has devoted himself to creating and publicizing happenings and establishing them as a viable art form.

Robert Rauschenberg
Nettle

c. 1959 Rauschenberg (1925–) is a leading figure in American Pop art, environmental art and experimental theatre. His early works include the 'combine' paintings of the late 1950s, which grew from modest collages of newspaper fragments and photographs into complex, three-dimensional creations. The most spectacular, *Monogram*, consists of a stuffed ram encircled by an automobile tyre; the base is splashed with paint and collage elements. Since the 1960s, Rauschenberg has produced kaleidoscopic silk-screened works which often include his own photographs, transferred via silk-screen. His 1991 show, 'The Rauschenberg Overseas Cultural Interchange', at the National Gallery in Washington, D.C., constituted a latter-day wrap-up of his work: over 125 paintings, sculptures and photographs created out of discarded materials in each of the many countries the artist visited throughout the 1980s.

Yves Klein
Venus Bleue

1960 Klein (1928–1962) was among the younger generation of artists who became known as the New Realists. He sought to express human sensibility though art and invented a colour of his own, International Klein Blue (IKB), through which this revolution was to be spread. The colour can be seen to great effect in *Venus Bleue*, illustrated here. The most publicized of Klein's paintings were the *Anthropometries* – canvases bearing the marks of paint-soaked female bodies – which extended his belief that an artist could undertake anything which would express his conviction that human beings could overcome their physical limitations. Although Klein had no formal artistic training, he developed elaborate metaphysical theories about art and was fascinated by the process of making it; his public demonstrations (in particular the *Anthropometries*) caused a sensation. One of the strongest of these, *The Large Anthropophagy – Homage to Tennessee Williams*, is an imprint of a female body in IKB blue paint.

Andy Warhol
Marilyn Diptych and Green Coca-Cola Bottles

1962 Warhol (1928–1987) was the founder of Pop art. In 1960, he produced the first of his paintings depicting enlarged comic-strip images, and he pioneered the development of the process whereby an enlarged photographic image is transferred to a silk-screen which is then placed on a canvas and inked from the rear. This technique enabled Warhol to produce the series of slightly varied, mass-media images that he began in 1962. Incorporating such items as Campbell's soup tins, Coca-Cola bottles and the faces of celebrities, these works can be taken as comments on the banality, harshness and ambiguity of American culture. Later in the 1960s, Warhol made a series of experimental films. He was obsessed with Marilyn Monroe, whom he saw as an icon of popular culture, and used her image repeatedly over the years, affording her an added cult status by making her one of the icons of Pop. His *Marilyn Diptych* was one of a series of works that reflected the emblems of modernity, which also included *Green Coca-Cola Bottles*. In these works, the same image is repeated across the entire surface of the canvas, and the aura of mass production is intensified by Warhol's technique rather than the serial repetition.

Naum Gabo
Torsion Bronze

1963 Born Naum Pevsner (1890–1977), Gabo changed his name to differentiate himself from his brother Antoine Pevsner, with whom he would later write the 'Realistic Manifesto' which marked the inception of Constructivism. Gabo's first constructions showed the influence of Cubism – Picasso in particular – but in post-Revolutionary Russia, he discovered a different agenda. The aim in launching Constructivism was to counteract the productivism of the state and underline the emotional and aesthetic values of art. Gabo was known in particular for his constructions in transparent plastics, which introduced a new idea of sculptural space. In the 1920s, he began to study the aesthetics of movement and was an early pioneer of kinetic sculpture, of which the Monument for the Institute of Physics and Mathematics was a prime example. Gabo lived in Berlin (1922–32) and in England (1935–46) before moving to the USA, where he continued to create new sculptures, including *Torsion Bronze*.

David Hockney
The Rake's Progress and Mr and Mrs Clark and Percy

1963; 1970–71 Hockney (1937–) is one of the key figures in contemporary art. He studied at the Royal College of Art in London, and his work first became widely known as a result of the 'Young Contemporaries' exhibition (1961–62). In Hockney's earliest, most irreverent phase, he treated popular imagery in a quirky, graffiti-like manner interlaced with visual puns. From the beginning, he showed that he was an artist of unmistakable originality. One of the finest draughtsmen of his era, Hockney has executed several series of prints, of which *The Rake's Progress*, inspired by William Hogarth, is the best known. His ambitious pictures of the 1970s were usually portraits; *Mr and Mrs Clark and Percy*, showing the British designer Ossie Clark with his wife and cat, is a highly finished, technically accomplished work which conveys a strong impression of the sitters' characters and the relationship between them and the artist.

Andy Warhol's portraits of Marilyn Monroe are among the most famous artworks of all time. He created the series in 1962, the year of her death.

Roy Lichtenstein
Whaam!

1963 New York City artist Roy Lichtenstein (1923–1997) was a Pop artist known for his painted enlargements of banal comic strips. After studying and teaching at Ohio State University, Lichtenstein taught at Rutgers University in New Jersey and held his first solo show in New York City in 1962. Comic-strip paintings like *Whaam!* transpose the simplified violence and sentimentality of popular culture into huge, almost abstract images with verve and unmistakable humour. Lichtenstein exploited pre-existing imagery and a crude colour-printing technique made up of Ben-Day dots in his huge blow-ups. *Whaam!* is worked at a larger scale than many of his earlier works, with two panels presenting a scene of violence and sentimental idealization. When Lichtenstein's painting first claimed wide attention in the early 1960s, it was because it was diametrically opposed to the then-dominant Abstract Expressionist style. His art was calculated in the extreme, leaving no room for the personal gestures and expressions of sensual pain to which critics and viewers had become accustomed. As a Pop artist, Lichtenstein reprocessed popular imagery, designing his work to shock. His later works applied his distinctive vocabulary of dots and lines to adaptations of compositions by such modern masters as Picasso. He also produced sculptural parodies of the decorative styles of the 1920s and '30s.

Claes Oldenberg
Soft Typewriter

1963 The work of Swedish Pop artist Claes Thure Oldenburg (1929–) is characterized by oversized replicas of ordinary objects that blur the line between the mundane and the aesthetic. In his early career, he became a planner of happenings, events involving the use of various media which were intended to break down the limits of art. By the late 1950s, Oldenburg had begun to exhibit props for these events as independent works – generally sculptures of everyday objects modelled from plaster or papier-mâché and heavily spattered with paint. Although he was linked with the American Pop artists, he tended more towards Surrealism, injecting a strongly personal, often humorous quality into his art. While his earliest sculpture transformed soft subjects into hard forms, during the 1960s this procedure was reversed. Hard objects were turned into soft, kapok-filled sculptures as, for example, in *Soft Typewriter*, which has an almost sensual, organic quality.

Whaam!, painted in 1963, is one of Roy Lichtenstein's most famous works. The famed pop artist was renowned for painting enlargements of comic strips.

encourage a sense of the refined spirituality and mysticism suggested by their colours and size. In *Stations of the Cross* (1958–66), he eliminated form and the illusion of depth, creating his effects solely through pure colour and the interaction between the field and narrow 'zips'. Newman created several noteworthy pieces of sculpture, including the steel *Broken Obelisk*, which consists of a pyramid on a shallow, square plinth, topped by an inverted obelisk.

Jasper Johns
Painted Bronze II: Ale Cans

1964 Johns (1930–) is a major American artist who re-examined the relation between works of art and physical objects. Between 1954 and 1955, he created a series of paintings of targets and of American flags. When they were exhibited in 1958 at his first solo show, they inspired a storm of protest. Johns used the ancient technique of encaustic to modify the traditional canvas surface and identified his images with the background or field, thus asserting the formal priority of the second dimension while at the same time insisting on the significance of the image. He also incorporated 'found' objects in his work. Some of Johns's sculptures use ordinary objects – the two beer cans of *Painted Bronze* are a notable example – to point out the ambiguous relationship between reality and the illusions of art. His use of these everyday materials influenced the growth of the Pop movement.

Barnett Newman
Broken Obelisk

1963–67 The Abstract Expressionism of New York-born painter and sculptor Barnett Newman (1905–1970) played a major role in the development of colour-field painting. From 1948, Newman painted huge canvases consisting of unified fields of pure colour interrupted by one or two narrow vertical stripes of another colour or tone. The stripes, which became known as 'zips', were a trademark of Newman's style. Newman sought to suggest a mystical abstraction in his paintings, to

Left: Barnett Newman sculpted Broken Obelisk *in the 1960s. The magnificent artwork was constructed out of steel.*

Right: Jasper Johns created his Painted Bronze II: Ale Cans *in 1967. They measure 137 cm x 20 cm x 11 cm.*

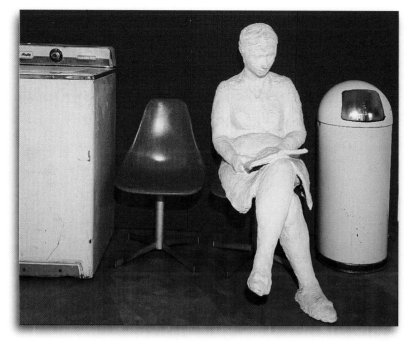

constructions, which Grooms made with a group of associates, satirize the worlds they depict.

Robert Smithson
Spiral Jetty

1970 One of the originators of earth art, Smithson (1938–1973) studied at the Art Students League in New York City. In his early work, he experimented with Minimalism and Conceptualism, but in 1967 he turned to enormous outdoor projects, which he termed earthworks. Smithson's most famous earthwork, *Spiral Jetty*, was a road 4.6 m (15 ft) wide spiralling out into Great Salt Lake in Utah. Companion works were his conical *Spiral Hill* (1971) and his 43-m (141-ft) half-submerged *Broken Circle* (1972), both near Emmen in the Netherlands.

Anselm Kiefer
Parsifal III

1973 The German artist Anselm Kiefer (1945–) attracted enormous attention in the 1980s, with his very large lead-and-straw-encrusted paintings, intended as savage criticisms of the country's Nazi past. Indeed, the theme of German culture is central to his work, and his paintings portray Germany as both a country of calamity and a place of grandiose and ridiculous pretension. Kiefer's themes reiterate the destruction wrought by the Nazis: tattered landscapes, burnt clothing and books. He was invited to exhibit in Israel in 1984 and in 1990 was awarded the Israeli Wolff Prize 'for a distinguished contribution to the betterment of humankind'. *Parsifal III* is a monumental example of Neo-expressionism, a style which emphasized the artist's reaction to an experience rather than the facts of the experience itself. Kiefer's later paintings involve mythical figures and themes.

George Segal
The Laundromat

1964–66 The American Realist George Segal (1924–) is known in particular for his life-size plaster figures. Segal attended New York University and Cooper Union and had his first show in 1956. During the early 1960s, he turned to making these figures – usually white and rough with an occasional prop or piece of clothing – and also participated in the early happenings. In his larger works, such as *The Laundromat*, the dead-white plaster figures are set in rooms with actual stools, counters and fixtures, as if they had been mummified in the course of their mundane pursuits. Segal's intention was to portray the anonymity of the daily actions imposed on us by society and to capture humanity's sense of alienation in the modern world. His portrayal of familiar activities which the spectator could relate to was typical of the Pop movement.

Red Grooms
Discount Store

In his larger works, such as The Laundromat, *George Segal sets his deathly white plaster figures in rooms with actual furniture, as if mummified.*

1970 Charles Roger 'Red' Grooms (1937–) was involved in the early happenings, including Burning Building (1958), in New York City during the late 1950s and early '60s before developing an individual, cartoon-like sculptural style. As an artist on the fringe of the Pop movement, Grooms is best known for his playful constructions such as *Discount Store* and *Ruckus Manhattan* (1975), huge, distorted models of people and buildings executed in papier-mâché, plywood and paint. These witty

Judy Chicago
The Dinner Party

1979 The American feminist artist Judy Chicago (1939–) has always been a controversial figure. Having studied in Los Angeles, California, she then set up the first feminist art course in America. Chicago's work in painting and sculpture is often sexually suggestive; she believes that women should celebrate and represent their sexual difference from men. Her most famous work, *The Dinner Party*, was made in collaboration with other women artists. It comprises a large, triangular table set for dinner. At each of the places is a chair embroidered with traditional needlework patterns and a dinner plate decorated with abstract whorls and patterns reminiscent of women's genitalia. Each place setting is named after a famous female cultural figure and marked by an image symbolizing creativity and openness. By the mid-1980s, Chicago's work was being criticized by younger feminists as essentialist (that is, as reducing women to a biological condition).

Keith Haring
electric billboard

1980s During his short but amazingly prolific life, the American artist Keith Haring (1958–1990) created a new lexicon of powerful visual images, bringing his graffiti-style art into the mainstream and earning the recognition of a huge international public. His idiosyncratic, cartoon-style images are instantly identifiable: the radiant baby, the barking dog, the brightly-coloured, faceless figures. Haring spray-painted these icons on to subway walls and buildings, later creating large designs of interlocking figures, vibrant with movement and colour. He went on to design electric billboards for Times Square in New York City, murals for schools and stage sets, as well as designs for T-shirts and watch faces. The apparent lightness of his style provides a foil for the density and complexity of the message.

Rebecca Horne
Peacock Machine

1982 The German artist Rebecca Horn (1944–) works across many media, including film and performance, but is best known for her spare and often disturbing installations, which attempt physical stagings of emotional experience. Horn's materials juxtapose the industrial with the earthy; she has used steel and copper pipes, coal, eggs and water in the same work, presenting a fascinating juxtaposition of the mechanical and the erotic. *Peacock Machine* is a fan of steel rods, a disturbing example of the artist's use of metal to portray life as machinery. Horn's work is influenced by Marcel Duchamp but also by the more personal work of the German artist Joseph Beuys. Some installations make reference to personalities such as Oscar Wilde, Franz Kafka and Buster Keaton, commenting on the private lives of artists who have struggled with the demands of modern society to maintain their integrity.

Gilbert and George
Finding God

1984; 1980; 1970 Gilbert Proesch (1942–) and George Passmore (1943–), two genuine English eccentrics, met at St Martin's School of Art in London in the 1960s and have lived and worked together ever since. They were first known as performance artists, producing works which they called living sculpture and which consisted of them posing in a gallery. Since then, Gilbert and George have worked in a variety of media, but their best-known works are enormous, vividly coloured photomontages combining photographs of themselves with other images, from both city and countryside, and of other models, mostly men. The two artists appear in almost all their own works, sometimes several times, presenting themselves as iconic figures emerging through the detritus of the world. Their work almost defies categorization, but its gaudy colours and large scale serve to debunk traditional art-historical values, giving it an affinity with Pop art.

Richard Long
Norfolk Flint Circle, Spring Circle

1990–92 Long (1945–) is one of Britain's foremost practitioners of environmental art. Since 1965, he has rejected the use of technology and consumer products in art, choosing to work with natural materials either transported into a gallery or installed at outdoor sites, which are then photographed. These might be geometric shapes made of stones or sticks, trees plaited with green stems, or patterns woven in cornfields or long grass. Viewers can participate in some of these works by walking through or around them. This aspect was taken a stage further when Long created actual walks based on the patterns of the land in certain gardens and on commons. His work makes an ecological point as well as a social comment about the ownership of the land.

The figures of Gilbert and George appear in almost all their own works, including this work entitled Finding God.

Photography

13

THE RAPID DEVELOPMENT OF PHOTOGRAPHY
INITIALLY CAUSED MANY PAINTERS TO REASSESS
THE ARTISTIC VALUES OF THE NINETEENTH
CENTURY. DURING THE TWENTIETH CENTURY,
THE MEDIUM AND PRACTICE OF PHOTOGRAPHY
HAS GROWN IN ACCEPTANCE TO BECOME ONE
OF THE MOST IMPORTANT AND INFLUENTIAL
VISUAL FORMS.

AUJOURD'HUI

Gertrude Kasebier
Camera Work

1903 Kasebier (1852–1934) was born in Iowa. After studying painting at the Pratt Institute in Brooklyn, New York, she began to photograph in 1893, becaming a founding member of the Photo-Secession in 1902. In 1897, she opened a highly successful portrait studio in New York City. Building up her compositions in contrasting tones, Kasebier created evocative, soft-focused platinum prints which far surpassed contemporary camera portraiture. Her works are charmingly inventive, using special qualities of light, shade, tone and texture to create fresh, romantic images. Of her pictures she wrote, 'I have longed increasingly to make pictures of people ... to make likenesses that are biographies, to bring out in each photograph the essential personality that is variously called temperament, soul, humanity'. One of the founders of the Pictorial Photographers of America, she continued to photograph until 1929.

Overleaf: Henri Cartier-Bresson's Sunday, Bank of the Marne, *was taken in 1938 (see page 180).*

Right: Clarence White employed only natural methods of lighting: here the naked woman is lit by the glare of the sun amid the shadow of trees.

Clarence H. White
Nude

1903 Born in Ohio, White (1871–1925) achieved an international reputation for his unique approach to photography, based on the intimate style of American Impressionism. White never used artificial light and was distracted by artifice in any form. He employed the back-lighting effect of sun through trees, and his subjects were usually female – romantic maidens in nightgowns or flowing garments – and set against hazy landscapes. White contended that good photography relied upon concentration and planning, and thought that by the continued use of the same subjects, he would come to a deeper understanding of their emotions.

Alvin Langdon Coburn
London

1909 Born in Boston, Massachusetts, Coburn (1882–1966) became a photographer at an early age and, as a friend of photographer Alfred Stieglitz, joined the Photo-Secessionists in 1902. When he visited London in the early 1900s, he took soft-focus photographs in which smoke, fog and sunlight create an eerie, Whistlerian effect. Coburn's Post-Impressionist gum-platinum pictures – prints on rough cream paper with serrated edges – were praised by George Bernard Shaw, who wrote, 'Coburn's work always sets out to convey a mood and not to impart information'. Coburn was best known for producing so-called 'vortographs', the first entirely non-objective photographs. In 1904, he began making portraits of London celebrities, including George Meredith (1904) and Bernard Shaw himself (1906). Coburn's 1913 pictures of New York City experimented with unusual perspectives.

Alfred Stieglitz
portraits of Georgia O'Keeffe

1924– Stieglitz (1864–1946) was the principal American force behind the recognition of photography as a fine art, and he was a champion of the avant-garde in all the visual arts. He trained in photographic technology in Berlin in 1883, returning to New York in 1890. As the editor of the periodicals American Amateur Photographer and Camera Notes, Stieglitz gained international recognition for many young American photographers. He married painter Georgia O'Keeffe in 1924, and over many years made thousands of portraits of her: no more comprehensive or intimate photographic essay has ever been made of one person. Influenced by avant-garde movements in Germany, Stieglitz organized an impressive display of the finest pictorial photography at the National Arts Club in New York City, an exhibition which gave rise to the photographers' group known as the Photo-Secession.

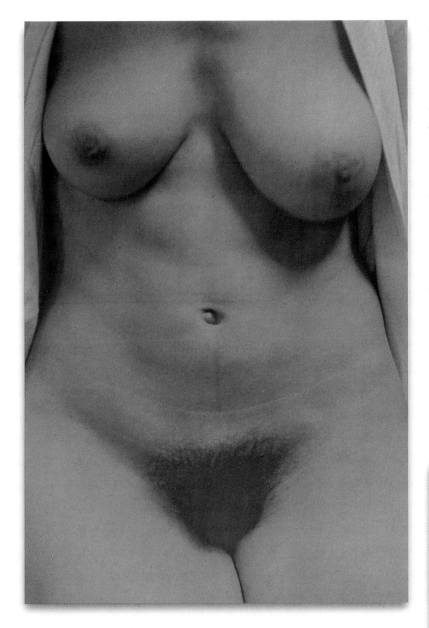

what he considered to be a reproductive technique to a productive medium. *The Shooting Gallery* uses shadows in an extraordinary and diverse way, providing a good example of his non-representational photography. He authored several pedagogical works, among them *Painting Photography Film* (1969), *The New Vision* (1932) and *Vision in Motion* (1947).

André Kertesz
Mondrian's Glasses and Pipe

1926 Born in Budapest, Kertesz (1894–1985) was one of the inventors of modern photojournalism, wandering the Hungarian streets to capture the unfamiliar from different angles. His compositions were unusual, often cutting off the heads and feet of his subjects. Kertesz moved to Paris in 1925, and three years later purchased a Leica miniature camera which enabled him to work with both speed and discretion. Kertesz contributed photographs to the first French picture magazines, including *Vu*. His ability to expose the significant details and communicate the essence of a subject determined future trends in journalistic photography. From 1936, Kertesz worked in the USA. His photographs can be seen in *Paris vu par André Kertesz* (1934) and *André Kertesz: 60 Years of Photography, 1912–1972* (1972). *Kertesz on Kertesz* was published in 1985.

Lászlo Moholy-Nagy
The Shooting Gallery

1925 The Hungarian-born Moholy-Nagy (1895–1946) was a painter, sculptor, stage designer, photographer and film maker and co-founder of the Constructivist movement. The immense influence of his art is partly due to his success as a teacher, both at the German Bauhaus (1923–28) and at his own New Bauhaus (1938–46) in Chicago, Illinois. By the 1920s, Moholy-Nagy had become well known in Europe for his photograms, created by flashing a light on everyday objects placed on sensitized paper. He was concerned about changing photography from

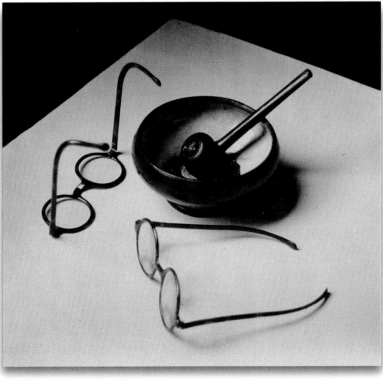

Left: photographer Alfred Stieglitz was married to the celebrated artist Georgia O'Keeffe. Throughout their marriage he made a series of portraits of her, comprising thousands of photographs.

Right: Kertesz's still life, composed of the artist Mondrian's personal effects, typifies the photographer's approach to his art and his ability to make others view objects in a totally new light.

Brassaï
Paris de Nuit

1933 Born in Hungary, Brassaï (Gyula Halasz; 1899–1984) began his working life as an abstract painter and sculptor. Under the influence of his friend André Kertesz, he approached photojournalism with an obsession for the night life of Paris and a taste for the strange, ambiguous and depraved. The American writer Henry Miller once called Brassaï the 'eye of Paris'. The photographer achieved success overnight with his revealing 1930s street scenes, published in 1933 as *Paris de Nuit*. The result was a new dimension in documentary photography, which became famous due to its combination of restrained sensuality, menace and tension. Brassaï's other books of photographs include *Camera in Paris* (1949), *Graffiti* (1961) and *The Artists of My Life* (1982).

John Heartfield
Zum Krisenparteitag Der S. P. D.

1935 Born in Berlin, Heartfield (1891–1968) was a master of photographic collage, using his razor-sharp gift for political satire in his work. The German playwright Berthold Brecht said of him, 'through this new form of art he exercises social criticism, steadfastly on the side of the working class'. Heartfield was a Communist, and his work is a pictorial expression of that ideology. He used photography because of its realism and its ability to convince, such as this arresting image of a 'respectable' man turning into a snarling beast. One of his most famous montages, depicts a German family eating ironwork, and is captioned, 'Hurrah, the butter is finished!', to illustrate Nazi Hermann Goering's saying 'Iron always makes a country strong. Butter and lard only make people fat'. Heartfield moved to England as a refugee from Prague in 1938, and his work appeared in the English periodical *Lilliput*. His books include *John Heartfield* (1936) and *John Heartfield Photomontages* (1969).

Margaret Bourke-White
Have You Seen Their Faces?

1937 Bourke-White (1906–1971) was a pioneer in the field of photojournalism. Her strength lay in her objective recording of social conditions, her intense vision allowing her to photograph harrowing scenes with complete calm. In 1936, she joined the staff of *Life* magazine as one of its first four photographers; she used to take many pictures in order to capture a single moment which conveyed the human drama of an event. In 1937, Bourke-White collaborated with the writer Erskine Caldwell on a documentary book, *Have You Seen Their Faces?*, which portrayed the terrible conditions in the American South, including black

German photographer John Heartfield used his medium to create political statements. This photomontage depicts a man turning into a wild animal.

chain-gangs and unimaginable poverty, in moving, pure and unfettered photos. *Dear Fatherland, Rest Quietly* (1946) records Bourke-White's experiences as American troops liberated prisoners from German concentration camps.

Henri Cartier-Bresson
Sunday, Banks of the Marne

1938 First and foremost a painter and draughtsman, the French photojournalist Cartier-Bresson (1908–) is known as the master of the expressive documentary photograph. His technique is based on previsualizing the finished print, waiting until the 'decisive moment', and then, with a single exposure, creating a photo which is both spontaneous

Paul Strand
*Buttress, Ranchos de Taos
Church, New Mexico*

1950 Strand (1890–1976), born in New York, was one of the twentieth-century's foremost photographers, known for his artistic blending of formalism and humanism. Stimulated by modern art, Strand made abstract close-ups of bowls, machine parts and rocks. Alfred Stieglitz was so impressed with Strand's work that he gave him a solo show, which was praised as being 'brutally direct ... an expression of today'. Strand's work reveals the humanity of his subjects and creates rhythm from natural forms. *Buttress, Ranchos de Taos Church, New Mexico* is a characteristically atmospheric piece, an intellectual work that goes far beyond the simple art of photography and brings 'honesty of vision' to living expression. Images from his wide travels were published in *Un Paese* (1955) and *Living Egypt* (1969).

and carefully composed. His finest evocations – of women praying in the mountains of Kashmir, of cripples and children at play in the crumbling streets of Valencia, and of many other groups of people oblivious to his presence – are unqualified examples of extraordinary technique. One of the founders, in 1947, of the co-operative photographic agency Magnum, Cartier-Bresson photographed in India, China, the USSR, the USA, Canada and Japan for the next two decades.

Minor White
Song without Words

1948 One of the most influential photographers of the twentieth century, White (1908–1976) is best known for his application and extension of Alfred Stieglitz's concept of 'equivalence', pursuing mystical or psychological readings of photographs. White developed a metaphorical and sequential approach to the medium, in which he saw photographs as equivalents for emotions and experiences, and he searched ceaselessly for the inner essence of the photographer. He recorded this deep love of self-analysis in *Song without Words*, which was exhibited at the San Francisco Museum of Art. White showed nature in a sensuous manner in small, sharp, impeccably printed images. He was a founder and editor (1952–65) of *Aperture* magazine and taught at the Rochester Institute of Technology (1955–64) in New York, Massachusetts Institute of Technology (1965–76), and numerous workshops across the USA.

Robert Frank
The Americans

1959 Born in Switzerland, Frank (1924–) worked as an apprentice to Hermann Eidenbenze in Basel and Michael Wolgensinger in Zürich. From 1947, he worked as a fashion photographer for *Harper's Bazaar* in the USA, and from 1948 he worked in South America and Europe. Frank is best known for his book of photographs, *The Americans* (1959), with text by Jack Kerouac. Kerouac wrote about Frank's images: 'After seeing these pictures you end up not knowing whether a jukebox is sadder than a coffin'. The first European to win a Guggenheim Fellowship, Frank travelled around America in 1955–56, producing the ironic, captivatingly realistic pictures which make up his famous oeuvre. He subsequently made a series of films, of which *Pull My Daisy* (1959),

Right: Paul Strand's work is typified by his close-up shots and accurate depictions of everyday American life.

Left: Henri Cartier-Bresson travelled extensively to build up his incredible collection of photographic scenes. depicting everyday life throughout the world.

a short classic about the authors of the Beat generation, with a screenplay by Kerouac, is the most successful.

Jerry N. Uelsmann
Untitled

1960s The American photographer Jerry Norman Uelsmann (1934–) had, for many years, been considered one of the most exciting and influential young American photographers. In his work, which he calls 'postvisualization', he employs innovative darkroom techniques to create photomontages which juxtapose disparate elements, some utilizing combinations of negative and positive images. Uelsmann has broken down the hegemony of the straight photograph: each of his pictures is a composite of many negatives, fused by incomparable darkroom magic into a seamless whole. Like Surrealist paintings, but with the impact of photographic truth, Uelsmann's pictures are intended to be 'careful records of dreams'. Like many of his photomontages, *Untitled* is about nature and landscapes, with double reflections which may surprise the viewer.

Right: Aujourd'Hui is one of a series of three gelatin silver prints, stylized by the addition of cut paper shapes applied to the photograph.

Opposite top left: Cindy Sherman is one of America's foremost postmodernist photographers. In Untitled Film Stills, she placed one woman's life in the context of scenes from movies.

Opposite bottom left: Sherman's photographs are often viewed as parodies of the anxieties and stereotyping of women in contemporary society.

Man Ray
portraits

1963 The Philadelphia-born Man Ray (1890–1976) was a pioneering painter and photographer in the Dada, Surrealist and abstract movements of the 1920s and 30s. After co-founding the Dada movement in New York, he moved to Paris, where he became portrait photographer to the intellectual and artistic avant-garde, including painters Georges Braque, Henri Matisse, Fernand Léger, Joan Miró and Pablo Picasso. At the same time, he experimented with cameraless photographic techniques. Man Ray's 'rayographs' were made by placing objects on sensitized paper which was then exposed to light. Solarization and

negative printing were other innovations. He was known for using superficial aids, trick printing and elongation by special lenses. Man Ray made several Surrealist films in the 1920s, including *Anemic Cinema* (1925–26) and *Star of the Sea* (1928). *Delightful Fields* (1922) is an album of rayographs.

Richard Avedon
fashion photographs

1968 Born in New York City, Avedon (1923–) worked in the photographic department of the United States Marines at the age of 19. By the age of 22, he had achieved success as a fashion photographer under the aegis of Alexey Brodovitch at *Harper's Bazaar*. Avedon's photographs were designed to show movement, and although not technically perfect, they created the impression he wished to portray of enthusiasm and delight. His stage and ballet photographs were also fascinating studies of movement. Avedon instigated many new fashion poses, often using a wind machine for dynamic effects. He claimed to have 'come of age' when he discovered the strobe light, which he used to capture light, shadow and detail in a split second.

Garry Winogrand
The Animals

1969 New York City photographer, photojournalist and teacher Winogrand (1928–1984) is best known for his active 'street photography', which appeared in magazines across the USA. Apart from his time in the army and at two teaching posts, Winogrand remained in Manhattan all his life, featuring the unusual and freakish in his pictures, with glimpses of the frightening and the funny. His photos formed part of the Museum of Modern Art's famous 'Family of Man' exhibit of 1955. *The Animals* portrays Winogrand's whimsical sense of humour, with unusual portraits designed to capture attention and, in many cases, to shock. His pictures of monkey's urinating into each other's mouths created some controversy in the United States, where they were deemed 'scabrous'. In 1980, he co-published *The Fort Worth Fat Stock Show* and Rodeo. His other books include *Women Are Beautiful* (1975) and *Stock Photographs* (1980).

Cindy Sherman
Untitled Film Stills

1978 The American Cindy Sherman (1954–) is considered to be the ultimate Post-modern photographer, recycling or plundering the past and reinvesting it with meaning in a new context. In each work, she sets out to introduce speculation about the significance of subject matter.

Untitled Film Stills is an extensive collection of photographs which feature a female figure in a broad, sometimes disturbing range of scenarios and which evoke speculation not only about the drama of the situation but also about the identity of the woman involved. In each case, the female figure is Sherman herself. Her lifelong fascination with make-up and her collection of costumes and wigs have contributed to the creation of her 'characters', who run the gamut of age, sex, historical period and emotional condition. They have been seen as representations of actual persons, as comments on, or parodies of, the anxieties – and the stereotyping – of women.

Irving Penn
Flowers

1980 Penn (1917–) is a commercial fashion photographer whose work appears frequently in *Vogue* magazine. His work is celebrated as 'likeness-in-depth', and he creates effects without gadgets, props or anything but the simplest of lighting – usually a one-source light coming from the side of the sitter. Penn has travelled widely, documenting the banal in unique, moving studies. His photographs, which have been exhibited at the Museum of Modern Art and Metropolitan Museum of Art in New York, are characterized by dramatic composition and striking imagery. His Flowers – close-ups of dew-spangled blooms – are extraordinary still-lifes, with flowers taken from their natural habitat and superimposed in the photographer's own environment. Penn's portraits are considered both daring and vigorous; his point of view is cool and refreshing. Penn has also published *Inventive Paris Clothes 1909–1939* (1978).

Robert Mapplethorpe
Tulip

1985 Mapplethorpe (1946–1989) began his career as an independent film maker and sculptor. He frequently used photographs in collages, and by the late 1970s had drawn considerable attention to his own photography: he is best-known for intense black-and-white compositions in which the subject appears as object, even icon. Mapplethorpe's gallery shows scandalized some viewers and critics with their juxtaposition of straight portraits and elegant still-lifes, such as *Tulip*, with overtly homoerotic, even sadomasochistic, male nudes. Mapplethorpe became successful as a commercial fashion photographer and celebrity portraitist. Learning in 1986 that he had AIDS, he used a series of self-portraits to help focus attention on the disease.

Below: Robert Mapplethorpe's Tulip *is a fine example of his intense study of flowers.*

Transport design

14

OVER THE LAST HUNDRED YEARS, TRADITIONAL MODES OF TRANSPORT HAVE UNDERGONE RADICAL CHANGE. THE HORSE-DRAWN CARRIAGE HAS BEEN REPLACED BY MACHINES UNIMAGINED IN THE NINETEENTH CENTURY SUCH AS CARS, TRAINS AND AEROPLANES. SOME OF THE KEY MOMENTS IN TRANSPORT DESIGN HAVE RESULTED IN THE PRODUCTION OF BEAUTIFUL YET POWERFUL VEHICLES.

Wilhelm Maybach
Mercedes motorcar

1902 The epitome of high-powered motorcars in the early years of the century was the Mercedes, originally developed by Wilhelm Maybach out of the succession of Cannstatt-Daimler models and put into limited production. Having evolved the lithe and elegant Mercedes, Maybach assumed the mantle of pace-setter to the motoring industry. The new model made its debut at Nice Speed Week, causing an immediate sensation with its expensively chic design and advanced technology: a pressed-steel frame, mechanically operated inlet valves, low-tension magneto ignition and a selective gate for gear-changing. Within a few years, there was a considerable market for the expensive car, which became an icon of wealth in the twentieth century.

Henry Ford
Model-T Ford

1908 The Model-T Ford motorcar was introduced in 1908, designed by Ford (1863–1947) as the 'car for the great multitude', and it was an immediate success. It had a four-cylinder, 20-horsepower engine and a simple planetary transmission operated by foot pedals. To meet the demand for the new car, the Ford Motor Company introduced the moving assembly-line technique for mass production. By 1919, nearly 60 per cent of all American motor vehicles and half of those in the entire world were Model-T Fords. While the Model T underwent nearly 20 years of consistent development, Ford's second most celebrated car, the V8, was launched in 1932. It was only then that his motorcars – previously designed for economy of scale – took on a more streamlined shape.

R. Buckminster Fuller
Dymaxion Car

1933 The futurist R. Buckminster Fuller (1895–1983) was one of America's most radical inventor-designers. Fuller worked from the premise that technological progress can, if unhampered by outmoded traditions and conventions, give all human beings a rich and satisfying life. Many of his major inventions were designed to reduce or eliminate barriers to mobility. His Dymaxion Car of 1933 brought economies similar to that promoted by his Dymaxion House to motorcar design. The Dymaxion was the ultimate in streamlined design, with three wheels and a tear-drop shape for which superior performance and a 60-per-cent saving in fuel were claimed. The car was revolutionary in concept and attracted international interest, but it carried many dangerous design faults and could not succeed as an alternative to conventional cars.

Carl Breer
Chrysler Airflow Car

1934 Commercially unsuccessful but extraordinarily influential, the Chrysler Airflow Car was based on the ideas of Carl Breer, the chief engineer with the company, who not only took styling seriously but also believed that in order to take a competitive lead, Chrysler must produce a radical project. The Airflow's structural arrangement and mechanical design provided the basis of this new effort, which was intended to provide both stability and comfort. Attempts were made to unify the design of the body by smoothing out its contours and providing a double-curved bonnet. The design was accentuated by the flowing line of the mudguards and running-boards. Breer introduced streamlining

Overleaf: the first flight of a Zeppelin airship – the LZ1 (see page 188).

Left: Henry Ford's Model T heralded a major breakthrough in car manufacture – the introduction of moving assembly lines to supply huge public demand.

Right: in spite of the Chrysler Airflow's limited commercial success at the time of being built, it is today regarded as one of the finest designs of the 1930s.

and a measure of ergonomics, by placing the engine over the front axle to create greater spaciousness throughout. The Airflow Car was launched with a massive marketing campaign, but the general feeling was that it was simply too innovative to sell. Despite this, it remains one of the best examples of 1930s streamlining.

Budd Manufacturing Company
Burlington Zephyr railway train

1934 In response to the 1930s obsession with streamlining, railways scrambled to produce new designs, one of the most successful of which was the Burlington Zephyr, produced by the Chicago, Burlington and Quincy Railroad. This innovative train was an articulated three-car unit with a light and powerful diesel engine. The body used a new technique of welding stainless steel, which required no

paintwork and provided a gleaming finish. The design team at Budd Manufacturing Company came up with a unique rounded front end, angled forward and with corrugations running above and below the windows to strengthen the cars and provide a unifying motif. The Zephyr appeared at the end of the Depression, and its radical new form was a symbol of the hope offered by progress and of better times to come. The Zephyr was the subject of a feature film, *The Silver Streak*.

featured an innovative recirculating lubrication system, with the main stand mounted on the rear of the frame. The radical styling was typified by the rounded oil tank, wrapped around the body; the distinctive knuckle appearance was created by the rocker covers. The Knucklehead demonstrated the practical technology and performance possible in a motorcycle while showing just how far styling had evolved from the early days.

Harley-Davidson
Knucklehead 61E motorcycle

1936 Motorcycles were first introduced towards the end of the nineteenth century, but it was only when Werner produced their model in 1901, with an advance braking system, that motorcycling became safe and practical. In 1936, Harley-Davidson introduced a model which set the standard for motorcycles to come. The Knucklehead 61E

R. J. Mitchell
Supermarine Spitfire monoplane

1936 The Supermarine Spitfire, which first flew in 1936, became famous as a mainstay of the Royal Air Force in the Second World War. It was designed by Reginald J. Mitchell on the basis of his experience with the Schneider Trophy series. The Spitfire was a huge technological achievement, with a superb, streamlined shape – the first 'beautiful'

The Spitfire is the best known of all military aircraft. It was designed by Reginald J. Mitchell and was first flown in 1936.

fighter plane. It was also the first all-metal British fighter and the best-known fighter ever built. The single-seat, low-wing monoplane had a Rolls-Royce Merlin engine and elliptical wings armed with eight Browning machine guns. Improvements on the Spitfire design culminated in the Mk. 24 model (1946) and the Seafire, which was developed for use from aircraft carriers of the Fleet Air Arm. The Spitfire was also used to pioneer unarmed photographic reconnaissance.

Ferdinand Graf von Zeppelin
Hindenburg Zeppelin

1936 The Zeppelin rigid airships were designed to be prestigious, their grandiose character and dramatic form making them abundantly suitable for marketing and propaganda purposes. When the National Socialists came to power in Germany in 1933, giant Zeppelins were used to hover over party rallies. The Hindenburg was a rigid airship built by the firm of Luftschiffbau Zeppelin in Friedrichshafen, Germany. Completed and tested in 1936, it was the world's first transatlantic commercial airliner. Accommodating more than 70 passengers, it had a dining room, a library and lounge with a grand piano, a cocktail lounge and promenades with large windows. The design was overwhelmingly opulent, in contrast to the commercial aircraft of the period. In 1937, the airship's hydrogen was ignited and the Hindenburg was destroyed by the resulting fire.

Pierre Boulanger
Citroen 2CV motorcar

1939 In 1936, Citroen conceived the idea of a low-priced car with a small engine to compete with the German 'people's car', the Volkswagen Beetle. The result was architect-engineer Boulanger's 2CV, launched in 1939. This economic and straightforward car was produced until 1990, when it was superseded by the lighter-weight AX. The Citroen 2CV completely rejected streamlined styling; its uncompromisingly functional bodywork was described by some critics as a product of the 'garden-shed school of auto design'. Nevertheless, its simplicity made it popular, and the 2CV introduced a new dimension in European small-car design. Supply never kept up with demand for this car, and it became a design classic, which visually or by association summed up the best of its time.

This picture illustrates the first flight of a Zeppelin airship, which took place on 2 July 1900 at Bodensee. The airship was called LZ1.

modern aircraft, with banks of multiple, high-backed armchairs. To avoid the feeling of overcrowding, lights were recessed, and hand-luggage storage, passengers' lighting and ventilation, and emergency equipment were built into continuous panels overhead. Plastic panelling, upholstery and carpets were in subdued tones, in an attempt to soothe passengers rather than stimulate them.

Ferdinand Porsche
Volkswagen 1200 Beetle motorcar

1952 Designed by Ferdinand Porsche (1935–) in the 1930s as the German people's car – a small motorcar which would be inexpensive enough for the average family – the Volkswagen was not put into large-scale production until after the Second World War. The decision was then made to concentrate on a single model, the Volkswagen 1200 Beetle, and to avoid annual model changes. The Beetle recalled Henry Ford's Model T in being simple in design, plain in style and economical to operate. It was unique in that its four-cylinder air-cooled engine was mounted over the rear axle. Sold internationally, the car became one of the best-selling models in automotive history. Porsche was a leading exponent of streamlining theory and practice, and the Beetle's distinctive body became the most widespread example of 1930s streamlined design. Porsche went on to design sports cars with his son, Ferdinand Porsche II.

Walter Dorwin Teague
Boeing 707 jet aeroplane

1950s Walter Dorwin Teague (1883–1960) was one of the earliest industrial designers who, along with Henry Dreyfuss and Raymond Loewy, helped to establish industrial design as a separate discipline and a recognized profession. His Boeing 707, designed in the 1950s, was meticulously worked out before production began, including a complete working interior mock-up costing more than half a million dollars. Teague's design established the layout which has become common in

Harley Earl
Cadillac Eldorado motorcar

1955 Harley Earl (1893–1969) was a styling pioneer who became known for breaking the mould of black, standarized cars set by the Model-T Ford. Employed by General Motors from 1925, he introduced the

Top: Pierre Boulanger designed the Citroen 2CV in the late 1930s. The car was France's competition to the German Volkswagen Beetle.

Bottom: Harley Earl's extraordinary space ship fins on the Cadillac Eldorado heralded an obsession with the post-war rocket age.

technique of designing with clay models rather than solely on the drawing board. Between 1927 and 1936, Earl progressively reduced the height and broadened the width of GM's cars, incorporating the engine and cabin as a visual whole. The Cadillac Coupe of 1948 was the first model to sprout tail-fins, which became the most controversial design feature of this period. The '55 Eldorado was advertised as 'styled in the mode of a jet aircraft'; one critic wrote that it never had 'been so hard to see the basic substance of a car'. Elderados became an icon of the wealth and power which suddenly seemed accessible to Americans in the post-war boom.

Honda
Supercub scooter

1958 In the post-war years, the style of motorcycles evolved to meet increasing demand. This process included technical improvements in design, materials, fuels and lubricants. Model ranges increased, creating more choice for motorcyclists, and it was the manufacture of smaller engines that led to the development of the scooter, which became the 'new force' on two wheels. Motorcycles were perceived as noisy, dirty, heavy and awkward to use, and the scooter seemed a more reasonable alternative. The Honda Supercub, a scooterette which combined weather protection and full-sized wheels in a package which millions could afford, appeared on the market in 1958. The Supercub became the most successful vehicle of all time, with sales of over 20 million world-wide. It was build in several sizes and was incredibly reliable.

Sir Christopher Cockrell
hovercraft

1959 The first air-cushion vehicle, or hovercraft, stems from work done in the 1950s by the British electronics engineer Sir Christopher Cockrell. Cockrell constructed a model from two coffee tins and a hair dryer and measured its lift with kitchen scales. The idea was patented in 1955, and in 1959 the first full-scale ACV, the SR.N1, was successfully tested at Cowes, England. Under British government sponsorship, the first commercial hovercraft, the SRN-4, went into service as a cross-Channel ferry. It could also run up on a beach and travel over flat or marshy terrain. The design was uncompromisingly practical but sleek and innovative, setting a standard for years to come.

Alec Issionis
Austin Rover Mini motorcar

1959 One of the best post-war examples of industrial transport design was the Austin Rover Mini, which became the motorcar of the 1960s. The brainchild of Turkish designer Alec Issionis, the Mini introduced front-wheel drive, 'audacious handling' and high speed to the mass market. Less than 4 m (13 ft) long, and with only 25-cm (10-in) wheels, the Mini was a clever piece of design, offering a lot of room in a very small space. It became a twentieth-century icon and one of the best-selling cars of all time. The Mini's size precluded its sale in the USA, where larger cars were favoured, such as General Motors' Cadillac, launched a few years earlier. But the Mini set a trend in small European cars which most manufacturers were unable to match.

Top: the Austin Mini was aimed at a fast-expanding young market. Issionis' design by Alex Issionis achieved cult status in the 1960s and it became the best-selling car of all time.

Bottom: the Hovercraft prototype began life on a very humble scale – created from kitchen implements and a hair dryer! Today the vehicle is a common sight on its cross-channel route from England to France.

Raymond Loewy
Avanti Studebaker

1962 The French-born Raymond Loewy (1893–1986) was one of a new breed of designers-as-stylists, describing design in terms that manufacturers could understand and producing designs which were both signature works and easily interpreted by the manufacturer. Loewy styled several of the pre-war American locomotives and the Greyhound buses of the 1940s. His Avanti Studebaker car was described by the engineer at Porsche as almost perfect in its streamlining, the result of 'design intuition'. Loewy's great achievement is that he proved that product design was about capturing the imagination of the public and understanding what they regarded as modern and exciting. He used the acronym MAYA for his design philosophy, meaning 'most advanced, yet acceptable'.

Ferrari
Dino 246GT sportscar

1969 A classic sportscar, the Pininfarina-designed Ferrari Dino 246GT was introduced as the Dino 206 in 1965, going on general sale in 1967. The engine capacity was increased in 1969, bringing the designation to 246GT. In the Dino, Ferrari had created the ultimate sportscar, with sleek lines and sunken headlights, the whole working to aerodynamic specifications. Ferrari was aiming at the upper end of the market, with expensive features and 'Rolls-Royce' styling. The Dino had exceptional roadholding, handling, and acceleration, making it a truly outstanding driver's car. Pininfarina, a motorcar design firm founded in Turin by Battista 'Pinin' Farina, is notable for its concern with research in design, and housed the first computer-aided design centre in Italy. Ferrari used Pininfarina for a number of its vehicles, including some of its most successful auto-racing models.

Sundberg and Ferar
BART, San Francisco, California, USA

1970s Although ergonomics and human-factor design were not thoroughly explored by industrial designers until the 1970s, there was a group of industrial transport designers whose work extended far beyond mere styling to combine flair with features which would match the needs of the public. The best example of this ergonomically astute yet carefully styled approach was BART, a mass-transit system put into operation in the early 1970s by the San Francisco Bay Area Rapid Transit District. Designed by Sundberg and Ferar, BART set a new standard in design for public transport and became the model upon which other systems were based. The trains were both modern and streamlined, with large, sloping windows and a unique rectilinear form which allowed large numbers of commuters to sit and stand in comfort.

Giorgietto Giugiaro
Volkswagen Golf motorcar

1974 Giugiaro (1938–) is considered to be the world's most influential motorcar designer. Having studied at the Turin Academy of Fine Arts, he joined the Fiat styling centre at the age of 17. In 1959, he became head of the styling department at Carrozzeria Bertone, where he worked on the BMW 3200CS (1961), Alfa Romeo Giulia GT (1963) and Fiat 850 Spider (1965). In 1967, Giugiaro formed Italdesign with Aldo Mantovani and Luciano Bosio, to offer pre-production services beyond straightforward design to motorcar industries. Services included styling, feasibility studies and the construction of models and prototypes. Among designs created under the Italdesign umbrella were the Volkswagen Golf (1974) and Fiat Panda (1980). The Golf offered the 'two-box' solution, with sharp-edged contours and a vigorous break between the engine compartment and the passenger area – a design solution which was much copied. The Golf replaced the Beetle in 1974.

When Ferrari launched their Dino 246GT, they had created the ultimate in sports cars designed to appeal to the car-buying élite.

Industrial design
15

THE INDUSTRIAL REVOLUTION OF THE
NINETEENTH CENTURY SOWED THE SEEDS OF
NEW STYLES IN ARCHITECTURE AND DESIGN AT
WORK. TOOLS AND WORKSPACES WERE
REQUIRED FOR NEW BREEDS OF INDUSTRIAL
AND OFFICE WORKERS. SOME OF THE BEST
TWENTIETH-CENTURY INDUSTRIAL DESIGNERS
RESPONDED WITH THE CREATION OF NEW
WORKING ENVIRONMENTS AND CLASSIC
DESIGNS FOR EQUIPMENT SUCH AS
TYPEWRITERS.

Peter Behrens
AEG Turbine Factory, Berlin, Germany

1908–9 As a fusion of architecture and engineering, the Turbine Factory became one of the most influential buildings of the 1910s. The main features are a classical façade, curved ends and, on the side walls, an early example of curtain walling (where the glazed walls are not structural but are suspended from a frame). The General Electric Company (AEG) commissioned Behrens (1868–1940) to design not only the building but also the electrical equipment and the firm's packaging and catalogues. The influence of industry on art is clear, but this was also an early attempt to humanize technology. The AEG wanted to produce objects which were sensitively designed as well as functional, and they wished to have this outlook reflected in the architecture of their factory.

Albert Kahn
Ford Motor Company Glass Plant, Detroit, Michigan, USA

1910–13 The German-born American architect Albert Kahn (1869–1942) is best known for his novel approach to factory design, especially for the assembly-line plants which he designed for the Ford Motor Company in the Detroit area. Kahn's buildings were based on the visionary ideas of Henry Ford, who revolutionized the automobile industry, combining all production under one roof. The Ford Glass Plant provided fundamental requirements such as good lighting and ventilation, and the uninterrupted, flexible interior through which the assembly line could be extended was based on a morphology of grid plans and simple, pleasing proportions. Kahn's factories were considered to be an 'index to the spirit of the new times' and set the pace for industrial design in the automotive industry for years to come.

Walter Gropius
Fagus Shoelace Factory, Anfeld an der Leine, Germany

1911 For three years following his training in architecture in Munich and Berlin, Gropius (1883–1969) worked in architect Peter Behrens's office. Later, he set up on his own as an industrial designer and architect, receiving his first major commission from Karl Benscheidt, who owned the Fagus Shoelace Factory. Gropius described the building as 'an artistic and practical design'. In contrast to the monumental effect of Behrens's Turbine Factory, the Fagus building seems weightless and transparent. The administration block was a particular breakthrough, with its frame and wall piers set back so that the glazing wrapped around with the appearance of a floating skin. Inside, Gropius incorporated the latest American industrial techniques of good ventilation and a logical, open plan to accommodate mass production.

Albert Kahn
River Rouge Ford Plant, Detroit, Michigan, USA

1917 Kahn's (1869–1942) River Rouge Ford Plant was planned as a single-storey structure, allowing the assembly line to proceed in a continuous flow from raw material to finished product. His elegant steel-framed factory designs inspired a new generation of industrial architects, including Walter Gropius and Mies van der Rohe. Kahn discovered many applications for concrete – then a new material – in factory, warehouse and even grain-silo design. The European avant-garde, seeing his work in photographs, referred to his factories as icons of a new, universal language of architecture. So great was his fame as an industrial architect that the Soviet government commissioned him to design hundreds of factories, which were built during the 1930s.

Overleaf: the 'Lettera 22', the first modern portable typewriter (see page 196).

Right: Walter Gropius made use of the latest American industrial techniques when he designed the Fagus Shoelace Factory.

Walter Dorwin Teague
Kodak 'Baby Brownie' camera

1926 Teague (1833–1960) was one of the earliest industrial designers who, together with Henry Dreyfuss and Raymond Loewy, helped establish industrial design as a separate discipline and recognized profession. In 1926, Teague designed the Kodak 'Baby Brownie', a simple, functional, highly successful camera aimed at the youth market. This invention established him as one of the most important and influential industrial designers of his age. Later, he created the 'Vanity Kodak' (1928) and the 'Bantam Special' (1936). Teague was renowned for his preoccupation with rationalism and measurement, exemplifying the American post-war 'functionalist' look. His major designs included motorcars, petrol stations, aeroplane interiors, household appliances, business machines and magazines.

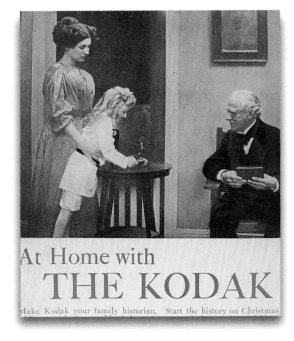

At Home with
THE KODAK
Make Kodak your family historian. Start the history on Christmas

Jacques Delamarre
radiator grille for the Chanin Building, New York, New York, USA

1929 The use of wrought-iron and metal for decorative purposes was popularized in Britain by William Morris at the end of the nineteenth century. Before his time, metal had been extensively used for railings and decorative gates, but it was the achievement of Morris and his contemporaries to transform it into an art form. Architects soon adopted the medium, and commissioned designers to make such articles as boot scrapers, fire irons, radiator grilles and lamp brackets to fit in with their decorative schemes. One of the most superb examples of Art Deco metalwork is Delamarre's radiator grille for the Chanin Building in New York City. Set in wood panelling and plated in brass, the grille masterfully encases the radiator pipes in to its design, with exquisitely curved metalwork leading up to the centre of the image, which repeats the shape of the building in ever-increasing dimensions.

August Dvorak
'Dvorak' typewriter keyboard

1936 The first practical typewriter was developed by Christopher Latham Sholes and patented in 1868. Six years later, Eliphalet Remington and Sons launched the first commercial typewriter, called the 'Remington'; it had a cylinder to hold the paper, and line-spacing and carriage-return mechanisms. There were many advances in typewriter capabilities, but the keyboard remained unchanged until 1936, when August Dvorak, cousin of composer Anton, designed a much more efficient arrangement of keys. With the 'Dvorak' keyboard, the right hand does equal work with the left, the strongest fingers do the most work, and 70 per cent of the typing takes place on the 'home row', where the fingers naturally rest. The 'Dvorak' keyboard is still used today.

Top left: the distinctive work of American architect Albert Khan provided inspiration for many avant-garde architects and artists in Europe.

Top right: when designing this factory for the Ford company, Albert Khan worked closely with the company's owner, the celebrated Henry Ford.

Bottom: Walter Teague's new cameras brought the art of photography into the home. This model, the 'Baby Brownie', was aimed at the youth market.

Henry Dreyfuss
'300-type' desk set for Bell Telephone, USA

1937 Dreyfuss (1903–1972) was an American pioneer in industrial design who influenced the shape, feel, look and, in some cases, the function of many manufactured objects used today. His work was successful since he paid meticulous attention to both rational design and good performance. A wide variety of objects, including telephones, refrigerators, typewriters, vacuum cleaners, petrol stations, prosthetics and aeroplanes were all reshaped by Dreyfuss. The '300-type' handset desk telephone, designed in 1937 for Bell Telephone, combined the mouth- and earpiece in a single unit. It was produced initially in metal, and from the early 1940s in plastic. Intended to be unobtrusive and suitable for use anywhere in homes and offices, it was reduced to its essential elements, with improved performance and a form which did not date rapidly.

Norman Bel Geddes
General Motors 'Futurama' display
for the 1939 New York World Fair, USA

1939 Bel Geddes (1893–1958) studied at the Art Institute of Chicago. During the early 1920s, he worked in theatre design and created shop-window displays in New York, constructing fabulous, multi-level arrangements with evocative lighting which changed the face of scenic design. Bel Geddes proposed, but never built, theatres-in-the-round, a non-proscenium theatre and various mechanized stage devices. For the 1939 New York World Fair, he designed General Motors' 'Futurama' exhibit, a futuristic pavilion showing a redesigned America – an advanced, super-technological utopia filled with highways, in which everything was clean and scientific. Bel Geddes did much to popularize the 'streamlined' style and is often acknowledged as having been influential in the development of the American highway system. By the 1940s, he was concentrating primarily on industrial design.

Marcello Nizzoli
'Lettera 22' typewriter for Olivetti, Italy

1950 Born in Italy, Nizzoli (1887–1969) worked as a freelance painter and designer, becoming associated with Futurism in Milan and Rome. In 1918, he established a design studio, working mainly on exhibition-design projects such as the 1934 Italian Aeronautical Exhibition in Milan. In 1936, he became chief consultant designer for Olivetti and set out to confirm the company's commitment to evolving a modern image for its production, from its publicity to its office machines. The 'Lettera 22', a portable typewriter, firmly established Olivetti's international reputation, with the visible mechanisms designed in balance with the bodywork,

The 'Lettera 22' was the first modern portable typewriter. It established Olivetti's international reputation.

which had graceful, rounded, solid features. With the 'Lettera 22', the general form of the modern typewriter was established, with an unadorned sheath split into two or three sections for ease of maintenance.

Mario Bellini
'Divisumma 18' electronic calculator for Olivetti, Italy

1972 Bellini (1935–), one of Italy's leading designers, studied architecture at Milan Polytechnic, joining Olivetti as a consultant in the 1960s. He created designs which were architectural rather than organic – using separate volumes and planes – and was responsible for many of the changes in style, colour and materials of Olivetti products between the early 1960s and mid-1980s. Bellini's 'Divisumma 18' electronic calculator is a landmark in design history, with a continuous, rubber-skinned flexible keyboard. The catalogue accompanying Bellini's retrospective in 1987 stated, 'The emphasis is not on calculating and power, but on stimulating a sense of pleasure'. Olivetti later used the same styling on products such as the DM range of electronic printers.

Sir Clive Sinclair
'Sovereign' pocket calculator

1972 The British inventor Sir Clive Sinclair (1940–) is a pioneer in the fields of microelectronics and industrial design, producing such items as a 340-g (12-oz) hand-held personal computer and a pocket-sized television set. Largely self-taught, Sinclair formed the Sinclair Radionics company in 1972 and produced some of the first multifunction electronic calculators and digital watches. His first pocket calculator was only 1 cm (1/2 in) thick and 12 cm (5 in) long. The most innovative and complex calculator of its time, it possessed a 7,000-transistor integrated circuit and was the first to be powered by a wafer-thin battery. After the company failed in 1979, Sinclair founded Sinclair Research Ltd., which produced the phenomenally successful ZX 80 computer.

Steve Wozniak and Steve Jobs
'Apple I' computer

1975 The electronics engineer Stephen Wozniak, (1950–), together with Steve Jobs (1955–), built a revolutionary microcomputer which formed the basis of Apple Computer Company's success and helped create the enormous personal computer industry of the 1980s. Wozniak and Jobs formed Apple in 1976, after building a prototype computer, 'Apple I', which was user-friendly, intended for single users, and the first personal computer to be sold complete with all the necessary elements, for use 'off the shelf'. One important aspect of 'Apple I' was the mouse, the hand-held controlling device which replicated hand movements to select services from the computer screen. The computer's styling was influenced by that of Mercedes Benz cars, resulting in soft lines but stark detailing. Apple's innovations paved the way for desk-top publishing (DTP).

Akio Morita
Sony 'Walkman'

1978 The 'Walkman', introduced by the Sony Corporation in 1978, represented a significant change in the Japanese industry's approach to styling. Until this point, companies had paid little attention to styling, which they believed added minimal value to a product. The 'Walkman' was the brain child of Sony chairman Akio Morita. Aimed at teenagers, the personal stereo – the ultimate personal accessory – used existing technology (the transistor radio), but repackaged it into a 'must-have' item, with a belt latch, colourful buttons and a pocket-sized format. The original 'Walkman's were metal, but by the mid-1980s, colourful plastic

became the standard. The 'Walkman' became an essential fashion accessory of the '80s.

Niels Diffrient
'Helena' office chair

1984 The American-born Niels Diffrient (1928–) worked in Milan on a Fulbright Fellowship and was a partner at Henry Dreyfuss Associates before establishing Neils Diffrient Product Design in Connecticut. Diffrient designed some spectacular products, involving engineering in his 'from-the-inside-out' approach (shared with Walter Dorwin Teague and Dreyfuss), in which the internal workings of a product are given equal importance to its external shape. After doing a great deal of work on American Airlines' Boeing jets, Diffrient concentrated on ergonomics, particularly in seating. The 'Helena' office chair, made in steel and leather for Sunar Hauserman in 1984, combines ergonomically sound design with a trend-setting black and metal frame – comfort and practicality in a contemporary design which was both expensively chic and highly acclaimed.

William Stumpf
'Ethospace' office system

1986 The American designer William (Bill) Stumpf (1936–) created the 'Ethospace' office system for the firm of Herman Miller, setting a new trend in flexible office design. Stumpf rebelled against the idea of an 'office system' – a concept previous designers had seen as the ultimate consummation of the theory that every worker needed his or her own geometric space. Stumpf believed in creating an office which worked as a 'civilized society', and he encouraged the idea that breaks from work were necessary for productivity. For example, a telephone might be placed near a window, so that workers could gaze out as they made calls, or a photocopier might be placed next to a coffee machine to encourage communication between workers. 'Ethospace' was designed as a high-quality, loose-fit system which was both comfortable and corporate, according to the demands of the client.

Sony released their Walkman in 1978, aimed at the teenage market. Today it is one of youth's essential symbols.

GLOSSARY

abstract Term applied to any work of art, made object or building whose form or decoration does not represent recognizable objects. Abstraction has become a characteristic feature of twentieth-century art styles.

Abstract Expressionism Art movement in New York from the 1940s to the 1950s, influenced by European Surrealists resident in America during the Second World War. It comprised two distinct styles: 'iconic' works characterized by a single form (e.g. by Mark Rothko); and 'calligraphic' works composed of many freely-painted forms (e.g. by Jackson Pollock).

Arts and Crafts Movement Founded in late-nineteenth-century England by William Morris in reaction to the mass production and commercialism brought about by the Industrial Revolution. The movement promoted a harmonious balance between artists and craftspersons. Furniture and everyday objects were beautifully hand crafted to complement their surroundings.

Art Deco Originating in the 1920s, Art Deco came of age in the 1930s. Exponents of the movement aimed to bridge the gap between fine art and mass-produced goods, by incorporating usable and highly modern forms of artistic expression into everyday objects.

Art Nouveau Art Nouveau ('New Art') began *c.* 1895, as a reaction against overbearingly traditional nineteenth-century art. The movement had a marked influence on all aspects of art, from architecture to ceramics. It was brought to an abrupt end by the Second World War, but enjoyed a revival of interest in the 1960s.

The Ashcan School Founded in America by Robert Henri in the early twentieth century. The Ashcan School, also known as 'The Eight', included artists such as John Sloan, George Bellows and George Luks. In rebellion against the softened, artistically re-created landscapes of Monet and other Impressionists, the Ashcan School attempted to truthfully depict the commonplace in unremarkable, even ugly urban scenes.

Ballets Russes In 1909, Russian Sergey Diaghilev formed the Ballets Russes, comprising the legendary dancers Anna Pavlova and Vaslar Nijinsky along with choreographer Michel Fokie. Despite its origins, the company based itself in Paris and never performed in Russia. With the aim of integrating other art forms with dance, music was commissioned from Rimsky-Korsakov and Stravinsky, and sets were designed by Picasso, Matisse, Roualt and Derain. In 1929, Diaghilev died and the company disbanded.

Bauhaus The Bauhaus ('building house') movement was begun in Weimar, Germany, in 1919. Its founder was Walter Gropius, an eminent architect, whose aim was to combine all elements of art under the canopy of architecture. His philosophies were greatly influenced by the Russian Constructivism movement (*see also* Constructivism).

Der Blaue Reiter A group of semi-abstract artists, founded in Munich, Germany in 1911. One of the founder members was Wassily Kandinsky (a Russian emigré), and it is from the title of one of his paintings ('The Blue Rider') that the group derives its name. The movement was short-lived, lasting only until the outbreak of the First World War in 1914.

Die Brücke A group of avant-garde artists that was founded in Dresden, Germany in 1905. The group's name is translated as 'The Bridge', and among its members were many of Germany's foremost Expressionist painters. The movement had come to an end by 1913 (*see also* Expressionism).

Constructivism Russian movement founded just before the Revolution of 1917. The group's aim was to explore individual elements of art such as construction, colour and surface. Constructivists experimented with, amongst other elements, architecture and clothes design.

Cubism Cubism was founded *c.* 1909, based on theories expounded by Paul Cézanne. The distinctive feature of this movement was the depiction of three-dimensional shapes on a flat canvas. Pablo Picasso and Georges Braque were both key figures of this artistic style.

Dada An 'anti-art' movement, set up in 1916 by a group of war-resisters in Zürich, Switzerland. It was deliberately given a non-sensical name, reflecting the members' disillusionment with a supposedly civilized western world that could still produce the First World War. Famous Dadaists included the Frenchman Georges Duchamp and the German Max Ernst.

De Stijl An art movement comprising architects, artists and designers associated with *De Stijl* ('The Style') magazine – a Dutch publication founded by Theo van Doesburg in 1917. The best-known De Stijl artist is Piet Mondrian.

Expressionism The term 'Expressionism' was first coined by the German art critic Herwarth Walden, publisher of *Der Sturm* – an avant-garde magazine based in Berlin, Germany and founded *c.* 1910. With primitive art being a key influence, Expressionism was the antithesis of Impressionism.

The Fauves A group of young artists based in France (most notably Henri Matisse) who first exhibited together in 1905. The group's name, which is translated as 'The Wild Ones', was first attributed to them by the critic Louis Vauxcelles.

Futurism An Italian movement founded in 1909 by the artist and poet F. T. Marinetti. The movement was built on the foundations of Cubism, and its exponents intended to drag traditional art forcefully into a modern age. Important aspects of Futurism are its stark, angular lines and the use of image repetition to convey motion (*see also* Cubism).

Glasgow School This name applies, confusingly, to two distinct groups of Scottish artists of the nineteenth and twentieth centuries. Here it refers to the artist-architect Charles Rennie Mackintosh and his circle. Influenced by Dante Gabriel Rosetti's Pre-Raphaelite Brotherhood, the group were strongly allied in artistic style and ideology to the Vienna Secession (*see also* Vienna Secession).

International Style An architectural term to describe an avant-garde style that emerged in Europe during the 1920s. This refers to architecture that focused on the inside of a building before working on the outside. International Style is also referred to as 'International Modern'.

Machine Age Begun in the late nineteenth century, with the introduction of mass production techniques, the Machine Age had its heyday in the 1920s and 30s. In absolute opposition to the Arts and Crafts Movement, the Machine Age's main characteristic was the replacement of individual craftsmanship with industrial design (*see also* Arts and Crafts Movement).

Memphis Italian group of architect-designers, led by Ettora Sokkasi, who produce furniture, fabrics, glass and ceramics. Their debut show was at the 1981 Milan Furniture Fair, where they received international acclaim. The Memphis style draws inspiration from eclectic sources that range from ancient art through to mass-produced 1950s designs.

Modern Movement The Modern Movement is also known as 'Modernism'. It is a general term used to describe the western world's many twentieth-century, avant-garde artistic movements, particularly those of fine art and architecture.

1900 & 1925 Paris Exhibitions In 1900, and again in 1925, Paris played host to a spectacular Exposition Universelle. Both events were celebrations of international culture and arts and the forerunners of today's EXPO exhibitions. Early exhibitors included Pablo Picasso and René Lalique.

Op Art A 1960s artistic movement that explored the effects of optical illusion on art and the observer. Op Art was created in stark black and white or vividly contrasting bright colours, with illusionist intentions. Op Artists included Bridget Riley and Victor Vasarely.

Orientalism A term to describe art by western artists depicting scenes from the East, particularly during the nineteenth century when the western world's fascination with the Orient was at its height. Orientalist artists let their imaginations run wild, creating lavish scenes of opulent palaces, erotic figures, mythology and ancient history.

Photo-secession A group of photographers founded in New York by Alfred Stieglitz in 1902. The group's aim was to establish photography as a fine art in its own right. Many photo-secessionist scenes are strikingly similar in content to paintings of the period.

Pop Art The Pop Art movement began in the 1950s, reaching its peak in the 1960s. Famous Pop Artists included Andy Warhol and Roy Lichtenstein in the US and Richard Hamilton and Allen Jones in the UK. The artists' works were inspired by everyday objects and popular culture (hence the name) and made ironic use of society's boom in consumerism and mass production.

Post-Modernism A term used (particularly with reference to architecture) to describe the extension and modification of the Modernist style . The term was first used in 1949, but did not become generally accepted until the 1970s with the publication of Charles Jencks' book *The Language of Post Modern Architecture* (*see also* Modern Movement).

Salon An exhibition of fine and decorative arts by living artists, held at the Louvre in Paris. The event originally took place every two years, but its popularity ensured it became an annual fixture. The term 'Salon' has now come to mean any exhibition modelled on the original Paris Salon.

School of Nancy (Ecole de Nancy) Founded in 1901 by Emile Gallé, the glass maker. The group, which was originally called the Alliance Provinciale des Industres d'Art, included book-binders, architects and artists. Their aim was to breathe new life into the French decorative arts industry.

Suprematism Developed *c.* 1913 by the Russian artist and Christian mystic Kasimir Malevich. The main exponent of the movement's characteristically geometric, abstract art, Malevich described Suprematism as a way of expressing the 'supremacy of feeling in creative art'.

Surrealism Created partly from the ashes of Dada, the movement was named in 1924 by André Breton, who also drew up a manifesto. Surrealists believed in letting the subconscious mind, especially dreams, dictate artistic style. Famous Surrealists included Salvador Dalí, René Magritte, Georges Duchamp and Max Ernst.

Vienna Secession An art group founded in 1897 by Gustav Klimt, in praise and imitation of the German Secessionists. The aim of Secessionists was to break away from traditional artistic moulds and to integrate varying elements of artistry. The Vienna Secessionists produced a magazine, *Ver Sacrum* ('Sacred Spring'), in which they expressed their desire to raise 'the level of artistic sensitivity in Austria'.

Wiener Werkstätte The Wiener Werkstätte ('Vienna Workshop') was set up in 1903 by Josef Hoffman and Koloman Moser. It was a showcase for works produced by artists associated with the Vienna Secession and a workshop used to train young artists in the Secession's techniques and artistic ideals. The Wiener Werkstätte was greatly influenced by the English Arts and Crafts Movement (*see also* Arts and Crafts Movement and Vienna Secession).

BIBLIOGRAPHY

Readers may contact The Eric Knowles Antiques and Collectors' Club at: Unit 3, Warstone Court, Warstone Lane, Birmingham B18 6JQ.

Architecture

Curtis, William J. R., *Modern architecture since 1900*, London, 1996
Giedion, Sigfried, *Space, time and architecture*, Cambridge, Mass., 1941
Lampugnani, Vittorio Magnano, *Encyclopaedia of modern architecture*, London, 1986
Sharp, Dennis, *Twentieth century architecture: a visual history*, London, 1991
Stevenson, Neil, Architecture: the world's greatest buildings explored and explained, London, 1997

Interior Design

Ball, V. K., *Architecture and Interior Design*, New York, 1980
Calloway, S., & Jones, S., *Style Traditions*, London, 1990
Hapgood, Marilyn Oliver, *Wallpaper and The Artist*, New York, 1992
Madden, Chris Casson, *Interior Visions: Great American Designers and the Showcase House*, London, 1988
Pile, John, *Interior Design*, London, 1989
Schoeser, Mary, *Fabrics and Wallpapers: Twentieth Century Design*, New York, 1986
Tate, A., and Smith, C. R., *Interior Design in the Twentieth Century*, New York, 1986
Völker, Angela, *Textiles of the Wiener Werkstätte 1910–1932*, London, 1994

Garden & Urban Landscape Design

Chen, Lixian, *Art and Architecture in Suzhau Gardens*, Nanjing, 1992
Evans, Bob, *Experts and Environmental Planning*, Aldershot, 1995
Jarvis, Simon, *The Penguin Dictionary of Design and Designers*, Harmondsworth, 1984
Karnavou, Eleftheria, *Urban Planning: Theory, Practice and Ideology*, London, 1978
Naylor, Colin (ed.), *Contemporary Designers*, Chicago, 1990
Vance, James E., *The Continuing City: Urban Morphology in Western Civilization*, Baltimore, 1990

Household Goods

Fraser, Hamish W., *The Coming of the Mass Market*, London, 1981
Hillier, Bevis, *The Style of the Century*, New York, 1983
Hine, Thomas, *Populuxe: The Look and Life of America in the 50s and 60s*, London, 1987
Meikle, Jeffrey, *Twentieth-Century Limited: Industrial Design in America*, Philadelphia, 1979
Sparke, Penny, *Japanese Design*, London, 1987
Sudjic, Deyon, *Cult Objects*, London, 1986

Decorative Arts, Ceramics & Glassware

Cameron, Elizabeth, *Encyclopaedia of Pottery and Porcelain: The Nineteenth and Twentieth Centuries*, London, 1986
Grayson, Michael (ed.), *Encyclopedia of Glass, Ceramics and Cement*, New York, 1985
Hawkins, Jennifer, *Scandinavian Ceramics and Glass in the 20th Century*, London, 1989
Lewis, M. M. (ed.), *Glasses and Glass-Ceramics*, Edinburgh, 1989
Klein, Dan and Margaret Bishop, *Decorative Art 1880–1980*, Oxford, 1986
McCready, Karen, *Art Deco and Modernist Ceramics*, London, 1995
Mentasti, Rosa Barovier, *Venetian Glass 1890–1990*, Venice, 1992

Fashion & Accessories

Howell, Georgina, *In Vogue – Six Decades of Fashion*, London, 1975
Mankey Calasibetta, Charlotte, *Fairchild's Dictionary of Fashion*, New York, 1988
Martin, Richard (ed.), *Contemporary Fashion*, New York, 1995
McDowell, Colin, *Directory of 20th Century Fashion*, London, 1987
McGrath, Jinks, *The Encyclopedia of Jewellery Making Techniques*, London, 1997

Costume & Set Design

Baker, Patricia, *Wigs and Make-up for Theatre, Television and Film*, Oxford, 1993
De Marly, Diana, *Costume on the Stage, 1600–1940*, London, 1982
Finkel, Alicia, *Romantic Stages, Set and Costume Design in Victorian England*, Jefferson, 1996
Hoover, Marjorie, *Meyerhold and his Set Designers*, New York, 1988
Kidd, Mary T., *Stage Costume*, London, 1996
Leese, E., *Costume Design in the Movies*, New York, 1990
Sklar, Robert, *Film: An International History of the Medium*, London, 1993

Furniture

Downey, Claire, *Neo-Furniture*, London, 1992
Fiell, C. & P., *Modern Furniture Classics since 1945*, New York, 1990
Garnier, Philippe, *Twentieth Century Furniture*, London, 1980
Garner, Philippe, *Emile Gallé*, London, 1990
Mang, K., *History of Modern Furniture*, New York, 1978
Norberg-Schulz, Christian, *The Baroque Age*, Paris, 1979
Sembach, K.-J., Leuthäuser, G. & Gössel, P., *Twentieth Century Furniture*, Cologne, 1988
Sparke, P., *Furniture – Twentieth-Century Design*, London, 1986

Furnishings, Wall Coverings & Metalwork

Conran, Terence, *The Soft Furnishings Book*, London, 1991
Heron, Norma, *Creative Textiles*, Oxford, 1989
Lynn, Catherine, *Wallpaper in America from the Seventeenth Century to World War I*, New York, 1980
Morgans, Marleen, *Exploring Textiles*, London, 1988
Purdon, Nicholas, *Carpet and Textile Patterns*, London, 1996
Randall, Justine, *Tapestries*, Winchester, 1992

Graphics & Typography

Barnicoat, John, *Posters: A Concise History*, London, 1972
Hollis, Richard, *Graphic Design: A Concise History*, London, 1994
Julier, Guy, *The Thames & Hudson Dictionary of 20th-Century Design and Designers*, London, 1993
Lewis, John, *Typography: Design and Practice*, London, 1978
McLean, Ruari, *The Thames & Hudson Manual of Typography*, London, 1980

Advertising, Logos & Packaging

Evans, Robin B., *Production and Creativity in Advertising*, London, 1988
Holme, Bryan, *The Art of Advertising*, London, 1985
Lasch, Christopher, *The Culture of Narcissism*, New York, 1979
Lip, Evelyn, *The design and feng shui of logos, trademarks and signboards*, New York, 1995
Moriarty, Sandra E., *Creative Advertising*, Hemel Hempstead, 1991

Painting, Sculpture, Prints & Environments

Duncan, Alistair, *Art Deco*, London, 1988
Duncan, Alistair, *Art Nouveau*, London, 1994
Gombrich, Ernst, *The Story of Art*, 15th ed., London, 1995
Hartt, Frederick, *Art: A History of Painting, Sculpture, Architecture*, 4th ed. London, 1992
Murray, Peter and Linda, *A Dictionary of Art and Artists*, Harmondsworth, 1984
Osborne, Harold, *The Oxford Companion to Art*, Oxford, 1970

Photography

Beaton, Cecil & Gail Buckland, *The Magic Image: The Genius of Photography from 1839 to the Present Day*, London, 1975

Gover, C. Jane, *The Positive Image: Women Photographers in Turn of the Century America*, New York, 1988

Green, Jonathan, *American Photography: A Critical History, 1945 to the Present*, New York, 1985

Patterson, Freeman, *Photography and the Art of Seeing*, Toronto, 1989

Tausk, Peter, *Photography in the 20th Century*, Prague, 1980

Transport Design

Butman, John, *Car Wars: How General Motors Built 'The Car of the Future'*, New York, 1991

Jervis, Simon, *The Penguin Dictionary of Design and Designers*, Harmondsworth, 1984

Jute, Andre, *Designing and Building Special Cars*, London, 1985

Stinton, Darrol, *The Design of the Aeroplane*, London, 1983

Thurston, David, *Design for Flying*, London, 1987

Industrial Design

Bayley, Stephen, *In Good Shape: Style in Industrial Products 1900 to 1960*, London, 1980

Heisinger, Kathryn, and George H. Marcus, *Design since 1945*, London, 1983

Heskett, John, *Industrial Design*, London, 1995

Lucie-Smith, Edward, *A History of Industrial Design*, Oxford, 1983

MacCarthy, F., *A History of British Design*, London, 1979

Pulos, Arthur, *Industrial Design*, Cambridge, Mass., 1989

PICTURE CREDITS

AUTHOR BIOGRAPHIES

Kevin Edge: *Introduction*

Kevin Edge lectures in art and design history at the University of Wales Institute. He previously worked as a curator of print and graphic design at the Victoria & Albert Museum in London where he co-curated the museum's Twentieth Century Gallery.

Deborah Gill: *Graphics & Typography*

Educated in India and England, Deborah Gill has worked in publishing for 15 years, writing on a variety of far-reaching subjects, including fine art and literature. She has written monographs on several artists including Magritte, Mucha and Klimt. She is married with two grown-up children, and lives in London.

Karen Hurrell: *Advertising, Logos & Packaging; Costume & Set Design; Household Goods; Industrial Design; Interior Design; Painting, Sculpture, Prints & Environments; Photography; Transport Design*

Karen Hurrell is a well-known author of a number of books on art and design-related subjects, including The Pre-Raphaelites, The Impressionists, Charles Rennie Mackintosh and Renoir. She writes widely for magazines both in the UK and Ireland, and lives in London with her two sons.

Eric Knowles: *Foreword*

Eric Knowles is the presenter of two of television's most popular antiques shows, *The Antiques Roadshow* and *Going for a Song*. He is director of the London auction house, Bonhams, the author of several bestselling books, including *Discovering Antiques*, and a leading authority on nineteenth- and twentieth-century antiques.

Robert Prescott-Walker: *Furnishings, Wall Coverings & Metalwork; Furniture; Decorative Arts, Ceramics & Glassware*

Robert Prescott-Walker is a freelance decorative arts and design consultant, lecturing part-time at Loughborough University College of Art and Design. He worked for eight years for the auctioneers Sotheby's, and Bonhams, where he was manager of the European Ceramics and Applied Arts departments. He has had published various books and articles including a collector's guide to Lalique glass.

Martin Raymond: *Fashion & Accessories*

Martin Raymond is senior lecturer in fashion journalism and fashion history at the London College of Fashion. Former editor of Fashion Weekly, he presents a weekly fashion advice clinic on BBC GLR, and is a regular contributor to *Woman's Hour*, *Mediumwave*, *Retail Therapy* and *Face Value*. He continues to write for *The Evening Standard*, *Options*, *Elle* and *ID* magazine.

Vicky Richardson: *Architecture and Gardens & Urban Landscape Design*

Vicky Richardson is senior reporter on the leading architectural monthly, *RIBA Journal*. She graduated in architecture at the University of Westminster in 1992 and studied journalism at Napier University in Edinburgh. In 1997 she was shortlisted for the International Building Press's Young Journalist of the Year Award.

SUBJECT INDEX